Revolt
in Prerevolutionary
France

Revolt in Prerevolutionary France

The Prince de Conti's Conspiracy against Louis XV,

1755–1757

✤ ✤ ✤

John D. Woodbridge

The Johns Hopkins University Press
Baltimore and London

© 1995 The Johns Hopkins University Press
All rights reserved. Published 1995
Printed in the United States of America on acid-free paper
04 03 02 01 00 99 98 97 96 95   5 4 3 2 1

The Johns Hopkins University Press
2715 North Charles Street
Baltimore, Maryland 21218-4319
The Johns Hopkins Press Ltd., London

Library of Congress Cataloging-in-Publication Data will be
found at the end of this book.
A catalog record for this book is available from the British
Library.

ISBN 0-8018-4945-4

Frontispiece: "Crime armed by authority tramples underfoot the
attributes of justice." © Bibliothèque Nationale, Paris.

To the memory of Dean Jacques Godechot,
esteemed teacher and friend to many

CONTENTS

Preface and Acknowledgments ix

ONE
The Huguenot Struggle for Freedom
of Conscience   I

TWO
Religious Political Disputes at Mid-Century   24

THREE
The "Secret" Negotiations between the Prince
de Conti and Pastor Paul Rabaut   48

FOUR
The Prince de Conti "Embroiled" in Damiens'
Attempt on the Life of Louis XV   72

FIVE
William Pitt and the Secret Expedition   94

SIX
The Failure of the Secret Expedition   115

SEVEN
The Conspiracy of the Prince de Conti against
Louis XV: The Aftermath   135

EIGHT
Epilogue: Of Revolt, the Conti Conspiracy, and
French Citizenship   161

Notes 185   Bibliography 217

Index 237

The conspiracy of the prince de Conti* against Louis XV has the makings of a cloak-and-dagger tale. Its bit players include spies and counterspies; its huge chorus encompasses English troops whom governmental strategists sent to invade the western coasts of France; as protagonist, it features the headstrong prince de Conti, the king's cousin and confidant, turned renegade and suspected of masterminding an extremely dangerous plot to topple Louis XV from the French throne; as supporting actor, it highlights William Pitt the Elder, ready to risk a brilliant political career on the launching of an English expedition to spark a Huguenot revolt against the French government or, that failing, to "rescue" French Protestants from Catholic France. All the elements of a fanciful imagination are here. But in this instance the components are actually related to a conspiracy concocted by a very real and desperate eighteenth-century prince.

If a well-placed English spy at the French court is to be believed, so "melancholic" did the conspiracy's target, Louis XV, become in the summer of 1757 that he seriously contemplated resigning the throne of France. In a coded message the spy forwarded this startling news to the English secret service, headed by Lord Holdernesse. This agency passed the intelligence report on to certain members of the English government. The attempt on Louis XV's life by a "domestique" named Damiens earlier in the year and French spies' alarmist reports about the Conti conspiracy apparently created much of the sinister context for His Majesty's dark thoughts. The spy indicated that Madame de Pompadour and other insiders at court frantically tried to dissuade Louis XV from resigning the throne. Would not the king thereby forsake his people in time of war and unleash frightful dynas-

---

*For convenience sake, "the prince de Conti" is used throughout, despite the initial confusion caused by the identical spelling of the French "*prince*" and the English "prince."

tic conflicts? Would not Madame de Pompadour lose her own highly prized political power?

The Conti conspiracy has benefited from a successful coverup. It was masterfully concealed behind Louis XV's polite public discourse about the prince de Conti, as well as behind the prince's own public and histrionic professions of loyalty to Louis XV. To this day, corners of the conspiracy (1755–57) disappear, swallowed up by archival lacunae.

Not only did several of the "conspirators" swear oaths to keep their activities an "inviolable secret," but Louis XV, who covertly tried to thwart the conspiracy, did his royal best to smother public knowledge of it. With France locked in a war against England and Prussia, a "melancholic" Louis XV dreaded the possibility that rumors about a Conti-led internal rebellion might circulate through his kingdom or make their way to foreign enemies. Louis XV had received spies' reports that "embroiled" the prince de Conti, a charismatic leader, in Damiens' attempt on his own life. Other reports variously pinpointed the prince as an agitator fomenting an "insurrection" of the people of Paris, stirring French Huguenots to revolt, and arranging for the English military descent upon France's poorly defended western coasts. These reports, if widely disseminated and believed, could stimulate further revolt against royal authority and give fresh resolve to France's external foes. For good reason, Louis XV sought to squelch information about his cousin's seditious schemes. Nonetheless, several rumors eluded the king's capacity to control their flight. In 1757, *mauvais discours* harvested by the Paris police from the people of the streets did carry news of a missed Fronde-like rebellion in which the prince de Conti starred as the principal agitator. According to one *mauvais discours*, Conti was to join his "discontented" partisans in Languedoc. According to another, the Protestants were to have taken up arms and joined France's enemies to "dethrone the king."

All in all, Louis XV and the prince de Conti were quite successful in their mutual enterprise of covering up the conspiracy. So concealed was the plot that G. Capon and R. Yves Plessis make no mention of it in their massive biography of Conti, *Paris galant au dix-huitième siècle: Vie privée du prince de Conty Louis-François de Bourbon (1717–1776)* (Paris, 1907). In his encyclopedic study, *Louis XV* (Paris, 1989), Michel Antoine describes aspects of the prince's machinations that rendered him a "dangerous and suspected personage" for Louis XV. But Antoine adds, these are "poorly known" (p. 721).

Cloaking the conspiracy even further, William Pitt the Elder, a politically adroit secretary in the Newcastle administration, felt sufficiently distraught about the negative entailments of the conspiracy's "failure" that he was willing to risk much political capital in exchange for keeping the involvement of George II's government with French Huguenots carefully disguised. In the fall of 1757, Pitt's earlier role in planning the "Secret Expedition" to the French coasts near Rochefort almost cost the minister his political career. But Pitt took solace in the fact that the English public never discerned the English government's own "secret" motivations (distinct from the publicly announced goals) for the "Secret Expedition": to spark a Huguenot rebellion against Louis XV and, if that failed, to assist thousands of French Protestants to escape France.

For their part, French Protestant leaders in 1756–57 attempted to fend off the monarchy's "mistaken" suspicion that some of their brethren had participated in Conti's conspiracy against the king and had colluded with the English. In the fall of 1757, French Protestants in the Saintonge and Guyenne complained bitterly that the government's retribution for this alleged sedition was so severe, Huguenot mothers, fathers, and children were trying to escape its punitive reach by hiding in the woods and caves of the "wilderness." In the nineteenth century, Edmond Hugues, a French Protestant historian who published a selection of revealing documents regarding the conspiracy, also tried to dismiss the idea that French Protestants had been responsive to the prince de Conti's solicitation to revolt (if the prince had actually made such). In general, French Protestant historiography has portrayed the Huguenots of the eighteenth century as loyal monarchists who disassociated themselves from anything that smacked of republicanism or the effervescence of the Camisard Rebellion. According to this historiography, French Huguenots would not have been sympathetic to any plans of revolt against Louis XV.

Taking a different stance, Philippe Joutard has convincingly argued that at mid-century many Protestants in the south of France were more disposed to take up arms in imitation of their Camisard forebears than contemporary Huguenot professions of loyalty would lead us to believe (*La légende des Camisards: Une sensibilité au passé*

[Paris, 1977], pp. 124–29). Joutard's close reading of a number of texts has led him to this conclusion.

Despite bold public appearances Louis XV, Madame de Pompadour, the lieutenant of police, Berryer, and a number of governmental officers in France privately took the conspiracy very seriously. But few enjoyed a vantage point from which to survey its wide-sweeping dimensions, to catalog its multinational cast of characters, or to determine with assurance what the conspirators' goals and stratagems might be.

Many conspiracies shoot through the political heavens like meteors, leaving little trace of their passage. The Conti conspiracy, however, marked political life in France and England in a significant fashion. Unless placed in the context of the conspiracy's shifting configurations, a number of actions by several of the principal figures of European politics in the mid-1750s, including the king of France, Louis XV, the prince de Conti, Madame de Pompadour, William Pitt the Elder, and the king of England, George II, become mystifying, if not bizarre.

This study takes us behind the scenes of political life in both France and England and into the very recesses of power, that is, the confidences of Louis XV, Madame de Pompadour, the prince de Conti, and William Pitt. It reveals the discrepancy that on occasion existed between the public discourse of these individuals and their private actions, fears, and concerns. The analysis is specifically intended to open vistas not only upon the conspiracy but more broadly upon the politicoreligious controversies in the 1750s with which the conspiracy was inextricably connected. These controversies combined with the Conti conspiracy rocked Louis XV's government to its foundations. Several contemporaries claimed that "revolt," or resistance to established authority, was widespread. Chancellor Guillaume Lamoignon, Seigneur de Blancmesnil, for example, expatiated that for a long time he believed that "our state was menaced by a revolution"; now he feared that he would have "the pain of witnessing it" (Jules Flammermont and Maurice Tourneux, eds., *Rémonstrances du Parlement de Paris au XVIIIe siècle* [Paris, 1888–98], 2: xxvi).

In the quest to discover the origins of the French Revolution, Dale Van Kley, Jeffrey Merrick, and others have convincingly demonstrated that the politicoreligious disputes focusing upon the bull *Unigenitus* and the refusal of sacraments to Jansenists acted as a driving force in the "unraveling" (Van Kley) and the "desacralization" (Merrick) of the *ancien régime* or the monarchy. The king's ideology, which posited that only Roman Catholics existed in France and that the sacraments of the Roman Catholic Church knit society into a whole, was dramatically challenged by a significant Jansenist and parliamentary victory that Van Kley locates in September 1757. The Parlement of Paris permitted Jansenists, Augustinian Catholics, to have access to the sacraments without running the gauntlet of *dévot* Roman Catholic opposition.

In this study I propose that the monarchy's ideology was also threatened in 1756–57 by the prince de Conti's Fronde-like rebellion involving French Huguenots and, tangentially, English troops. The Jansenist triumph and the Conti conspiracy were not totally unrelated and occurred almost in tandem. Conti worked closely with the leadership of the *parti janséniste* in the Parlement of Paris while he simultaneously curried "seditious" relations with a government suspect, the Reformed pastor Jean-Louis Gibert, to whom many Huguenots in the south looked for both spiritual and military guidance.

After his traumatic encounter with the genuine threat of a Fronde-like revolt thought to be directed by the prince de Conti and including large Huguenot contingents and English military forces, a much-relieved Louis XV began to recognize the presence of at least those Protestants who had remained faithful to him during the time of the crisis. A de facto toleration began to emerge for Protestants. It belied the king's formal rhetoric that he intended to enforce the anti-Protestant legislation on the books. Louis XV's actual toleration of Protestants contributed to the further undermining of the monarchy's ideology that only Roman Catholics existed in France and that only they could be legitimate citizen-subjects.

By the eve of the French Revolution, this ideology had fallen into palpable disrepute. Politicians with various ideological orientations called for a new definition of citizenship that excluded religious affiliation as a criterion. The Huguenot struggle for freedom of conscience that for a time was linked to the prince de Conti's conspiracy against Louis XV had played a major role in eliciting this new definition of who could be a French citizen (see Chapter Eight).

Perhaps a word about the genesis of this inquiry might be appropriate. My interest was piqued in the late 1970s when I reread a notebook of the lieutenant of the Paris police, Berryer, in which he had copied in a meticulous hand conversations he had personally garnered from Herrenschwand, a spy for madame de Pompadour. The spy attributed shocking statements to the prince de Conti and his confidant, Jean-Louis Le Cointe, concerning a rebellion against the monarchy; the notebook also included references to Conti's seditious relations with French Huguenots. The prince de Conti's sub rosa involvement with French Huguenots was more extensive than I had earlier surmised when, as a graduate student, I had first stumbled on the notebook and read secondary literature on the topic.

Even after my 1979 reading of Berryer's notes, I did not understand their import. But the more I pondered Conti's vexed comments about acting to protect what amounted to his "frondish" ambitions and the interests of his family if the throne of France became empty, the greater the allure of probing the rhetoric covering the prince's own seditious plots. I began to sense that the prince was engaged in a high-stakes conspiracy against his cousin, the king of France. But why? Did the prince actually intend to "dethrone" Louis XV? Did he have a hand in Damiens' attempt on the life of Louis XV in January 1757? As the byzantine story of intrigue began to unfold, I came to realize that the conspiracy was far more complex and expansive than I had ever envisioned. By bits and pieces, and over a period of a decade, the basic story-line of the conspiracy was teased out, although even now gaps remain here and there.

The story line of the conspiracy is the central thread linking the chapters of the present study. In framing a context for the conspiracy, the first chapter discusses in some detail the Huguenot struggle for freedom of conscience. The prince de Conti's first secret overtures to the Huguenot community concerned how he might help them win religious toleration. Even though in the mid-eighteenth century the prince was an exceedingly powerful personage, well esteemed in many European courts, today he remains a neglected historical figure. Chapter Two offers an introduction to the prince's turbulent life and enigmatic character. It isolates several critical issues that drove Conti to conspire against Louis XV: Madame de Pompadour's success at excluding the prince from controlling France's foreign policy and the prince's perception that Louis XV had trampled upon France's "fundamental laws" in the refusal of sacraments controversy (including the serious dispute over the rights of the princes and peers). This chapter also sets the stage for the Conti conspiracy by tracing the Jansenists' struggle for freedom of conscience as a backdrop for the politicoreligious strife at mid-century. Chapter Three explains the circumstances in which the prince de Conti entered into secret negotiations with Pastor Paul Rabaut, a principal leader of the Reformed churches in the south of France. Chapter Four discusses the prince de Conti's alleged involvement in Damiens' attempt upon the life of Louis XV, as well as the prince's seditious relations with French Protestants. Chapter Five moves the scene of action to England. It analyzes William Pitt's clandestine efforts in planning the "Secret Expedition" to the coasts near Rochefort. This expedition, which encompassed one of the largest armadas of the Seven Years' War, represented an offshore phase of the larger Conti conspiracy. Chapter Six describes the French government's retribution upon some French Protestants for their alleged conspiratorial activity with the English. It also chronicles the political turmoil that the failure of the "Secret Expedition" provoked in England during the fall of 1757. Chapter Seven assesses the aftereffects of the conspiracy upon Louis XV, the prince de Conti, William Pitt, and the French Huguenots. Chapter Eight places the Huguenot struggle for freedom of conscience, which for a time was enmeshed with the Conti conspiracy, into the context of later battles waged by philosophes, Jansenists, and magistrates in the parlements of France over the "constitution" and the "fundamental laws" of France.

This study, then, attempts to penetrate the public discourse of Louis XV and the prince de Conti to uncover the basic configurations of Conti's conspiracy against Louis XV during the years 1755–57. It seeks to provide another vantage point from which to take the measure of the surprisingly widespread presence of politicoreligious revolt in the 1750s against Louis XV. It also broaches issues regarding what it meant to be a French "Citoyen" in the closing years of the *ancien régime*. In particular, it treats the question of how the French people moved from being the citizen-subjects of a divine right monarch to being the citizens of a nation.

In research of this kind, special debts are incurred. I am very pleased to acknowledge my own. For more than a decade Dale Van Kley has provided me with sage counsel and timely encouragement. Not only did he graciously give me pertinent research materials, he also made insightful criticisms of earlier drafts of this study and suggested ways to draw out its significance for the prerevolutionary period after 1757. His magisterial analyses of Jansenism and politics are essential background reading for students of eighteenth-century France. Jeffrey Merrick has also afforded wise counsel on this project and offered many astute suggestions and criticisms of an early draft of the manuscript. His essays on the nature of citizenship as it relates to the sacraments of the Roman Catholic Church inform the present study, which also addresses this issue. Timothy Tackett offered helpful advice for trimming certain sections of the manuscript with a view to keeping arguments focused. His comments confirmed once again the depth of his knowledge of eighteenth-century France and his masterly skills as an editor. Orest Ranum, a remarkable scholar and a generous friend to so many students of French history, read an early draft of the manuscript and provided keen insights into the political life of France during the *ancien régime*. Sarah Maza graciously read two drafts of the manuscript and perceptively recommended a number of important emendations for the study. Raymond Birn turned my attention to the writings of Keith Baker, Mona Ozouf, and Roger Chartier on the subject of "public opinion" in the second half of the eighteenth century. These writings prompted more sustained reflection about the place of the Protestants' campaign for toleration in the larger debate regarding criteria for determining citizenship on the eve of the French Revolution. Thomas Kaiser, Julius Ruff, Jacques Le Brun, Robert Lerner, and John O'Connor provided references to pertinent materials. To these colleagues and others, I express my sincere thanks. Obviously, whatever errors remain within this volume are my own. They should in no wise be attributed to those who with such a generous spirit read earlier drafts of this work.

I would also like to thank librarians and archivists at the British Museum, the Public Record Office, the Bibliothèque Nationale, Archives Nationales, the Bibliothèque de la Société du Protestantisme Français, Bibliothèque de Port-Royal, the Arsenal, the Ministère de la Guerre, Archives du Ministère des Affaires Etrangères, departmental, city, and church archives in France, the Herzog August Bibliothek, the Bibliothèque de l'Université de Genève, the Newberry Library, and Northwestern University Library, for their diligence and courtesy in helping locate and duplicate materials.

I am especially grateful to my wife, Susan, who, around dinner tables in France, Germany, and the United States, listened to stories about the prince de Conti's exploits, after her husband had returned from yet another trip to an archive or a library. Her kindly encouragement and suggestions about how the final manuscript might be improved are deeply appreciated.

Revolt
in Prerevolutionary
France

ONE

The Huguenot Struggle
for Freedom of Conscience

✤ ✤ ✤

A spirit of reflection, of great wisdom and especially of a martyr
. . . prepares us and disposes us to lose our lives courageously . . . if
Providence calls us to this.

A definition of *l'Esprit du Désert,* by Antoine Court

The French Huguenots who reconstructed the Reformed churches of the "Church of the Desert" in the eighteenth century often did so at great personal risk.[1] Convinced that no less than God himself had enjoined them to worship publicly, they defied the king's law by holding open-air religious assemblies in the ravines and rugged mountains of the Cévennes, or on the wind-swept barren shores along the Atlantic coastline, or in any other secluded spot that might elude the prying eyes of spies or the notice of His Majesty's soldiers. The Huguenots who dared attend these services knew what might befall them if they were apprehended: perpetual sentences to the galleys for the men and life imprisonment or the convent for the women. The Reformed pastors who led these meetings understood very well that they might be put to death. Refusing to abandon the Calvinist faith, a good number of Huguenots were either executed by hanging or killed by gunfire; some were subjected to torture or forced to pay onerous fines. Many also suffered the anguish associated with membership in an oppressed religious minority.

The Huguenots were descendants of the French Reformation. In the early sixteenth century this Reformation had taken root in ground cultivated by reform-minded Christian humanists within Roman Catholicism. These humanists enjoyed the support of partisans in the

French court including Marguerite, the duchesse d'Alençon, the sister of King Francis I. Jacques Lefèvre d'Etaples' emphasis on justification by faith alone, amplified by the evangelical preaching of Guillaume Briçonnet's "Meaux circle," and Erasmus' call for a return to a New Testament faith based on the "philosophy of Jesus," helped create an ambiance in which, at least initially, the doctrines of Martin Luther did not seem incompatible with the humanists' own reforming programs.[2] Towards 1519, Lutheran teachings began to penetrate Paris. In the 1520s the printed page greatly abetted their dissemination. Not surprisingly, early Protestants in France were called "Lutherans." Although governmental officials scented heresy, they did not always understand what the nature of "Lutheran" beliefs actually was. For that matter French clerics did not always distinguish carefully among heresy, heterodoxy, and orthodoxy.[3] Nonetheless, "Lutherans" were persecuted. A weaver from Meaux was burned in 1524, the first Protestant martyr.

By the 1550s, the disciples of John Calvin had become the dominant Protestant group in France. They engaged in determined evangelistic activity. Some one hundred pastors trained in Geneva covertly slipped into France and helped direct church-building efforts.[4] Calvin himself kept up a correspondence with pastors and the laity in France. For example, he tried to encourage the "five prisoners of Lyon" who in 1552 faced possible death. By 1555, a Reformed church had been established in Paris.

In 1559, French Calvinists held their first national synod in Paris and drew up a Confession of Faith, later revised (1571). A number of Calvinists were convinced that their beliefs were going to spread throughout the kingdom. Jean Morély predicted: "We have, thanks to God, churches in nearly all the cities of the realm, and soon there will be scarcely a place where one has not been established."[5] Given the missionary zeal of Calvinists, this sentiment did not seem fanciful. The Calvinist population had already exploded to approximately two million, or 10 percent of the total French populace.

The aggressive evangelistic activities of these "heretics" and the little respect they evidenced for the traditions and practices of the Roman Catholic Church understandably fueled deep-seated resentments within the Roman Catholic population. Barbara Diefendorf reminds us that the spread of Protestantism represented more than a "religious" challenge for contemporary Catholics: "The 'Lutheran heresy' was not for sixteenth-century Parisians a mere failure of religious orthodoxy; it was a threat to the social order and a danger to the entire community. The Protestants were believed to be not only religious deviants, but also immoral and seditious."[6] Especially after the affair of the rue Saint-Jacques on September 4, 1557, spontaneous riots flared frequently in Paris. In their wake, societal order seemed to break down. Eventually a series of agonizing and enervating civil wars broke out, which bled France badly. Religious hatred boiled over, creating the impetus for heinous acts of violence perpetrated by the various sides.[7] In 1562–63, Protestants in pitched battles attempted to take and hold cities like Rouen, Tours, Blois, Grenoble, and Lyon. Later, led by the prince de Condé, they tried to capture the king himself (1567–70). Politicoreligious war followed upon politicoreligious war.

Military losses incurred during the civil wars and the events surrounding the Saint Bartholomew's Massacre on August 24, 1572, blunted the Calvinists' political and military advance.[8] During the massacres some three thousand Protestants were killed in Paris, including the flower of the Protestant aristocracy, with another eight thousand Huguenots losing their lives elsewhere in France. The Huguenots were thrown on the defensive as Roman Catholic forces gained the upper hand in the civil wars. Mark Greengrass observed "that a protestant church militant gradually became a protestant church under the cross, disciplined . . . , defensive and distrustful of royal authority."[9]

When one of their own, Henry of Navarre, became king of France, the Calvinists' political situation took a turn for the better. Henry had earlier converted to Roman Catholicism, but, once king, he did not forget his former coreligionists. In 1598, Henry promulgated the Edict of Nantes, which gave them not only political rights but also freedom of conscience. Article 6 stipulated that the king's subjects of the Reformed Religion were permitted "to live and dwell in all the Cities and places of this our Kingdom and Countreys under our obedience, without being inquired after, vexed, molested, or compelled to do any thing in Religion, contrary to their Conscience."[10] Under the Edict of Nantes, Protestants had full civil rights and could practice their public worship in certain designated cities within the kingdom. They could also fortify specified Protestant enclaves.

However, in the first three decades of the seventeenth century Huguenots lost much of this newly acquired political power. Failed rebellions against the Crown in the 1620s had precipitated the capture of important Protestant strongholds like La Rochelle (1628). The Paix d'Alès (1629) preserved Protestants' religious liberties but took away political and military privileges they had previously exploited in their uprisings.[11] Nonetheless, between 1630 and 1660 life in France was bearable for Protestants. In fact, in certain communities Huguenots retained dominance as economic and intellectual leaders. Moreover, most Huguenots remained true to their faith despite mounting religious, political, and economic pressures to abjure it. After painstaking research on the "demographic fate and customs" of the Huguenots, 1600–1685, Philip Benedict argued that the confessional community "successfully retained the attachment of the majority of its members throughout the period running from the Edict of Nantes to its Revocation."[12]

In 1661, with the debut of the personal reign of Louis XIV, signs of an assault on the Huguenots' corporate existence emerged.[13] Between 1661 and 1664 alone, more than 150 Protestant churches or temples of worship were demolished, with a total of 650 to 700 razed or "abattu" by 1685.[14] The cadence of anti-Protestant legislation increased after 1661 — more than 400 royal edicts, arrêts, regulations, and declarations preparing the way for and amplifying the Revocation of the Edict of Nantes (1685).

The French monarchy's attitude towards Calvinism was rubbed raw by remembrance of old griefs and renewed fears engendered when English "Protestants" (Calvinists) executed Charles I (1649). The monarchy continued to adjudge Calvinism heretical and opprobriously designated this faith the "Religion Prétendue Réformée" (self-styled Reformed Religion). But the monarchy and the clergy also suspected that Reformed political assemblies that began in 1573, as well as "Reformed" church discipline with its reliance on synods, served as carriers for the venom of republicanism — an ideology deemed subversive to a monarchical state.[15] A number of Catholic writers made this charge explicit by rehearsing the history of Calvinism as a litany of seditious activity. Had not Calvinists tried to undermine the monarchy during seven distinguishable wars of religion in the sixteenth century? In that same century did not the existence of Huguenot armies, separate coinage, and propaganda advocating a decentralized France demonstrate a rebellious and independent spirit? Had not their founder, John Calvin, indicated that if kings "happen to issue a command contrary to God's will, it should be disregarded. The dignity of their high office must not be taken into account in such cases"?[16] Did not the unknown Calvinist author of *Vindiciae contra tyrannos* (1581) argue that even a single individual has the right to resist oppressive legislation of a prince who disregards the law of God? Did not the thrust of Protestant political theory after the Saint Bartholomew's Massacre support political resistance to divine right monarchy?[17] Had not Huguenots created a "United Provinces of the Midi" (Janine Garrisson's term), similar to the Protestant federation in the Netherlands? Even if Calvinist apologists of the seventeenth century repeatedly professed allegiance to an absolute monarchy, sincere Roman Catholics often suspected that Huguenots still harbored a spirit of rebellion and sedition.[18] Huguenot political rhetoric sheltered sedition "with a vocabulary of loyalty and devotion."[19] Roman Catholic apologists took it upon themselves to "demask" Huguenot propaganda.

Encouraged by his advisors, including Madame de Maintenon, Louis XIV felt fully justified in implementing laws curtailing the rights of his Huguenot "subjects." As their employment opportunities and personal liberties became increasingly restricted, Protestants reacted in different ways. Some Huguenots belonging to religiously mixed families decided to convert to Roman Catholicism to prove their royalism and to escape further harassment. Conversion brought little change in their lives: "To convert is not to change your continent, it is to change your street."[20] Even before 1661, various communities of the Propagation de Foi had been established in France. In 1659 the archbishop of Lyon indicated that the community in his city was "to work . . . for the conversion of heretics and other strays from the faith."[21] In November 1676, Paul Pellison-Fontanier, a former Calvinist, began to administer the Caisse des Economats, which furnished funds to recompense Huguenots who converted to Roman Catholicism. Much-publicized conversions ensued.

Between 1681 and 1684, oppression became more systematic and violent. Thousands of Huguenots yielded to forced conversions before the king's *dragonnades*. The *dragonnades*, prosecuted by Marillac, the intendant of Poitou, were a frightful affair. As Elisabeth Labrousse explains, ill-tempered soldiers lodged in Huguenot homes were "incited to do whatever it took to bring about the abjurations of their involuntary hosts," excluding murder and rape.[22] Approximately thirty thousand conversions occurred in Poitou beginning in May 1681. During the years 1684–85, other waves of *dragonnades* swept through Poitou, Béarn, Languedoc, and Dauphiné with thousands of conversions in their wake.

Moreover, according to a law of 1681, children could abjure Protestantism if they had reached the age of seven. Thereafter they would live in homes run by the Roman Catholic clergy. On occasion, Protestant children were simply stolen away, with girls put summarily in convents and boys in Jesuit colleges.

Rather than convert to Roman Catholicism, many Protestants decided to emigrate from France in search of more hospitable lands in the United Provinces, England, Prussia, the cantons of Switzerland, the New World, and elsewhere. In 1679 the exodus began to accelerate. In July 1682 the government attempted to stanch this hemorrhaging by forbidding Huguenots to emigrate without royal permission. But this interdiction was, if anything, only partially successful. Brilliant intellectuals like Pierre Bayle had earlier left France for the United Provinces in 1681; other Huguenots escaped the kingdom after July 1682. The exodus reached its apex after the Revocation of the Edict of Nantes, between 1686 and 1689. The emigrants had recourse to a range of stratagems to facilitate evasion: sometimes they wore disguises, pretending to be beggars; sometimes they traveled by moonlight, wending their way through icy mountain passes; sometimes they stowed away in the cargo holds of ships. Many of these emigrants were willing to risk all, so disheartened had they become by recent developments in their homeland.

The best estimate of the number of persons who decided to emigrate from France in the years before and immediately after 1685 is 200,000 (out of an estimated Reformed population of 750,000 in 1680).[23] The greatest percentage of these (40%) came from regions nearest the kingdom's northern borders, whereas a much smaller percentage (16%) emigrated from the south, or the Midi. They felt obliged to join the "Refuge"—a movement whose members contributed significantly to the cultural life of their newly adopted countries.[24] Among the refugees were found the vast majority of the 873 pastors in France in 1685. Another 140 pastors, or 16 percent of the pastoral corps, abjured their faith and remained in France.[25] A much smaller group also stayed and tried to keep the Reformed faith alive in underground meetings.

The Revocation of the Edict of Nantes

What Henry IV had given Protestants in the late sixteenth century, his grandson, Louis XIV, took away in the late seventeenth. Louis XIV's Revocation of the Edict of Nantes (1685) represented the culmination of his concerted campaign to assure an absolute monarchy in which only one law, one faith, and one king existed. According to Jean Orcibal, Louis XIV viewed Calvinists as members of a dangerous republican, or antimonarchical, sect that was undermining unity in his kingdom.[26]

Whatever Louis XIV's motives, the revocation achieved by the Edict of Fontainebleau pushed Protestants to the very margins of French society; they were forbidden to practice their religion (Articles 2 and 3); their pastors could no longer exercise their functions (Articles 4, 8, and 9); they were forbidden to leave France or to transport their goods out of the kingdom, under penalty of the galleys (Article 10). Interestingly enough, Article 12 stipulated that Protestants would be permitted to live in France without being molested for their faith "while awaiting the time when it might please God to enlighten them like the others" and on the condition that they not assemble to practice their religion under the pretext of coming together for prayer or worship.[27]

For those Protestants who remained in France, painful choices had to be made. How could they reconcile their duty to obey the king, who forbade them to worship God publicly, with God's command to meet for such worship? Under enormous pressures, the overwhelming majority converted to Catholicism.[28] But they often gave formal adherence to Roman Catholicism while apparently practicing their "former" faith in private (*culte domestique*). A very small minority took another tack. Especially peasants and workers from the lower economic classes in southern France committed themselves to resist-

ing missionary efforts to convert them. Despite the risks, they tried
to sustain their worship practices in forbidden public meetings.

Before the turn of the eighteenth century, the successful efforts of
Pastor Claude Brousson to revive and reorganize church life, even if
it was obliged to survive in a clandestine fashion, had demonstrated
that a few pastors could create an underground church. But Brousson's work was prematurely cut short. He was captured in Béarn and
taken to Montpellier, where Bâville, the intendant of Languedoc, had
him put to death on the wheel on November 3, 1698. Other pastors
had preceded Brousson in martyrdom; twenty were executed in the
Midi between 1684 and 1698. These executions compounded by the
emigration of pastors from France led to the nearly total disappearance of a pastoral corps by the first years of the eighteenth century.

Deprived of guidance by a trained pastoral corps, a number of Calvinists in the south fell prey to a movement of radical prophetism
which had been simmering for more than a decade; it eventually
enticed them into fanatical activities. In the Vivarais, the Hautes-
Cévennes, as well as the Dauphiné, these Calvinists believed quite
literally the words of several illuminist prophets who foretold liberation from oppression in the last times. They saw themselves as a people of God, identifying their plight with that of the Children of
Israel. Moreover, they were prepared to die for the cause. In explain-
ing their demands to the authorities on December 15, 1702, one Camisard leader proclaimed: "We are ready to die rather than renounce
such a wonderful belief which Our Savior Jesus Christ has assured
for us in the death that he suffered, the just for us the unjust."[29]

A few prophets encouraged Calvinists to take measures into their
own hands in bringing about the expected liberation, even if this
meant resorting to physical violence. A conflict known as the Guerre
des Camisards on occasion turned the south into an armed camp, as
neither the prophetic leaders of the Calvinists, nor governmental
officials, nor members of the Roman Catholic population disdained
the use of arms.[30] The hostilities were particularly inflamed when
the abbé du Chayla was murdered at Pont-de-Monvert on July 24,
1702, by fifty Cévenols whose leaders were two "prophets," Abraham Mazal and Esprit Séguier.[31] The war cries of the Camisards
reveal their economic and religious goals for the rebellion: "point
d'impôts" (no taxes) and "liberté de conscience" (freedom of con-

science). Ultimately governmental military might triumphed, as the last major contingent of warring Calvinists, called *Camisards*, was forced to flee to Switzerland in 1704. However, as late as 1710, Abraham Mazal was slain after he tried once again to incite the Protestant population of Vivarais to take up arms. More emigrations took place during the Guerre des Camisards. The war strongly reinforced the impression that had existed since the sixteenth century that French Protestants were rebellious and republican. Not easily dispelled despite concerted efforts by Protestant apologists, this suspicion continued for decades to hang heavily over the reputation of French Huguenots.

After the tragedies associated with the Guerre des Camisards the situation of French Protestants became worse, at least from a legal point of view. As he approached his deathbed in 1715, Louis XIV, who was inclined to demonstrations of personal orthodoxy in this dire circumstance, created the legal fiction that there were no longer any Protestants in France.[32] According to this fiction, any person residing in France must be a Catholic because Catholicism was the only religion tolerated in the kingdom.

Philippe d'Orléans, the regent who followed Louis XIV, assumed a more tolerant attitude. He even contemplated a plan that some Huguenot emigrants might be permitted to reside in Douai. The duc de Saint-Simon disabused him of interest in this proposal, however, by declaiming that after the Edict of Nantes, Calvinists had formed "a separate, well organized republican government . . . in a word, a state within a state."[33]

Despite Philippe d'Orléans' more lenient attitude, penalties for participation in the religious life and public meetings of the Reformed churches remained onerous. The death penalty continued to be meted out to pastors arrested by the king's officers. Between 1718 and 1762 another fifteen pastors were put to death.[34]

In 1724 the duc de Bourbon decided to reinforce the policies of Louis XIV. The Declaration of 1724 bolstered the anti-Protestant legislation by reinforcing articles of the Edict of Fontainebleau (1685) and the declaration of December 13, 1698. Upon the Roman Catholic clergy alone was conferred functions deemed essential to maintaining the institution of the family. The monarchy upheld the principle that only the sacraments of baptism, marriage, and extreme unction performed by a priest of the Catholic Church were valid. Couples married by a Protestant minister were living in sin; their offspring were automatically considered bastards with no legal right of inheritance. Further, it was required that their babies be baptized by a Roman Catholic priest within twenty-four hours of birth. As in the past, no public records of births were kept except in parish registers. The Declaration of 1724 stipulated that Protestant parents were responsible for sending their children to "schools and to catechisms until the age of fourteen." Young persons between fourteen and twenty were to attend religious instruction, which took place on Sundays and festival days. A French person who did not receive the last sacrament of the Church was considered relapsed and liable to the penalties for that state. A Calvinist who refused this rite could suffer the indignity of having his body thrown into a refuse heap and his property confiscated. The Declaration of 1724, renewing a stipulation of the Edict of Fontainebleau, demanded that all persons seeking access to public office, to the legal and medical professions, and to a university education furnish certificates of Catholicism. This ruling was especially designed to cut Protestants off from these avenues of advancement. As Charles Dardier observed, the anti-Protestant legislation did not allow members of the Reformed churches the elemental rights of birth, of life, and of dying in peace.[35]

At least 10,724 persons of the Reformed population (estimated at 593,307 in 1760) suffered the full brunt of persecution between 1685 and 1787: they included 219 men and 32 women executed, 635 killed by gunfire or other means, 3,484 men and 3,493 women taken prisoner, and 1,940 persons who served on the galleys. Thousands more Protestants felt the burden of heavy fines.[36]

The Restoration of Reformed Churches

Irony would have it that the very year Louis XIV died, 1715, the restoration of the Reformed churches of France once again began in earnest. Antoine Court, a young man of twenty years, transformed a meeting of a few pastors held at Monoblet in the Cévennes into the first synod of the Desert. Later, in Switzerland, he outlined his plan of action for the churches. Among other goals, he wanted to disabuse the Calvinist population of the "infection" of fanaticism which had spread like a raging epidemic during the Guerre des Camisards.[37] To do this, he hoped to raise up trained men who would pastor flocks without shepherds, stifle the flames of fanaticism, and become willing martyrs if God called them to this lot.

In 1726 a seminary was established in Lausanne, Switzerland, which offered a secure and hidden-away place where young Frenchmen aspiring to the ministry could be trained.[38] The historian Jules Michelet would later call the seminary "l'étrange école de la mort"—an apt expression, given the fate of several of its students.

The seminary was placed under the aegis of two committees: the Committee of Geneva and the Committee of Lausanne. Composed of eminent Calvinists, the Committee of Geneva sought funds from Protestant countries for the French seminary; it received a generous pension from England between 1750 and 1785 and other sums from the Estates General of Holland, the court at Hesse, the king of Sweden, and the Republic of Berne.[39] The Committee of Lausanne was composed of pastors and professors who oversaw the housing of the students and acted as guarantors to local town officials for their conduct. This committee also maintained a correspondence with pastors back in France.

Antoine Court, who had emigrated to Lausanne in approximately 1729–30, directed the operations of the seminary until his death in 1760.[40] Moneys that the committees had received from foreign Protestants were funneled to Court, who in turn often paid the expenses of the students and professors and forwarded sums to support pastors in France. He gave advice to young students about what they might expect in their ministries. Moreover, his counsel was often sought by pastors back in France, especially by Paul Rabaut, one of the most influential leaders of the Church of the Desert.

The vast majority of the pastors of the Church of the Desert received their relatively brief theological education (from six months to more than two years) at the underground school in Lausanne. The contrast between student life in the security of Protestant Lausanne and the uncertainties of a vocation in Catholic France was striking to many of these young Huguenots. Undaunted by the dangers that lay ahead of them, they generally relished the day they could return to their homelands to minister to what they perceived was a suffering people.

Not that French Protestants in the south of France faced unremitting persecution after 1715. In La Rochelle, for example, well-to-do Protestant families were able to maintain important interests in commerce despite their religion: "Elite Protestant families suffered only occasional harassment. By and large, local authorities — secular and religious — left them alone on matters of faith. Presumably their great wealth, commercial influence, and proven loyalty to the crown buffered the Protestant families against the law."[41] In Paris, Protestant "Messieurs" with good political connections lived rather comfortably. In the provinces wealthy Protestant "notables" often entertained amicable relationships with their Catholic business associates and neighbors. They sometimes viewed their brethren who were engaged in outlawed church-building activities as dangerous and fanatical.[42] They feared that these church-building efforts might provoke a backlash among the Roman Catholic clergy and governmental officials against all Protestants, thereby endangering the circumscribed but real breathing space they personally enjoyed. Genuine class distinctions based on wealth existed in the Reformed community. They created one context for the bitter differences of opinion regarding the ultimate legitimacy of defying the monarchy's interdiction against public worship assemblies.

The actual level of persecution that a given group of Protestants endured in one province might differ from what their brethren were confronting in a neighboring province. Among the variables affecting the experiences of a particular group of Protestants were the willingness of an intendant or subdelegate to enforce anti-Protestant legislation; the availability of troops to impose the dictates of an intendant; and the attitudes of the local Catholic clergy.

Furthermore, the vicissitudes of France's foreign relations and Louis XV's own attitudes towards the Protestants often affected national patterns of persecution. During the War of the Austrian Succession, for example, Louis XV and his officials feared that French Protestants were in contact with advancing Austrian armies and with the English king, George II. These suspicions were not allayed, even though Protestant leaders volunteered young men to serve in Louis XV's armies. In these circumstances, in which the monarchy could little afford an internal rebellion, French Protestants enjoyed a period of relative toleration. The anti-Protestant legislation on the books was sometimes not enforced with as much rigor. Three pastors, however, did not escape it and were executed: Louis Ranc, in 1745; Jacques Roger, in 1745; and Matthieu Majal, in 1746.[43]

The year 1750 found Reformed pastors witnessing a recrudescence of systematic persecution particularly in evidence after the War of the Austrian Succession ended in 1748. During the war, Roman Catholic clergymen had complained to the government about the boldness with which Protestants were rebuilding their churches. In 1745, one bishop lamented this upsurge of audacity: "We are losing in less than two years, the care and the strenuous efforts which it took during fifty years to win back these poor souls; we see ourselves as having almost returned to the days in which we were before the Revocation of the Edict of Nantes."[44] The Assembly of the Clergy of 1750 called upon the king "to have the edicts executed which had been drawn up against the self-styled Reformed persons and particularly the declaration of 1697 and that of 1724, a monument so respectful of his religion." In response, Louis XV observed that he had just given "the most precise orders to have the Declaration of 1724 executed in Languedoc and that he would voluntarily have it executed in other provinces."[45]

Indeed, an ordinance of January 17, 1750, signaled the king's intention of bringing about the suppression of all Reformed assemblies.[46] There was, however, strong opposition. On March 28, 1751, a group of about four hundred Calvinists, holding a service in the Cévennes, were surprised by a detachment of the king's soldiers attempting to enforce the Ordinance of 1750. A scuffle broke out in which several young men attempted to free their Reformed companions whom the soldiers had taken captive. Governmental officials claimed later that the affair was minor; the Reformed pastors countered that five young Calvinists had been slain and several others seriously wounded. In any case, this incident touched off murders and reprisals that turned the years 1751–52 into terrifying ones for Protestants and Roman Catholics alike in parts of the south.[47]

Despite the exhortation of most of their pastors, a number of Calvinists resorted to violence against the Catholic population, apparently in reprisal for the persecution. A series of murders of Catholic priests and laymen shocked both communities. On June 11, 1751, several Catholics found the body of Guillaume Lefebvre, who had been slain, rumor had it, because he was an informer against the Protestants.

In August 1752, two Reformed pastors, Coste and Vesenobre, were openly charged by the bishop of Uzès with having deliberately fired upon three priests, one of whom later died.[48] The same year the bishops of Languedoc indicted the Protestant pastors for usurping the prerogatives of the priesthood and for becoming accomplices to the murder: "It is no longer only a question of assemblies, of Baptisms, of Marriages made in the Desert by ministers and preachers who usurp the functions of the Ministry, and who spread fanaticism and revolt in the minds of the people. . . . Today, we have about reached the times we had feared. These preachers that had been represented as dangerous seducers on account of their artifices and violent ways are now placing themselves at the head of murderers."[49] The climate of terror created by the assassinations prompted a number of Catholic priests to flee the countryside in the Languedoc.

Members of both the Roman Catholic clergy and the local governments believed that the Protestant pastors were ultimately at the root of the laity's resistance to campaigns to close down the assemblies and to enforce compulsory baptisms. In 1751, Soulier de Puechmille, sometimes called Lafage or Lagarde, a spy whom the state had engaged on the recommendation of the archbishop of Avignon, proposed a simple solution for breaking the Protestants' will: "Chase from this kingdom a rather considerable number of ministers and of proposants from this sect," for then the assemblies of the Desert "would terminate for lack of preachers."[50] The method for doing this was as simple as it was treacherous: "It is merely a question of forcing them [the pastors] to leave the Kingdom by seizing the wives of those who are married and the fathers of those who are not. Relegate the first to a convent and the second ones to a citadel, and let them be convinced there that they will be freed only when their husbands and their sons have left France."[51] Puechmille attempted to help the government implement his plan by providing the addresses of the pastors' relatives in question. Fortunately for the pastors, Lenain, the intendant of Languedoc at the time, did not prosecute the scheme in a determined manner.

Nonetheless, two pastors, François Bénézet and Molines, called Flechier, were arrested. After admitting that he was a pastor, Bénézet was executed on March 27, 1752, at Montpellier; for his part, Molines abjured the Reformed faith and was transferred to a Catholic seminary in Viviers.[52] During this tense period several pastors traveled with armed escorts, having judged that necessary for their safety.

Indeed, 1751 and 1752 were horrendous years for the Calvinist populations in various corners of the south. From the point of view of many Protestants, the new wave of persecution was so distressing that they had doubts concerning Calvinism's very survival in France: "It can be said, that there are no people in Europe so maltreated as the Protestants in France. There is no kind of affliction they have not suffered since the fatal epoch of the revocation of the Edict of Nantes; but the rigors that have been exerted against them in recent days, feeding upon previous ones, are carried to such an excess that it appears it has been resolved to bring about their total ruin, and that in order to lead them to it in a sure fashion and with some semblance of justice, it is wished to throw them into the depths of despair."[53] Paul Rabaut echoed these sentiments: "The persecution is becoming stronger from day to day; and for quite a while we have had so many reasons to cry: Lord, save us, for we are perishing." Emigration again became a real temptation for French Calvinists of the south.

Saint-Florentin, the governmental official whose duties included responsibility for Protestant affairs, realized that the situation had become so perilous in the south that revolt might break out. He called upon the *procureur général* to the Parlement of Paris, Joly de Fleury, for his advice on the explosive yet delicate Protestant question. In response, Fleury drew up a memoir in which he defended the thesis that the Calvinists usually rebelled after each new anti-Protestant ordinance. The present unrest followed naturally on the promulgation of the Ordinance of 1750, which struck not only at the Protestant assemblies but at Protestant marriages as well. To calm the situation, Fleury suggested that Protestant marriages be blessed by Catholic priests, giving the marriages civil but not religious sanction. Pleased with this insight, Saint-Florentin ordered Saint-Priest on February 17, 1753, to refrain from "all executions and all acts of authority" issuing from the Ordinance of 1750. He chided Roman Catholic clergymen who were applying the anti-Protestant legislation too rigorously.[54] Peace was restored to the Languedoc in 1753, but the calm lasted only a brief time.

On February 16, 1754, the duc de Richelieu, who had recently arrived in the Languedoc to take control of the military command, published a new ban against the Protestants, perhaps on the order of

Louis XV himself.[55] The intention of Richelieu was to close down the religious meetings of the Protestants at any cost and with any means required. He instructed his commanding officer to eliminate the pastoral corps, for according to this strategy the leaderless assemblies would then cease to exist; the assemblies ought to be surprised, so that "those who are found there might be arrested by the troops, especially the ministers or the preachers, upon whom one might fire in case they take flight by horse. . . . It will be easy to recognize them by their clothing and by the care which the N.C. [*Nouveaux convertis*] take to help them escape and to secure their safety.[56] The despairing testimony of Pastor Paul Rabaut is telling: "Troops fill up absolutely all the villages where there are some Protestants. . . . There are as many spies as there are flies. . . . We [pastors] wander in the Deserts without knowing where to repose our heads."[57] But Pastor Teissier did not elude the troops; after his arrest, he was executed on August 17, 1754, at Montpellier.[58]

The two pastors governmental officials most wanted to capture were Jean-Louis Gibert and Paul Rabaut. Both major actors in our story were correctly perceived to be skillful organizers and opinion makers in the Protestant communities. Gibert had a large following in the Saintonge and in the Cévennes, and Rabaut was generally recognized as the leader of the Reformed churches throughout the south. If these two could be arrested, governmental officials knew that they would have delivered a devastating blow to the Reformed churches in the south.

Jean-Louis Gibert and a "Camisard Spirit"

Jean-Louis Gibert (June 29, 1722–?) had studied at the seminary in Lausanne between 1746 and 1749.[59] As an effective preacher and organizer, Gibert stood out as a prime target for the intendants. He was despised and feared by members of the Roman Catholic clergy. On several occasions he barely evaded carefully devised traps, once outracing the king's soldiers on horseback. In the latter incident, his correspondence and sermons fell into governmental hands. On July 14, 1756, the intendant Jean Baillon delivered an *arrêt* that declared that Gibert was "duly attained and convicted of having pursued the functions of a minister for several years in the province of Saintonge, of having convoked and held assemblies of *religionnaires* there, of having preached there, of having offered the Eucharist, of having baptized and married." He was ordered to appear before the Church of Saint Barthélemy of La Rochelle, where he would watch his papers, books, and sermons be burned and where he would be hanged, after which his body would be exposed on the gallows.[60] At liberty, Gibert (and his brother, Etienne, who had been condemned to the galleys) wisely chose not to attend this ceremony; so he was hanged in effigy.

What kind of person was Jean-Louis Gibert, who so agitated the authorities in the Saintonge by his bold church-building activities? According to a "wanted" notice of the early 1760s, the government suspected the pastor of being an English agent. The notice described him as a large man ("extrêmement gros") who wore a wig, had small legs, and was a handsome figure on horseback. He was allegedly "audacious, enterprising," given to plots, and "equal to all the excesses that fanaticism is capable of inspiring." He spoke with facility and with much fire.[61]

From other sources, we know that Pastor Gibert was driven by an unshakable commitment to his faith and interested in millenary doctrines, especially prophetic beliefs about the thousand-year reign of Christ over the world at the end of this present age. Gibert called others to risk their possessions and their lives for the Reformed Gospel and to brook no compromise with Roman Catholicism. In January 1755, a Protestant from Tremblade complained to Pastor de Superville in Rotterdam about the alleged intolerance of Gibert, who had excommunicated him because he did not want his child baptized by the pastor and ultimately had the child baptized by a priest. De Superville then wrote to Antoine Court about the problem and added: "I have learned from other sources several other things which all confirm the fact that the zeal of Monsieur Gibert is not always directed by wisdom nor tempered by charity. It is even said that his doctrine is not entirely pure and that he greatly insists upon the opinions of millenarians."[62]

Troubled by this and other reports, Antoine Court asked Pastor Pierre Dugas, on March 2, 1755, to go to the area where the dispute was unfolding, sift out the true from the false, engage Gibert in friendly discussions, and seek to bring him back to more moderation in his comportment. Court indicated to Dugas that this was the only way to handle the problem because writing to Monsieur Gibert "is lost effort."[63]

Pastor Gibert did not relish these measures. He protested bitterly to pastors in the Cévennes that he was merely upholding the discipline of the Reformed churches. On September 1, 1755, Pastor Henri Cavalier, called Latour, wrote to Antoine Court about the potential legitimacy of Gibert's grievance: "M. Gibert wrote a letter to our synodal assembly in which, as a member of our synod [Gibert had just left the area], he is asking for justice vis-à-vis you and M. de Superville about the unfavorable judgments that you have charged to his account without understanding him and based upon this false report made by several badly intentioned persons from the area where he is now, in complaining about his excessive rigor in exercising discipline against scandalous sinners." Latour noted that the controversy had created much anguish for the assembly of pastors in the Cévennes.[64]

On September 18, 1755, Pastor de Superville's consistory in Rotterdam wrote to various churches in the Saintonge, urging them to follow a policy of moderation in the application of discipline. Pastor Gibert would have none of this interference or counsel. Between December 24 and 27, 1755, he defiantly led a colloquy of churches that dispensed strong doses of discipline to erring Reformed church members in his area.

In many regards Gibert exemplified a more uncompromising form of French Protestantism than did Antoine Court or Paul Rabaut, the latter deemed an "homme modéré" even by several governmental officials. Seemingly imbued with the Camisard spirit, Gibert was rejecting Court's admonitions for moderation at the very time (the last months of 1755) that, as we shall see, the prince de Conti was making his bid to become their military leader.

The government in Paris began to receive intelligence reports that targeted Jean-Louis Gibert as one of the most dangerous men living in France, a fanatic prone to hatch plots. For many Protestants of the Saintonge and in the Cévennes, however, he was a man of God who boldly encouraged them to construct church buildings (*maisons d'oraisons*) in 1755, despite the dangers this enterprise engendered, and who seemed unimpressed by the personal risks he braved on nearly a daily basis.[65] He was a man they could trust and follow. And they apparently did so by the thousands.

Paul Rabaut and Antoine Court, "Moderate" Spokesmen

Called by one of his colleagues "the most celebrated minister of the kingdom," Paul Rabaut was indisputably the most notable Protestant pastor during the second half of the eighteenth century.[66] Born at Bédarieux at the foot of the Cévennes, on January 29, 1718, Rabaut was the son of a "marchand drapier." For six months, he studied at the seminary in Lausanne, where he met Antoine Court, who later said about Rabaut, "I can do nothing without him."[67] Rabaut exercised his active ministry at Nîmes between 1741 and 1785. In the mid-1750s, he, like many other pastors, was a hunted man and often did not know where to find safe shelter on a given night. He, too, was engrossed by millenary doctrines.

Rabaut and Protestant pastors of the Church of the Desert faced a perplexing problem. On one hand, they were engaged in the taxing task of rebuilding the Reformed churches of France. On the other, they knew that legislation sanctioned by the kings of France outlawed their activities. How could they justify transgressing the king's laws? In their apologia, French Protestants gave a rather standard response to this question: The monarchs of France have no more loyal citizens than members of the Reformed churches of France. And yet the king's law forbids public worship, a practice commanded by God himself. In this one instance, Protestants must obey God's commands and not the king's. They do so not in a spirit of revolt or independence, but because they must submit to the divine will.

The Protestant literature, particularly from the pens of Antoine Court and Paul Rabaut, then, generally portrayed the members of the Reformed churches as loyal monarchists who for conscience sake had to disregard an ill-considered demand of the anti-Protestant legislation.[68] At least formally, this stance put the French Protestant pastors on the side of Pierre Bayle, who in the last decades of the seventeenth century shrewdly argued the case for religious pluralism *and* submission to the monarchy against the more explosive "republican" theses of Pierre Jurieu.[69] The cruel memories of the Guerre des Camisards were too vividly etched in many apologists' minds for them to advocate the idea of armed revolt against a monarchy that denied them freedom of worship. The Camisard Rebellion and earlier failed republican conspiracies (Van den Enden, the comte de Linange) against the monarchy had demonstrated the folly of that approach.[70] The war had enticed Protestants into fanatical and reprehensible behavior.

Several difficulties encumbered this "moderate" stance associated with Antoine Court and Paul Rabaut. First, the caveat that Protestants submitted to the monarchy's authority except when it forbade public worship permitted foes to impugn the sincerity of the Protestants' repeated professions of loyalty. The Protestants were depicted as seditious because they made allowance for this one important exception. Not only did Roman Catholic apologists drive home this point, but wealthy Protestants in Paris, Bordeaux, and La Rochelle conceded that the nonnegotiable demand for public worship services could be rightly interpreted as a sign of rebellion or defiance. In *Lettre sur les assemblées des religionnaires en Languedoc* (Paris, 1745), Pastor François-Louis Allamand .from Switzerland also seconded this stance, downplaying the significance of public worship services. So troubled was Antoine Court by this criticism that he felt obliged to draft *Réponse à la lettre sur les assemblées* (Geneva, 1745). Armand de la Chapelle also tried to answer Allamand in *La necessité du culte public* (The Hague, 1746).

A second inconvenience troubled the "moderate" position of Court and Rabaut. Whereas their stance advocating public worship displeased some Protestants who thought it too provocative, its emphasis on loyalty to the monarchy displeased other Protestants who thought it too long-suffering. Philippe Joutard, who has carefully studied the history of evolving perceptions of the Camisards in the Protestant community, finds a greater appreciation for the Camisards among the Protestants of the south than the "official" position of Court and Rabaut suggests.[71] Whereas Court and Rabaut, wary of charges of republicanism and rebellion, attempted to distance the Protestant community from anything that evoked memories of the Camisard Rebellion, many peasants, workers, and pastors, such as Gibert sensed a continuity in the frustrations they personally experienced and those that had vexed Camisards decades earlier. The Camisard revolt was not forgotten by these Protestants. They could grasp why the Camisards, in desperation, might have believed that recourse to arms was the only means left to them in their quest for freedom of conscience. For these Protestants in the mid-1750s, the right of self-defense was as much approved by God as was the teaching that pub-

lic worship should be practiced at all costs. The formal pronounce-
ments of Court, Rabaut, and other "moderates" did not fully represent their views.

A third difficulty of the "moderate" stance advocated by Court
and Rabaut was that it contained an ambiguity of no small portent.
Although they rejected any gesture that blessed fanaticism and rebellion, the two spokesmen frequently placed an only slightly veiled
threat in their carefully worded declarations to governmental leaders.
If the officials would not relax the enforcement of the anti-Protestant
legislation, then new emigrations of French Protestants could be expected. These emigrations would further deprive France of needed
merchants and skilled workers. According to this argument, the loss
of thousands of French Huguenots (Protestant apologists as well as
the philosophes often exaggerated their numbers) had already severely
damaged the economic well-being of the country.[72] Not only did
Antoine Court frequently hold this Damoclean sword over governmental officials, he was willing to formulate plans for an emigration
(1752) when the Protestant plight seemed insupportable.[73] Because
emigration by Protestants was forbidden, the "moderates" Court and
Rabaut were paradoxically championing a policy that countermanded
their claim of submission to the monarchy.

In the mid-1750s, the "moderate" position advocated by Court and
Rabaut did not want for critics in both the Roman Catholic and the
Protestant communities. For *dévot* Roman Catholics, spiritual descendants of the *sainte union* of the late sixteenth century, who tended to
be ultramontanist rather than Gallican Catholics and partisans of the
Jesuits, it represented a subterfuge designed to cover up a spirit of
rebellion and sedition. For more wealthy Protestants it demanded
too much freedom (freedom of worship), given the religious and
political realities of French society. For many suffering Protestants, it
demanded too much patience and placed too much trust in what
might eventually prove to be the illusory good will of the king or
governmental officials.

The French Protestants, then, engaged in rebuilding their churches
in southern France, confronted a trying and complex situation on the
eve of the Seven Years' War. They had recently been the victims of
one of the most systematic campaigns of persecution experienced by

the Protestant community in the eighteenth century. A number of them had resorted to violence, which had fueled the fires of hostility in the Catholic community. A local Roman Catholic clergy appeared traumatized; it believed that unless a dramatic campaign against the Protestants were mustered, their brazen church-building activities could never be checked. At any moment Protestants risked losing their esteemed leaders Paul Rabaut and Jean-Louis Gibert, who might be seized by soldiers and put to death. And most troubling, their family life was still racked by the effects of the anti-Protestant legislation. In a 1756 *placet* to Louis XV, Pastors Alexandre Vernet and Jean Blachon of the Vivarais and Velay lamented that His Majesty, the father of his people, did not understand the extent of the torments some of his children were experiencing: "The entire Kingdom shares our alarms and grimaces in secret regarding the evil that is being hidden from You and is greater than one might think. This province, Sire, is filled with marriages which Your laws do not recognize. This is for us a great source of tears and grief. . . . Our wives are treated like concubines. . . . To avoid this ignominy, we can only live in forced celibacy, which is so prejudicial to the welfare of the State; our children are regarded as bastards and cannot succeed us, which is the reason for many legal trials and the ruin of this province."[74] Protestant "notables" often scorned the members of the churches of the "Désert" and feared what reprisals might fall on their own heads if these determined church-builders became fanatical and demanding. The pressures upon members of the Church of the Desert were frequently enormous.

When the Seven Years' War broke out, many Protestants, only too tired of daily harassments, perceived a possible benefit stemming from the conflict. They understood that the central government would not have at its disposal as many troops as before to enforce the anti-Protestant legislation, owing to the manpower requirements of the war. Indeed, the notion that several Protestant pastors wanted to "profit" from or take advantage of the war was reported back to governmental officials. Not surprisingly, this report made governmental officials in the south anxious.

It is surprising, however, that these pastors also had the opportunity to seek relief from an unexpected quarter. In 1755 their correspondence had already begun to convey clipped comments about secret negotiations in process which might bring about an improvement in their precarious situation. In the summer of 1755, Pastor Paul Rabaut had met the prince de Conti, the powerful cousin of Louis XV, in two head to head secret meetings in an abandoned *hôtel* along the Seine in Paris. Hopes began to build among pastors aware of these clandestine contacts that this prince might be able to provide succor for their people, many of whom had suffered about as much as human beings could bear. It is to the intriguing career of the prince de Conti that we now turn.

Religious Political Disputes
at Mid-Century

✤ ✤ ✤

In the midst of all these little literary squabbles . . . I received the
greatest honour that literature has ever brought me, and one by
which I was greatly moved, in the two visits which the Prince de
Conti condescended to make me.

Jean-Jacques Rousseau, *The Confessions*

At mid-century, the prince de Conti figured as a very popular combatant in the religious political disputes so prevalent in Louis XV's France.[1] A prime architect of France's foreign policy from 1745 to 1756, an accredited military hero, a patron to the Parlement of Paris, a confidant and advisor for his cousin, Louis XV, the prince de Conti acted as an effective power broker dispensing advice and protection. Then, in the fall and winter of 1755–56, he lost favor with the king. Few contemporaries grasped what had provoked the deep alienation between the two cousins. The prince de Conti would henceforth spend the rest of his days (d. 1776) as an "exile" of sorts from the court. He never fully regained the highly ratcheted political leverage he had exercised before 1756–57.

Who was this dashing prince of the realm, and what personal and religious political concerns shaped his thinking in the mid-1750s when he entered into negotiations with Paul Rabaut, the Reformed pastor of Nîmes? What factors would lead him to treat the Protestants of France in the quixotic way that he did? These questions do not admit of easy answers. The prince was a complex person. Projecting affability and dignity, he could appear the paragon of statesmanship and loyalty. He could speak persuasively and eloquently. At the same time he could be haughty and cruel. He could mock an opponent with ridicule and contempt. Reveling in the art of dissimulation, he could nurture grandiosely subversive schemes. In a word, the prince de Conti could be or do most anything. The prince de Ligne astutely observed: "He is a composite of twenty or thirty men. He is proud, he is affable, ambitious and philosophe, at the same time; frondeur, gourmand, lazy, noble, debauched, the idol and example of good company, not liking bad company except by a spirit of libertinage, but caught up in much self-love."[2] The prince de Conti defied facile descriptions of his character.

Moreover, the prince went to great lengths to keep his own counsel. He rarely vented his personal feelings to confidants who would in turn describe them to others. When he did write about sensitive matters, he did so on occasion with pinpricks or he asked his correspondents to burn his letters. Then again he tried to destroy any evidence that might incriminate him in one scheme or another.

Louis XV, who himself regularly had recourse to secret stratagems in directing his own affairs, appreciated the similar disposition in this talented prince of the blood. Beginning in 1740–41, the king secretly turned to his younger cousin (by seven years) for trusted counsel. Louis XV admired the military daring and quick mind of the prince. He met with his cousin in clandestine sessions, thereby giving Conti extraordinary political influence.

Louis-François de Bourbon, the prince de Conti, was born into a family of nobility and privilege on August 13, 1717. The prince's forebears included Louis II de Bourbon (Grand Condé) and his brother, Armand de Bourbon, the prince de Conti, both major participants in the mid-seventeenth-century Frondes.[3] Conti's father, Louis-Armand II, adjudged avaricious and mentally unstable by some contemporaries, nonetheless provided him ample opportunity to receive a good education at the *collège* Louis-le-Grand. But his mother, the princesse de Conti, disliking his treatment there, withdrew him after a relatively brief stay. The prince was then tutored by the Jesuit preceptor, Antoine du Cerceau. Later he was taught by another Jesuit, Simon de La Tour, who became a principal at Louis-le-Grand and ultimately served as an important confidant and advisor for the prince.

As a youth, Conti enjoyed the financial means to pursue his personal version of pleasure. Sensational anecdotes reveal corners of his

"terrible adolescence," his cruel and ruthless personal behavior and
his libertinage in sexual mores. He shot and killed one of his precep-
tors, Father du Cerceau. Soulavie, who examined papers regarding the
case, indicated that the shooting could have been premeditated, but
the judgments on it were contradictory. Louis Dutens, a great admirer
of Conti, assured his readers the shooting was an accident and that the
prince had become disconsolate about the horrible mishap.[4]

On another occasion, the young prince de Conti and the prince
d'Epinay engaged in a heated altercation, and blows were exchanged.
Apparently to gain revenge, Conti invited the prince d'Epinay to his
residence at the Isle Adam, where a room was especially prepared for
the unsuspecting guest. When the impressionable young man awoke
in the middle of the night, he saw "death masks" illuminated by can-
dles advancing towards him and then receding into the darkness.
D'Epinay became so frightened, he could not speak. He later claimed
he had a bad dream. In reality, the prince de Conti had set up a con-
traption with which he could manipulate the ghoulish display.[5]

The prince's "terrible adolescence" passed, and he married Louise-
Diane de Bourbon-Orléans. Contemporaries recognized a definite
improvement in his demeanor as the years went by, although he did
not forsake sexual libertinage. He was known to be winsome, the
type of person capable of eliciting deep loyalties from those who
knew him well. He combined generosity to the less fortunate with
displays of prodigality for his equals. This led to his frequent need to
find sufficient funds to support his accustomed way of life. According to one anecdote from the 1740s: "The prodigality of the prince de
Conti sometimes reduced him to expedients. One day, his horseman
came to him and said that there was no longer forage for his horses;
he called his intendant, who excused himself by indicating there was
no more money in the treasury and that he could not get credit from
the treasurer. 'All the others refuse credit too,' he added, 'except your
rotisseur.' 'Eh bien,' said the prince, 'then give fattened pullets to
my horses.'"[6] Etienne-François, the duc de Choiseul, later a distinguished foreign minister, believed that Conti's prodigality stemmed
from his libertinage: "The princes of the blood had attained a degree
of debauchery and brutishness almost equal to that of the king. I have
never known a man more prodigal of his substance than the prince de
Conti, who ruined himself with girls — among others, with the Du-

rancy girl."[7] In 1755, Louis XV attempted to rescue his cousin from debts by giving the prince 1.5 million livres to cover them all. Perhaps Monsieur de Paumy's assessment of Conti provides an even-handed summary of prince's disparate qualities: "fierce, generous, a dangerous enemy; a good friend and zealous protector of those for whom he has affection."[8]

For his countrymen the prince's reputation rested not so much upon vagaries of character but upon his well-known daring exploits as a military leader. He became a *maréchal de camp* on June 15, 1734, and a lieutenant general on July 6, 1735. In 1742 he defied Louis XV's ban on princes of the blood taking part in active military service and attached himself to Maillebois' army during the War of the Austrian Succession. The prince's victories in the Piedmont brought him great renown. On July 31, 1744, one diplomat in Paris wrote: "For the last two days they have forgotten in this town that there are other countries in the world besides Piedmont. The only talk is of the brilliant success which the Prince de Conti has had there and which very far surpasses all hopes that had been formed for it." So popular did Conti become among his troops that on one occasion they cheered: "Vive le Roi! Vive le Prince de Conti, le père des soldats et de l'armée." Louis XV offered a toast to the health "de mon cousin le grand Conti."[9]

In a startling reversal, however, the prince's fortunes began to sag. His troop losses in the Italian campaign against the Austrians became known. In 1745 the maréchal de Saxe declared: "The feats of the Prince de Conti in Italy have not gone down very well here. Since his return the officers of his army have arrived and the public is informed that he has fruitlessly lost two-thirds of it. So he is no longer called the invincible Conti."[10]

The maréchal de Saxe entertained his own reasons for scoring the prince. Conti had berated him for not moving his troops during a particular battle. The prince refused to serve under Saxe's command in the Austrian Pays-Bas and returned to Paris. The court sided with the maréchal against Conti, and at Madame de Pompadour's urging, Saxe was appointed the head of the army. Conti complained bitterly to Louis XV but happened to do so when Madame de Pompadour was present. According to Louis Dutens, Madame de Pompadour interrupted their intense conversation: "Do you never lie, Monsieur?"

He responded: "Pardon me, Madame. Sometimes . . . to the ladies."
Then he turned away and continued his discussion with Louis XV.
Troubled by recent events, the prince de Conti quit the army on September 1, 1745.[11]

By this stage in his career, the prince had emerged as a figure of considerable reputation but he had also accumulated a bevy of enemies, including the formidable Madame de Pompadour, against whom he intrigued at court for years to come.

Conti's voracious ambition was not thwarted by these setbacks. Choiseul noticed this, as did Louis XV.[12] The king attempted to feed his cousin's appetite for power by abetting his appointment to the throne of Poland, a position Conti's grandfather had narrowly lost to August II, elector of Saxony, in 1697. The imminent vacancy of this kingship appeared to create a situation into which the prince could pour his considerable energies and talents and in which he might receive another round of acclaim. As the comte de Broglie later (1774) explained to Louis XVI, the origins of the "secret du roi" dated back to 1745.[13] Early that year, several Polish lords came to Paris to apprise Conti of their desire to have him elected king of Poland. Louis XV allowed the prince to listen to these overtures and to take whatever measures were necessary to bring about the election. Because the maréchal de Noailles and d'Argenson were quick to counter the aspirations of the prince de Conti (who did not belong to the Conseil of the king), the prince decided to set up a "secret correspondence" that would allow him to seek election to the Polish throne without members of the government being informed. But another justification for the "secret du roi" also proved persuasive: Conti emphasized "the utility that His Majesty would gain from being informed by several different routes, and by this to be more sure of the truth."[14]

Thus was born a clandestine information-gathering apparatus parallel to the ones that the French diplomatic corps used. Towards 1748, Conti placed the comte des Alleurs at Constantinople, the marquis d'Havrincourt in Sweden, and the chevalier de La Touche at Berlin. The chevalier d'Eon, one of Conti's favorite agents who later donned women's clothing as a matter of course in his religion, provided this perspective on the secret labyrinth of agents: "At the time of the negotiations concerning the aspirations of the Prince de Conti to the throne of Poland and to the hand of the Empress Elizabeth [of

Russia], a secret correspondence had been organized between the King, the Prince, M. Tercier, Count Voronzov, the Chevalier Douglas and myself. M. Monin, the Prince de Conti's secretary, was not only in on the secret but he was also the most active agent in touch with Chevalier Douglas, myself, and M. Tercier, who had complete confidence in him."[15] With Louis XV's support, Conti manipulated this "secret correspondence" to his own advantage.

The prince became a dominant force in developing France's foreign policy through his regular but secret sessions with the king about foreign affairs. In January 1748, the marquis d'Argenson wrote in his journal: "People are always astonished by the intervention of the prince de Conty in the affairs of state. . . . This prince often carries great letter-cases to the king's quarters and works with His Majesty." But what he did with the king and why they met so regularly remained a mystery for many at court. On February 1, 1754, the duc de Luynes observed: "M. the prince de Conty was here; he worked about an hour and one-half with the King. People still do not comprehend what the nature of this work is; for M. the prince de Conty has the portfolio of a minister, and people do not see, however, that he is in charge of anything."[16] If the nation had a chief strategist or "minister" for foreign affairs between 1745 and 1756, it was the prince, who was working sub rosa. He helped create the northern alliance between France and Prussia which the famous "diplomatic revolution" (1756) overthrew.

Louis XV's Favorite, Madame de Pompadour, was chagrined by the prince de Conti's mysterious meetings with the king and she asked the prince why he and Louis XV spent so much time together. Conti resolutely refused to enlighten her, thereby engendering even further rage in the marquise. The comte de Broglie later suggested to Louis XVI that this hostility had a direct bearing on creating her desire to control France's foreign policy:

> Madame de Pompadour, admitted to the court beginning in 1745–46, did not lose time in gaining a baneful and absolute influence there. Although she had been presented by madame the princesse de Conti, from whom the deceased King had demanded this mark of submission, she was not able to procure for her son the friendship of the new favorite; she [Madame de Pompadour] viewed with jealousy the work

of the prince about which the deceased King always left her in the dark, and she did not pardon the prince de Conti. Madame de Pompadour did everything possible to discover what it was, without success. . . .

She felt that inasmuch as she was not a witness of affairs, in putting one of her favorites in the department of foreign affairs, she would only influence these affairs in part. To succeed, she was persuaded that there should be a general revolution in the system of politics in Europe.[17]

For years Madame de Pompadour and the prince de Conti tried to siphon off each other's credit with the king and at court by engaging in backhanded slights, outright insults, and ingenious plots.

When royal ceremony or the king's wishes brought the two into close physical proximity, they sometimes feigned polite conversation or impolitely refused to say a word to each other. On July 10, 1754, the duc de Luynes reported: "M. the prince de Conty ate dinner with the King last night; but he did not have dinner at Madame de Pompadour's. He has no contact with her. They look at each other, that is all."[18] Madame de Pompadour tried to countermand the activities of those individuals whom she suspected to be Conti's agents. For his part Conti in early 1756 attempted to topple Madame de Pompadour from her lofty perch at court. According to the *Mémoires sécrets* by Duclos, the prince de Conti plotted to have Madame de Coslin, with whom he had a close relationship, replace Madame de Pompadour as the king's favorite. Madame de Coslin helped spoil the scheme by asking the king for too many presents and by submitting too readily to his physical desires. Louis XV promptly lost interest in her. For her part, Madame de Pompadour had facilitated Madame de Coslin's undoing. She had arranged that the king read a forged letter that implied that her rival, Madame de Coslin, would require a small fortune ("un million") a year to be kept happy.[19] This was too high a premium even for Louis XV.

The king's dalliance with Coslin reflected his growing fatigue with Madame de Pompadour. Feeling insecure about her position at court, Madame de Pompadour, again according to Duclos, realized that she could not hold power much longer as a mistress and "resolved to make herself into a minister."[20] This desire obviously set her once again on a direct collision course with the prince de Conti, the unofficial first "minister" of the king. Thus one of the prince's major sources of vexation in the mid-1750s issued from his bitter warfare with the king's favorite.

Conti was simultaneously involved with Jansenists and the parlements in religious political controversies that eventually pitted him against Louis XV. These seemingly intractable disputes generally opposed Jesuits and the bishops of France against Jansenists in internecine warfare and Roman Catholics against Protestants in interfaith conflict. Jansenists wanted recognition of their Augustinian theology and practices as fully orthodox; Protestants wanted the right to worship God as they pleased and legitimation of their births, marriages, and deaths. These demands butted up against an allegedly inviolable premise of the monarchy: that Roman Catholicism is the only religion of France.

With deft strokes, Jeffrey Merrick has argued that in the prerevolutionary period, French jurisprudence was based on the premise that the unity of the kingdom resided only in the king, not in the hypothetical sovereignty of a people bound by a social contract. French citizens were subjects of their king. Contemporaries used the words *citizen* and *subject* interchangeably.[21]

The government continued to propagate the legal fiction that all Frenchmen were loyal subjects and Roman Catholics. Malesherbes offered a succinct description: "The status of citizen is attested in France only by certificates of birth, marriage, and death furnished to Catholics by their priests." The sacraments of the Roman Catholic Church, then, were intended to serve as threads binding the kingdom into a social and political whole. Merrick writes: "The Most Christian King, in other words, promoted outward confessional uniformity not only by criminalizing heresy but also by forcing his people to have recourse to the offices of the national Church 'in order to have the prerogatives of citizens of France in their full measure.'"[22]

At mid-century, Jansenist and Protestant demands for toleration could not be easily accommodated to Louis XV's sacramental ideology.[23] For example, if Protestants received civil rights, that concession would destroy the monarchy's basic premise that loyal orthodox Roman Catholics alone were the subjects of His Most Christian Majesty. It was this fiction that Jean-Pierre-François Ripert de Monclar — a jurist from the Parlement of Aix, who was among the promoters of toleration for Protestants — essayed to overthrow. In his controversial work, *Mémoire théologique et politique au sujet des mariages clandestins des protestans* (two editions, 1755, 1756), Monclar wrote: "According to the present jurisprudence of the kingdom, there are no Protestants in France when there are more than three million. These beings, who are claimed to be imaginary, fill the cities, the provinces and the countryside, and the capital of the kingdom alone contains sixty thousand of them. A strange illusion one more time." Monclar was well aware that bishops were "complaining about the profanation of the sacraments by Protestants." He attempted to devise a means whereby the births, marriages, and deaths of the "imaginary" Protestants would possess a minimum legal status and yet the civic implications of the sacraments of the Roman Catholic Church would not be diminished in importance.[24] For *dévot* bishops, this kind of compromise had to be rebuffed on two accounts: it vitiated the monarchy's sacramental ideology; and it implied that parlements had some jurisdiction over the external control of the Church's sacraments—an issue hotly contested in the controversy over the refusal of sacraments to Jansenists.

The prince de Conti's intimate ties to the Jansenist faction in the Parlement of Paris and his willingness to work with Pastor Paul Rabaut for improving the Protestants' legal status in France gave him access to two potential constituencies but created the grounds for genuine discord between himself and his cousin, Louis XV. Quite simply, the prince had befriended groups the king's sacramental ideology could not countenance. As the bishops frequently complained, Jansenists and Protestants systematically defrauded the sacraments.

What the prince de Conti, a Mason, believed personally about religion is difficult to establish. Several of his contemporaries assumed that he was an atheist. The story goes that he once told a priest that he never went to mass. The priest replied that he never offered mass. Conti responded in turn that the priest was the type of man of the cloth he really liked.[25] That he could be advised by both a Jesuit (Simon de La Tour) and a Jansenist lawyer (Adrien Le Paige) is yet another clue that he had few scruples regarding the actual theological issues in the long-standing conflicts between Jesuits and Jansenists. During his dealings with French Protestants, a number of pastors came to believe that the prince was going to convert to Protestantism.[26] At the end of his life he sought neither reconciliation nor solace from the Roman Catholic Church.

The prince de Conti does not appear to have been motivated by an appreciation for the narrowly defined theological distinctives of the Jansenists or the Protestants. What, then, was his interest in them? Undoubtedly, his "generous" spirit, so admired by his partisans, prompted him to want to improve the status of these suffering "outsiders." But once backed into a corner, he quickly refocused his attention on the protection of his own self-interest, often identified with the preservation of his political power and the defense of the rights of his family and those of the princes and peers. As a patron to the Parlement of Paris and as a prince, he attempted to defend the "fundamental laws" of the kingdom which allegedly guaranteed the rights of the parlements of France and those of the princes and peers against perceived royal encroachment.[27]

Jansenists and Huguenots Mutually Seek Freedom of Conscience

Although in the seventeenth century Jansenists obdurately denied they shared either doctrine or political theories with Calvinists, by the middle of the eighteenth century it was clear that both groups advocated the principle that neither the Church nor the state should violate the consciences of an oppressed minority. Jansenists finally realized, as Charles O'Brien has written, "that their predicament in France resembled significantly that of the Huguenots, a small, virtually powerless, and legally prohibited minority."[28]

Jansenists took their name from Cornelius Jansen or Jansenius (1585–1638), a professor of theology at the University of Louvain and bishop of Ypres for a time. In France, Duvergier de Hauranne, the abbé de Saint-Cyran, a close friend of Jansen's, acted as a successful evangelist for the movement in Parisian circles and especially at the convent of Port-Royal des Champs.

Jansen articulated a particular interpretation of Saint Augustine's theology as a nonnegotiable benchmark of Catholic orthodoxy. In his *Augustinus*, published posthumously in 1640, Jansen believed that he was defending the majesty of God against the bogus claims of the sovereignty of human autonomy. He insisted that since Adam's fall, human nature has been thoroughly corrupted by sin. So twisted are human motives, we are not able to perform any pure acts of love.

Only God's efficacious grace can bring about our salvation. God bestows this grace on the elect, for whom alone Christ died. Salvation is dispensed not according to any merits the elect have earned but according to God's own hidden counsel and mercy. This grace given to the predestined is irresistible. Their wills are so transformed, love of God rather than love of self dominates them. The elect act freely, moved spontaneously by their transformed wills to perform acts of charity. Still the elect struggle with concupiscence, which must be patiently overcome through a life of sincere contrition, lengthy penitence, and a careful attendance upon the sacraments. But the more their wills are conformed to the will of God, the more they are inclined to want to do what God wants them to do.[29] It is grace that inspires pure love for God and neighbor.

Jansenists represented a foil to any form of Roman Catholicism that gave "sinners" a principal role in their own salvation or encouraged a wide-ranging participation in the activities and delights of this world—witness Pascal's critique of "diversions." They accused the Jesuits of engaging in reprehensible casuistry and crude worldliness and of advocating the values of classical pagan culture. They also castigated the Jesuits' Molinism, a theology based on Molina's *De concordia liberii arbitrii cum divinae gratiae donis* (1588). He had proposed the theory that "sufficient grace" provides us with all we need to do good, but this good is only accomplished when we act using our free will.[30] God predestines us according to his foreknowledge of what merits we will earn using free choice.

In the Jesuits' eyes, Jansenism resembled unquestionably the predestinarian theology of the despised Protestant heretic, John Calvin. This Jesuit criticism was profound; it was also myopic. Early Jansenists' views on the all-important role of God's grace in salvation and the predestination of the elect mirrored the doctrines of their Augustinian relatives, seventeenth-century Calvinists. But there existed genuine differences: "Jansenism nonetheless remained self-consciously Catholic and profoundly different from Calvinism because, rejecting the assurance afforded the Calvinist by the doctrines of justification by faith and the perseverance of the saints, the typical Jansenist's spiritual vocation remained more anxiously preoccupied with the working out of his individual salvation than that of his Protestant Augustinian cousin."[31] Jansenists viewed themselves as "authentic," if not the best, Catholics; they categorically rejected aspects of Calvin's teachings.

Like Protestants, Jansenists were frequently regarded with suspicion by the monarchy and the papacy. Jansenists' enemies, including the Jesuits, attempted to paint them as crypto-"republicans" who cloaked rebellious attitudes towards the king and the pope with austere piety and devotion.[32] The Crown suspected Jansenists of complicity in the Fronde. In 1653, Pope Innocent X condemned five propositions allegedly drawn from Jansen's *Augustinus* as undermining the Church's doctrine of free will. The condemnation also associated Jansenist theology with the heresy of Calvinism.

In his *Apologie pour les Religieuses de Port-Royal* (1665) the Jansenist leader Antoine Arnauld, who had enlisted Pascal to write *Lettres à un provincial* against the Jesuits, defended resistance to papal condemnations: "One must do all that one can in good conscience for the peace of the Church, and one is absolved from this obligation only if an act which appears in itself to be to the advantage of the Church offends his conscience."[33]

A commitment to the inviolability of conscience emerged as a major component of Jansenist and French Huguenot ideology. In his instructive study of Arnauld's apologetic for the rights of conscience, Jacques Le Brun concludes that Arnauld's arguments resembled those of Protestants more than his denials of this similarity might suggest. Arnaud had maintained that the Jansenist quest for toleration from ecclesiastical authorities who as humans could err was of a totally different order from the campaign of "heretics" whose "error" was to believe "that the Ministers of the Church are not able to make laws obligatory for the conscience." Le Brun observes that although an exact parallelism did not exist between Jansenist and Protestant theories, "one should not purely and simply ignore the comparison, for things were less clear than the declarations of the *religieuses* and Arnauld would lead one to believe."[34]

The Constitution *Unigenitus Dei Filius*

In the last decades of the seventeenth century, few signs indicated that Jansenists had developed an appreciation of French Protestants as suffering "outsiders."[35] For example, when Louis XIV revoked the

Edict of Nantes in 1685, Arnauld, though himself exiled in Brussels, approved the measure. Reformed apologists deeply resented the sustained attack of the Messieurs of Port-Royal.

More generally, Jansenists were concerned about a severe threat to their own well-being. Pasquier Quesnel had broken afresh the silence the papacy had demanded of Jansenists: he published *Réflexions morales sur l'ancien et le nouveau Testament* (1699). This importunity was heightened for the monarchy and the papacy because a powerful churchman, the cardinal de Noailles, the archbishop of Paris, had approved the book when he was serving as bishop of Châlons. On July 13, 1708, Pope Clement XI, who in *Vineam Domini Sabaoth* (July 15, 1705) had condemned the premise that one could reject Jansen's five propositions while keeping "respectful silence" on whether they were indeed found in the *Augustinus*, now condemned Quesnel's *Réflexions morales*.

Urged on by Madame de Maintenon and the Jesuit confessor Père Tellier, the successor to Père de la Chaise, Louis XIV ordered some twenty Jansenist *religieuses* to be deported from Port Royal des Champs on October 29, 1709. In 1711, he commanded that the buildings of this important Jansenist center be destroyed. Louis XIV's anti-Jansenist campaign was in high gear.

Upon the solicitation of the aged monarch, Pope Clement XI on September 8, 1713, signed the constitution *Unigenitus Dei Filius,* which condemned 101 propositions allegedly taken from Quesnel's *Réflexions morales*. This action set off more dissension. Whereas several of the propositions condemned did represent controverted teachings of the Jansenists regarding sin, grace, true penitence, and free will, others were such that even non-Jansenists could approve. Louis XIV sought to have the bull registered by the Parlement of Paris. Lobbied by the archbishop of Paris, this body resisted the king's request. Using a distinction created earlier by Antoine Arnauld, the dissenters often argued that the bull erred not "in fact" (*fait*); it rightfully criticized a number of phrases attributed to Quesnel. Rather, the bull erred "in law" (*droit*), because it also disapproved doctrines that were authentically Augustinian.[36] The Parlement of Paris refused to register the bull, or constitution, until the bishops of France had done so. But the bishops were themselves divided on the bull's merits, 112 ready to accept it while 9 backed Noailles' refusal. Louis XIV was enraged; he had promised Clement XI unanimity of support for the bull. The king tried to extract a unanimous episcopal verdict in favor of it. Following a suggestion by Fénelon, he even contemplated holding a national council. The Parlement of Paris in silence eventually registered the bull (February 17, 1714). But the king died without securing the over-arching unity of support for the controversial constitution. The issue of the acceptance of *Unigenitus* by members of the Jansenist clergy and their followers remained a thorny one for the Roman Catholic Church and the state long after Louis XIV's death in 1715.

On March 5, 1717, four bishops made an appeal that the bull *Unigenitus* be discussed at a general council. Thereafter, other "appellants" to a future ecumenical council joined them in common cause. In 1718, Clement XI retorted by excommunicating about three thousand appellants out of a clergy of perhaps one hundred thousand.

The regency and the papacy expended enormous energy in attempting to quash the efforts of the clerical minority of appellants and their supporters in the Parlement of Paris. Many French bishops had come to believe that the bull was a "rule of faith" and thereafter implied that those who did not yield to the bull's teachings were heretical.[37] However, a royal declaration of March 1730, registered by the Parlement, described the constitution somewhat differently: it was a "law of church and state."[38] This angered the bishops, who rightfully perceived that the designation might provide a warrant for either the king or the Parlement to claim ultimate authority over the external affairs of the Church, including the monitoring of the use of the sacraments.

In the next decades, wrangling over the exact status of the constitution often reflected a bitter power struggle among the Crown, the Parlement, and the bishops. Jansenists found themselves at the center of this storm. In fact, post-*Unigenitus* "Jansenism" took on new multifaceted dimensions that combined theological Jansenism, Gallicanism, and parliamentary constitutionalism. The majority of Jansenists eventually came to advocate Gallicanism, loosely defined as the complete independence of the king from ecclesiastical control in the kingdom's temporal affairs and the rights of the king and the bishops of France to resist encroachments of the papacy in the nation's religious life. As the number of bishops sympathetic to Jansenism diminished, moreover, politically sophisticated Jansenists looked to various barristers of Paris and to the parlements as buffers against alleged papal usurpations of power in France.[39]

By the 1730s, a number of Jansenists who would not accept *Unigenitus* were refused the sacraments of the Eucharist and extreme unction. Despite this ruinous sanction, Jansenists gained a larger following among Parisians. Their popularity was enhanced by astounding miracles that occurred in association with the ministry of Jansenist appellants. In 1725 and more frequently after 1727 this outbreak of miracles seemed to confirm for some contemporaries that God himself was on the side of the persecuted minority. Especially from May 1727, when multiple healings of cancerous tumors, fevers, and blindness took place at the tomb of the pious Jansenist deacon, François de Pâris, in the cemetery of Saint-Médard in Paris, until 1733, the Jansenists attracted throngs of supporters. By an edict of January 27, 1732, an alarmed government closed the cemetery and then in 1733 forbade even private manifestations of convulsionary spirituality. The "convulsionary movement" eventually was discredited and never represented a serious challenge to the bishops and the Crown.[40]

Continued harassment obliged Jansenist authors to ponder more seriously arguments for the inviolability of conscience and against forcing religious conformity upon a minority. As sincere "Catholics," they confronted many difficult issues. Could they create an argument for toleration that did not at the same time promote what was for them the horrific idea that all religious beliefs were equally valid?[41] And could they strengthen their case for resisting the oppressive majority, even if that majority were Roman Catholic?

Unlike Protestant apologists who repaired to other arguments in favor of toleration, Jansenists were fortified by their particular reading of a conciliarist tradition that demanded unanimity of opinion from the faithful of the Church and, at the same time, paradoxically upheld the rights of the minority. A number of Jansenist writers argued that unanimity could not exist if a minority of the truly faithful challenged it. In the present instance this meant that an allegedly corrupted majority supporting the bull *Unigenitus*, including the pope, the ultramontane bishops, and the Jesuits and their allies, could and should be challenged by the authentic defenders of Augustinian Roman Catholicism, the Jansenist minority.

Even before mid-century, it was abundantly clear that Jansenists had enlisted important allies in the parlements. Often influenced by a *parti janséniste* in its midst or by Jansenist lawyers who worked for its members, some magistrates in the Parlement of Paris defended their own form of parliamentary constitutionalism against the king and the ultramontane bishops with elements of the same tradition.[42] But conservative tendencies remained within the Parlement as well.

The Prince de Conti and the Refusal of Sacraments Controversy

The allies faced a painful situation because the laceration caused by the refusal of sacraments controversy was roughly reopened. In the first phase of this new round of the controversy (1749–54), Louis XV largely supported his bishops who wanted to refuse sacraments to Jansenists against his parlements who thought they could and should prevent these refusals.[43] In 1749, Christophe de Beaumont, the archbishop of Paris, promoted a measure according to which a Jansenist who had not acquired a *billet de confession,* acknowledging the bull *Unigenitus,* would be refused the Holy Viaticum. Charles Coffin, former rector of the University of Paris, fell victim of this ruling. In 1750 the Parlement of Paris tended to give moderate support to the Jansenist cause. By 1751, however, the Parlement, influenced by members with Jansenist sympathies, reacted strongly against what it thought was an ultramontane power-grab and staked out its right of jurisdiction over the external affairs of the Church.[44] On April 18, 1752, it claimed for itself the right to assure citizens the opportunity to take the sacraments, whether they were Jansenist or not. In *letters-patentes* of February 22, 1753, the king ordered that all matters having to do with the refusal of sacraments be relegated to his Conseil. The Parlement declined to register these letters. The king then exiled the Grand' Chambre of the Parlement of Paris to Pontoise. The exile lasted from May 9, 1753, to September 4, 1754.

As the chief advisor for Louis XV and coincidentally a principal strategist for the Parlement of Paris, the prince de Conti found himself drawn almost ineluctably towards the vortex of the politicoreligious storm. During the summer of 1753 the prince struggled to patch together an accommodation between the king and the Parlement. The father of Choiseul observed that "the Prince de Conti being the sole intermediary between the king and his parliament, even the ministers are no longer taking a hand in it."⁴⁵

The prince tried to persuade his cousin to recall the Grand' Chambre, but Louis XV was not willing to accede to this advice. He sent other members of the Parlement to Soissons. But finally the king yielded and reinstated the Parlement in September 1754. The prince de Conti received many accolades for his role in bringing about this rapprochement between the Parlement and Louis XV.

In a second phase, September 1754 to March or April 1755, and as the crisis darkened further, the king did an about-face and supported his parlements against the bishops. On October 8, 1754, he promulgated a "law of silence" concerning the subject of *Unigenitus*; it forbade use of such terms as Jansenist and Molinist. Christophe de Beaumont, the outspoken leader of the *dévot* party, broke that silence, sharply criticizing the "law of silence" itself and claiming that the Church alone could administer the sacraments and set forth doctrine. The king exiled him to his country house on December 3, 1754.

The king's inconsistent policies were partially dictated by his desire to have the Parlement approve his borrowing of money. In any case, his "menagements" did not bolster confidence that he could quell the disturbances. In 1755 the royal historiographer Moreau looked back upon the controversy's debilitating effects: "In 1714, it was a matter of knowing whether Father Quesnel had explained the nature and effects of grace well in a very devout and rather boring book. In 1753 it was a matter of knowing whether the king was master in his realm. All authority was compromised, all order was disturbed."⁴⁶ By the 1750s the debate over the constitution *Unigenitus*, a *soi-disant* "religious" document, left some contemporaries with the distinct impression that the monarchy was being shaken to its foundations, that revolt was in the air.

In a third phase, April 1755 through December 1756, the king tried to strike some kind of balance between the parlements and the bishops. At the Assembly of the Clergy of 1755, the bishops found themselves divided regarding what significance they should attach to lack of submission to the bull *Unigenitus*. With Louis XV's permission, they asked for guidance on the matter from the urbane and conciliatory Pope Benedict XIV. In *Ex Omnibus*, a carefully worded encyclical, the pope attempted to carve out a middle path: priests were to warn the dying that, if they were Jansenists, they would be damned; but then again priests, at their own peril, could give the dying the Eucharist.[47]

To Louis XV's utter dismay, the encyclical pleased few magistrates in the Parlement of Paris; nor did it completely satisfy all of the bishops. On December 7, 1756, the Parlement of Paris suppressed the encyclical. Undaunted by criticism, Louis XV decided to force his royal will on the Parlement. On December 10, 1756, he issued an edict, adapted from the encyclical, which not by chance failed to stipulate that *Unigenitus* was a "rule of faith"—an omission that could only please the Parlement and infuriate the bishops. This implied that opponents of the bull *Unigenitus* were not heretics. But what the edict did say angered members of the Parlement and Jansenists. It denied the Parlement the right to enjoin priests to administer the sacraments. Furthermore, the king struck down two chambers of inquests and crippled the Parlement's capacity to function in other ways. Then, in a very strained session at the Palais de Justice on December 13, 1756, the king forced the Parlement to register his edict by using a *lit de justice*.[48] A number of the members of the Parlement promptly abandoned their posts.

As a patron to the Parlement of Paris, the prince de Conti was cut to the quick by the king's actions. From his point of view, Louis XV had once again trampled upon the fundamental laws of the realm by dismissing cavalierly the Parlement's legitimate claim to deal with the sacramental questions at hand. Conti was not alone in being furious. Many of the people of Paris were also partisans of the Parlement. Few if any cries of "Vive le Roi" greeted the royal carriage when it clattered through the streets of Paris to the fateful session on December 13, 1756, at the Palais de Justice.

France's Fundamental Laws

Critics of the prince de Conti claimed that his unbounded hostility had been stirred by Jansenist lawyers. Indeed, the prince had recently become interested in an ideology vigorously propounded by an advisor he had acquired towards 1752–53, the Jansenist Adrien Le Paige. As Daniel Carroll Joynes clarifies, Le Paige had emerged as one of the chief strategists for the Parlement of Paris, which was attempting to "transform itself from a corporate judicial body, visibly dependent upon the monarchy for its authority, into a body endowed with independent legislative and political powers, and constitutionally coequal with the crown."[49] One of the Parlement's tactics was to give itself additional accreditation by inviting the princes and peers to join with it to deliberate weighty matters.[50] According to Le Paige, the princes and peers represented an authority that was as ancient as the king's and the Parlement of Paris had an authority apparently independent of and equal to that of the monarchy. In his *Lettres historiques sur les fonctions essentielles du parlement; sur le droit des pairs, et sur les lois fondamentales du royaume* (1754), Le Paige had collected the tracts by the parliamentary writers of the Fronde and drawn up a lengthy history of the French nation to demonstrate the validity of these claims. The Parlement was portrayed as a deliberative body that, above all else, was the court of the princes and peers. It was the "successor" to and "representative" of the Merovingian assemblies at the Champs de Mars. According to Le Paige, "no edict has the force of law unless . . . examined and registered at the Parlement." The Parlement was not a special court of the monarchy. The princes and peers could join the Parlement to consider critical matters if they so desired. The Parlement was "the reciprocal tie between the Sovereign and the Subjects."[51]

Le Paige's political apologetic for the high authority of the parlements of France and of the princes and peers furnished the prince de Conti with a perspective that had earlier transformed several commands of the king into manifestations of outright tyranny. A jurisdictional debate between competing legal bodies, the Parlement of Paris and the Grand Conseil, had turned acerbic between October 1755 and April 1756. It concerned the allegedly innovative claim of the Grand Conseil that it "had the privilege of judging cases involving its own members."[52] The Parlement of Paris invited the princes and peers to join it as councillors in protest against the claim of the Grand Conseil. Probably worried about the potentially "frondish" implications of this invitation, Louis XV forbade the princes and peers to join the Parlement of Paris.

On February 20, 1756, the duc d'Orléans, in the name of the princes and peers, presented a reclamation, bearing the imprint of the Jansenist Le Paige's thinking, to the king. It was argued therein that the king's interdiction struck a devastating blow against the rights of the peers — rights that "were as old as those of the Monarchy."[53] So angered was Louis XV by the reclamation that he threw it into the fire. Madame de Pompadour was convinced that the prince de Conti had provoked this conflict. But by April 1756, the king had to back away from his support for the Grand Conseil, and the Parlement emerged victorious. Louis XV simply could not dispense with the Parlement's cooperation in registering his financial requests.

The prince de Conti's personal account of this highly emotional dispute reveals his belief that the king had trampled upon the fundamental laws of the nation. The narrative, recorded in a handsome volume, includes an "allegorical" drawing (see frontispiece) apparently created at a later date in which the prince stars as the savior of the nation in a perilous time. The caption for the drawing reads:

> Crime armed by authority tramples underfoot the attributes of justice.
>
> France, weeping, calls upon the help of his Altesse Sérénissime Monseigneur the Prince de Conty.
>
> The Prince, holding in one hand the torch of truth, stops with the other hand Themis [the goddess of justice and prophecy], who was going into exile.[54]

In the background the vacant throne of the king of France is clearly visible. As we shall see, Conti could well envision that very scene, the collapse of the monarchy in political turmoil.

In August 1756, Le Paige also sent a letter to the prince in which he set forth what guidelines allegedly existed in earlier centuries regarding the monarch's use of a *lit de justice*.[55] In bygone years, if a monarch wanted to have a piece of legislation registered by a *lit de justice* at the Parlement, His Majesty did so in consultation with the Parlement and with its approval. The king benefited from the "inestimable advantages" of this kind of consultation. Today, however, the king simply asked the Parlement to acquiesce. The resultant evils were devastating. Le Paige put the matter bluntly: "Today, in a *Lit de justice* all ends in an act of absolute power."[56]

In light of Le Paige's writings and the prince de Conti's own acrid disputes with the king, it can be seen why Louis XV's exploitation of a *lit de justice* some months later, in December 1756, constituted such an affront to the prince's political thinking and personal sensitivities. Not only was Louis XV pressing upon the Parlement of Paris an encyclical that its members with Jansenist sympathies found abhorrent, but the king had done so without any apparent recognition of the Parlement's prerogatives to debate the encyclical's merits and to give its consent if it so chose. The prince's parliamentary constitutionalism, heralding the parlements of France as the repositories and guardians of the "fundamental laws" of the kingdom, clashed directly with Louis XV's allegedly innovative and "despotic" perception of the king's supreme authority to interpret those laws without consultation.[57] Conti was convinced that his own theories captured how the monarchy had functioned in the earliest centuries when kings supposedly upheld the fundamental laws of the realm. The prince's perception of this past, mediated by the Jansenist Le Paige, included its own generous share of mythology.

Believing that Louis XV had exceeded the royal prerogative and had consciously slighted and dishonored him, the prince de Conti angrily spurned his cousin in December 1756. At the time, the king sadly acknowledged that he was losing an irreplaceable advisor— and this, at the height of the political crisis.

In the context of his struggle with an allegedly tyrannical king (1756–57), another issue apparently played on the prince's mind. The ideology of Le Paige that elevated the authority of the parlements and of the princes and peers at the expense of the monarch had roots in the thinking of the frondeurs, who a century earlier had attempted to regain the nobility's "lost" power from the king. The prince de Conti could look back to his forebears, Louis II de Bourbon (Grand Condé) and Armand de Bourbon, the prince de Conti, as leading frondeurs of the seventeenth century. During the frondes of midcentury, a plan by Oliver Cromwell, that English soldiers might join "republican" Huguenots in the area around Bordeaux, was presented to the earlier prince de Conti for his consideration. At first he enthusiastically welcomed the proposal, but, on the advice of the abbé de Cosnac, he ultimately rejected it.[58]

The prince de Conti of our interest may have been prompted by familial remembrances of that earlier prince in his own bout with a "tyrannical" king, or he may have recalled the activities of the Condé. The prince de Ligne observed that Conti wished "to play a role" as a power broker in the kingdom similar to the way the Grand Condé, his frondeur forebear, had exercised authority.

If a reenactment of a Fronde could be mounted, the French Protestants might represent a constituency upon which to rebuild his power base. Or could he not create an independent Protestant republic in the south like the "United Provinces of the Midi" of the 1570s? Would not the English government send military forces to lend support to this righteous cause? Extreme as these ideas might appear, they were certainly not new. Moreover, during the revolt of the princes in 1614–17 and in the 1620s, had not the duc de Rohan and other Catholic nobles, known as the "great malcontents," ignored religious differences and attempted to exploit the Huguenots for political and military purposes? Did not Richelieu complain that Rohan had turned the Huguenots into a "corps of rebellion"?[59] As to the Jansenists, Conti's concern for their cause may have been enhanced by his memory that some of his forebears had belonged to "Jansenist" families.[60]

In the summer of 1755 when the prince de Conti entered into face-to-face negotiations with the Reformed pastor Paul Rabaut, he had not yet experienced his severe falling-out with Louis XV. Rather, the prince was still confident that he exerted significant sway over the thinking and actions of the king, his cousin, and apparently told Rabaut as much. But unbeknown to the prince, forces were in motion elsewhere which would soon further damage his capacities to wield decisive political power.

Madame de Pompadour and the French-Austrian *Rapprochement*

Also in the summer of 1755, the Austrian ambassador George Adam von Starhemberg, who represented Maria Teresa of Austria, looked to the French court to determine which person he should approach about better relations or an outright alliance between Austria and France. He assessed the relative political clout of Madame de Pompadour and of the prince de Conti. With insightful advice from the comte de Kaunitz, Starhemberg concluded that he should approach Madame de Pompadour because her power was recognizably on the ascendant.[61] On September 3, 1755, Starhemberg met with her and her advisor, the abbé de Bernis, in secret at her country house adjacent to Bellevue. These meetings, along with a flattering letter from Maria Teresa, helped convince Madame de Pompadour, now in the throes of validating a newly acquired penchant for piety, that she should labor diligently to put together a Roman Catholic, French-Austrian alliance. Fearful that France might be isolated by agreements between Prussia and England in January 1756, Louis XV also favored this rapprochement with Austria.[62] On May 1, 1756, France and Austria agreed to the first Treaty of Versailles.

The prince de Conti, who had helped establish the earlier alliance between Prussia and France — the one that the diplomatic revolution was overthrowing — found himself "scrupulously excluded from the confidentiality of this negotiation which destroyed in one day his work of twelve years."[63] Only by the spring of 1756 did he begin to discern that a treaty between Austria and France was in the offing. By that time, however, his counsel on foreign affairs was no longer really heeded by Louis XV. Rather, the king and the prince had already squared off to do battle over whether the princes and peers had the right to join the Parlement of Paris to discuss the political crisis of the day. The prince de Conti's anger only intensified as he began to learn that Madame de Pompadour, his old nemesis, had skillfully blocked him from having any effective say about French foreign policy — an area he had treated as his own special preserve. Moreover, Madame de Pompadour had also foiled the prince's scheme to have her replaced by the charming but shallow Madame de Coslin in the favor of Louis XV.

The prince de Conti was capable of quietly retreating to the Isle Adam, his residence. He was also capable of launching a no-holds-barred campaign to recoup his political losses. Thinking himself justified by adherence to a time-honored doctrine of kingship, he chose the latter alternative.

Between late 1755 and the summer of 1757 many people undoubtedly viewed the prince as a loyal servant of the king. But Louis XV and Madame de Pompadour thought otherwise. They suspected that the intemperate prince had plunged into seditious conspiracies — this time, against them. Reports from well-informed spies and their own dealings with the prince only deepened their suspicions. Madame de Pompadour became literally obsessed with the fear that the prince had set his sights on overthrowing not only her but the king as well.

In the summer of 1755, Pastor Paul Rabaut correctly assumed that the prince de Conti, a potential benefactor for the French Protestants, exercised enormous influence over his cousin, the king of France. What Rabaut could not have anticipated was that Conti's political stock would soon drop precipitously. The pastor could not have known that the prince, feeling dishonored and desperate, would concoct an alluring conspiracy in an attempt to exploit the Protestant community as a power base for his own desperate ends.

On the eve of the Seven Years' War, a number of the Protestant pastors, aware of Rabaut's negotiations with the prince de Conti, were anticipating a halcyon era of tranquillity ushered in by their new benefactor's efforts. Rather, a number of them were soon to be swept up in the dangerous maelstrom of the prince de Conti's conspiratorial activity against the king of France, Louis XV.

The "Secret" Negotiations between the Prince de Conti and Pastor Paul Rabaut

✦ ✦ ✦

*Finally, this all seems to be a general crusade of the Catholic party
against the Protestant in Europe, and France is the treasurer of
this crusade.*

An assessment by the marquis d'Argenson,
November 22, 1756

The outbreak of the Seven Years' War created a genuine dilemma
for many French Protestants in the south, severely testing their
loyalty to the monarchy. During the reversal of diplomatic alliances,
the former antagonists England and Prussia agreed to the Westminster Convention in January 1756. These two major Protestant powers
thus formed a "defensive" alliance. In May 1756 France joined Austria
in what appeared to be a Catholic coalition. In their frustration,
some French Protestants needed no prompting to view this conflict
narrowly as a war caused by religious antagonism.

For Huguenots in southern France, this perception of the war
spawned a question that deeply troubled and divided their communities. Should they remain loyal to a Catholic state that persecuted
them, especially when that state was engaged in warfare against Protestant countries? Or should they rebel against the monarchy and seek
help from Protestant governments to do so?

Several governmental officials simply assumed that many Protestants would not be loyal, despite the familiar refrain of Protestant
apologists: Louis XV has no more loyal people than members of the
Reformed churches. Spies gave officials examples of alleged Protestant disloyalty: Protestant pastors were recruiting soldiers for Freder-

ick II; the Prussian king's "emissaries" had possibly attended a synod of pastors; Roman Catholics knowing of Protestants' real feelings taunted them as "Prussians" or "the English"; Protestants were praying for the "glory and the success" of Frederick II, whom they called "the hero"; pastors were circulating a brochure that overestimated the troops at Frederick II's disposal.[1] Thomond wrote to Saint-Florentin that in their assemblies Protestants also sang a song that asked God to grant success to their "dear Liberators," the king of England and his soldiers:

O le dieu fort arbitre de la guerre
Fais triompher les armes d'Angleterre
Donne puissance et victoire à son roy,
Le défenseur de ta divine loy

Puisque c'est lui qui doit rompre la chaîne,
que nous portons dès long tems avec peine;
nous te prions de le favoriser
par ton saint nom, et l'éterniser.

Ferme les yeux et trouble le courage
des meurtriers qui gardent le rivage;
pour empêcher nos chers Libérateurs
de prendre bord pour vaincre nos vainqueurs.[2]

These flat lyrics made it plain to Thomond where the sympathies of some French Protestants lay. With incriminating reports like this circulating during the war, it is no wonder that Huguenots were under suspicion.

Governmental officials, however, often lacked the manpower necessary to suppress Protestant assemblies or seize Reformed pastors. France needed soldiers to fight against its foreign enemies more than to police its Protestant communities in the Cévennes or along the Atlantic coast. The government's vacillation on the Protestant question was partially due to its recognition of this crippling logistical problem.

Higher-echelon governmental figures, such as the comte de Saint-Florentin, the secretary responsible for the affairs of the "Religion Prétendue Réformée," recognized still another issue. In 1756 they began to hear rumors that the prince de Conti might be intriguing with the pastors of the Church of the Desert. Why he was engaged in these exchanges came to haunt the thinking not only of the comte de Saint-Florentin but of Madame de Pompadour and Louis XV himself. They did not believe that Conti's dealings with the Protestants boded well for the king. Fearing the worst, Madame de Pompadour, who despised the prince, industriously sought to discover what kind of coup he was contemplating.

The Prince de Conti and Pastor Paul Rabaut

In 1751, the prince de Conti had received rights to lands in the Cévennes, where the population was overwhelmingly Protestant.[3] How Pastor Paul Rabaut of Nîmes first learned the prince might be sympathetic to Protestant solicitations is difficult to establish. Jean-Louis Le Cointe, an adventuresome soldier friend of Pastor Rabaut's, may have suggested to the pastor that the prince might be willing to defend the Protestant cause. Le Cointe served in Conti's regiment at Paris, considered himself a confidant of the prince, and was a Nîmois.[4]

In any case, in the spring of 1755, Rabaut wrote his closest pastoral colleagues both in France and in Switzerland about his hopes that this prince would serve their cause well. A flurry of correspondence ensued. On April 11, 1755, Rabaut wrote to Conti himself: "If through your auspices, Monseigneur, His Majesty could be instructed of the abuse that is being made of His authority to crush a people which burns with zeal for His service and for His glory, without doubt he would have compassion upon them and would make for them a bearable situation."[5] Rabaut also sent a memoir in which he outlined "nos malheurs" to the prince. He addressed the memoir to an infantry officer [Le Cointe] he knew to be "a very good subject of the King." On May 16, 1755, Rabaut wrote to Monsieur Monin, the prince de Conti's secretary in Paris and a prominent participant in the secret of the king: "You, Sir, who possess such a high sense of beneficence, help us to obtain the proper resolution of our just demands. Your spirit, your erudition, and the confidence with which you are honored by the king and Monseigneur the prince de Conti, put you in a better place than anyone to render successful the most wonderful and useful project there ever was." Also in May 1755, Le Cointe informed

Rabaut that he was going to have a conference with Conti about the Protestant question. On May 29, Rabaut wrote to Antoine Court that this conference might precipitate important negotiations. In early June, Rabaut received two letters from Le Cointe in which he described his meeting with the prince de Conti. Le Cointe indicated that the prince evinced good will and had asked the Protestants to be unified and keep the negotiations an "inviolable secret."[6] On June 11, Rabaut wrote to the prince, noting "that there was a greatness of soul, Monseigneur, of magnanimity, of heroism in the fine project that you have created. If Henry the Great could be instructed about it, he would applaud without doubt the nobility of the views of Your Altesse Sérénissime and the wisdom of the arrangement which it wishes to take. . . . In awaiting, Monseigneur, the time when we might celebrate your virtues and make known our gratitude, I believe that I can assure Your Altesse Sérénissime that it will be easy to observe the secret and keep harmony." Rabaut would write his colleagues but only to give them reason to hope and to dispose them to "our views." He concluded: "Full of confidence in you, Monseigneur, I will await your orders with impatience and I will execute them with as much promptness as fidelity."[7]

The prince de Conti had stipulated three conditions: that the Protestants (1) agree concerning what they wanted; (2) keep their dealings with the prince an "inviolable secret"; and (3) be willing to follow the prince's instructions. Rabaut promptly forwarded these conditions to Antoine Court in a letter dated June 23. On the same day he sent a memoir to the prince de Conti outlining "nos démandes."[8]

Later in June, Le Cointe urged Rabaut to journey to Paris to have face-to-face talks with the prince.[9] Rabaut hesitated to do so. On July 15, he informed his intimate friend Pastor Jean Pradel that he would go only if Pradel approved the venture. He asked for a quick response. He also told Pradel that he had written to Pastor Jean-Louis Gibert regarding these secret negotiations. Then on July 18, Rabaut wrote to Pradel: "I leave this evening, because it is necessary to do so, full of confidence in God and very hopeful that the trip will not be unfruitful."[10] In Paris, Rabaut attended two clandestine meetings with the prince in an abandoned hôtel on the quays of the Seine. The melodrama surrounding these secret talks between an outlawed minister of the Church of the Desert and a mighty prince of the realm was patent. By August 15, Rabaut had returned to Nîmes.

After his face-to-face conversations with the prince de Conti, Rabaut was ebullient. Lofty hopes for the end of oppression run through his correspondence during September and October 1755. On September 12, Rabaut wrote to Court de Gébelin, the son of Antoine Court, regarding his meetings with the prince: "Thanks to the Lord, I had the very best success and everything points to the conclusion that our affair cannot be lost. What an excellent *rapporteur* [the prince de Conti] we have found. He is a close relative of the principal judge [Louis XV], and the one who has the most influence over his thinking and the one with the most dexterity to maneuver him. I had two conferences with this illustrious man, and I was enchanted by all that I saw and heard. He spoke to me with goodness and openness of heart such that I could not help admiring him. He is entering into our troubles and will do everything he can to obtain as favorable a judgment for us as soon as is possible."[11] To Paul Moultou at Geneva, Rabaut gave this optimistic assessment on October 24: "Already the irons are in the fire and if the next development is similar to the happy beginnings, as I think it will be, the Spring will not pass before something very advantageous for us takes place."[12] Rabaut even contemplated bringing his sons back from Switzerland, so confident was he that Protestants would soon live in relative peace. From his own accounts and those of Antoine Court, it seems that the conferences with the prince de Conti had been a splendid success.

The prince de Conti had convinced Rabaut that he was willing to take the appropriate steps that would allow Protestants to worship publicly and bring about changes in their legal status. This is exactly what the pastor had sought, as he wrote in a "note" of August 7, 1755: "After having thought about the expedient to take concerning the subject of public worship, I find none other than the one which I took the liberty of proposing to Your Altesse Sérénissime. It is certain that my constituents would not be satisfied with house worship [*culte domestique*]. . . . It is ridiculous to pretend that there is only one religion in France. It is a notorious fact that Protestantism is believed and professed by a considerable number of His Majesty's subjects. To wish to make them Catholics is to attempt the impossible, as long experience has demonstrated. Is it necessary to deprive them of the exercise of their religion?" Then Rabaut concluded that Protestants must make the nonnegotiable demand for freedom to worship publicly.[13]

The Opposition of the "Messieurs de Paris"

Despite the optimism he expressed to colleagues in Switzerland, Rabaut was aware that the Conti "project" faced real difficulties. Notes in his diary about letters written and received reveal this. Incoming news from Paris was sometimes encouraging, sometimes disturbing. In a letter of September 14, 1755, Le Cointe indicated that the prince was working on "our affair" and still "full of good will." On September 22, Rabaut informed Le Cointe that requested moneys were being sent to the capital. But by September 26, Rabaut had learned that some "Messieurs de Paris" had become incensed upon finding out about the "secret" negotiations with the prince de Conti. In early October 1755, Le Cointe wrote several letters to Rabaut and lamented the rumor being spread in the Guyenne that Conti was "à nôtre tête." More positively, Le Cointe also indicated that the prince wanted a memoir drawn up regarding marriages performed by pastors of the "Desert." Le Cointe believed such a memoir would afford a "pretext" for the prince to speak about "our affair" to the king. In his response to Le Cointe's letters, Rabaut noted that the Messieurs de Paris had leaked the rumor to hamper the negotiations with the prince. Still unperturbed, Rabaut thought he could quash the rumor by means of appropriate letters.[14]

In November and December 1755, Rabaut's outlook became much less sanguine. Concern if not panic had traumatized the Messieurs de Paris regarding the negotiations with Conti. For one thing, they distrusted the Protestant negotiator, Le Cointe. He was too headstrong and given to dangerous and ill-considered plots. Indeed, several pastors from the south shared this negative evaluation. For another, Rabaut, many pastors of the Midi, and Antoine Court wanted the prince de Conti to seek outright freedom of worship for the Protestants; the more socially secure Parisians, however, urged piecemeal tactics, so worried were they about provoking a governmental or Roman Catholic clerical backlash. Conti should ask for the legitimization of the marriages and baptisms performed by Protestant ministers.[15] The Parisians' stance, with its more restricted objectives, received support from influential Protestants at Berne and Zurich. They believed that if complete toleration were granted to French Protestants, then Catholic minorities in their own regions could call for toleration, citing that very example.

The serious division of opinion splitting French Protestant ranks pained Rabaut. This concern surfaces in his diary. Had not the prince de Conti demanded that the Protestants be unified as he approached either the Parlement of Paris or the king? Was he not in fact receiving two sets of contradictory advice, one from Le Cointe and the other from the Messieurs de Paris? Rabaut had good grounds to be anxious, even though he received a letter (dated November 8, 1755) from Pradel, indicating that Conti was still planning to meet with the king to discuss the Protestant question.[16] But the prince understood that all the conditions for his intervention were not being met. The Protestant community was torn apart by disunity. He decided to ask the Protestant pastors for their specific advice regarding what requests he should bring to Louis XV. In a letter dated December 1755, to Antoine Court, Pastor Pradel described what amounted to directives by Conti: "The brothers Blachon from the Vivarais, Paul [Rabaut] and I had the honor to see at N.[îmes] our agent with M.L.P.D.C. [Monsieur le prince du Conti] who told us that this illustrious Prince, our chairman, was of the opinion, that a *requête en plainte* should be addressed to him for which he furnished a minute regarding marriages, baptisms, and worship; that measures should be taken between now and the month of March or April for the holding of a national synod the goal of which would be to establish good communication, perfect concert between all the Protestant churches of the Kingdom."[17]

In December 1755, Pastor Duval (called La Nible), who represented the Bordelais and the Rochellois, joined an effort to heal the breach between the Messieurs de Paris and the pastors of the Midi. Duval despaired that the negotiations between Conti and the Protestants were floundering, but the efforts at conciliation failed.[18] In early January 1756, Rabaut observed in his diary that the Protestant ranks could not agree on a proper strategy. He commented cryptically: "Wrote to M. Debosc the fifth of January 1756. Reasons for my silence. The plan of the memoir demanded by the *rapporteur* [the prince de Conti] and the plan of the one which he sent to us. How much more preferable is the system in question to that of the Messieurs of Paris."[19]

Despite the dissension, the prince de Conti did attempt to speak with Louis XV about the Protestant question. Only shadows of this discussion can be discerned in the Protestants' correspondence. In a letter dated February 1, 1756, Antoine Court and his son Court de Gébelin advised Rabaut that they believed that a national synod should be held (Conti had proposed this), even if the Parisians were going their own way. Moreover, the Courts pointed out: "It appears, however, that the storm in which you are enveloped issues from a higher source than these respectable friends [the Parisians] think." The Courts then cited a letter apparently from Paris which indicated that Conti had encountered difficulties: "A memoir was considered in the presence of the Judge [Louis XV] but all failed due to his son and because the Bishop of Pui, who last year wrote an alluring pastoral letter against the Protestants, proposed to refute the memoir."[20] Presumably, Conti's efforts were countermanded by the dauphin and by an advisor, Lefranc de Pompignan.[21] The letter also included several ominous comments: "No matter what the case, nothing is more pressing than to warn the P[rince] so that he can engage the Judge [Louis XV] to parry the coup with which he is being menaced." The Courts again cited the letter from Paris: "It is to be feared that our hopes are ruined, and that which has brought this about is the reckless enterprise of a man as imprudent as he is great."[22] Apparently, Conti's rash move had come to the attention not only of Protestants in the city but to members of the government.

The Prince de Conti Solicits a Protestant Rebellion

The prince de Conti was fully capable of becoming involved in ill-conceived plots at this juncture, so disturbed was he by the unexpected turn of recent events. Conti's political fortunes were falling into disarray in the early months of the new year. Madame de Pompadour was intent upon wresting the control of France's foreign policy from him and her political strength was growing. On January 13, 1756, d'Argenson commented: "The party of the marquise de Pompadour influences more than ever the government, and the King seems to be submissive to this corps of favorites."[23] The prince de Conti tried to topple her through the Madame de Coslin imbroglio. At the same time, it will be recalled, the prince was engaged in a raging debate with Louis XV regarding the rights of the princes and peers to join the Parlement to consider the growing political crisis. He was convinced not only that Louis XV had violated the "fundamental laws" of the realm but also that he, Conti, was France's potential savior from tyranny.[24]

Believing that the king had betrayed the Parlement of Paris, the princes and peers, and the people of Paris, the prince de Conti opted for a daring and dangerous gambit. He attempted to lure French Protestants into an open rebellion against his cousin, Louis XV.

Between late November 1755 and late January 1756, Conti sent to Rabaut a memoir in which he outlined what he wanted the Protestant representatives to approve at the national synod. He may have met Rabaut in Paris once again to discuss these measures. On November 15, 1755, Pastor Dulthiez wrote to Antoine Court about this projected meeting: "He [the prince de Conti] asked for instructive memoirs regarding the principal demands that the . . . [Protestants] would make in order to obtain a less intolerable situation. M. P [Rabaut] furnished them and the chairman promised him to give him certain general directives in the near future regarding how we should conduct ourselves. . . . M. P. told me in leaving that he was planning to return to the capital at about the same time for these negotiations."[25] Whether Rabaut actually went back to Paris for a second round of conferences with the prince is not known.

In any case, the import of the new directives that the prince de Conti proposed was nothing less than seditious: the Protestants should (1) determine what their total population is; (2) establish how many of their men could bear arms; (3) specify the quantity and quality of the arms that each Protestant family has in its home; (4) draw up a list of the "gens de condition" belonging to the "Religion prétendue réformée"; and (5) note what their capabilities (*facultés*) were. Not only did Conti outline these tasks for the synod, but he also instructed Rabaut what he should say at the synod: "M. Paul Rabaut will open the Synod by a discourse, in which he will prove the antiquity and utility of synods; he will demonstrate the insufficiency and lack of utility of the means Protestants have employed until now for the procurement of the best state; he will insist strongly on the neces-

sity to change the system and to have recourse to the means insinuated in the following memoir; and finally he will conclude with an
emotional exhortation to the members of the synod with the view to
have them promptly embrace these means with enthusiasm."[26] The
prince de Conti was asking French Protestants to rebel against Louis
XV at the very time France was sparring with two Protestant powers, England and Prussia, and Madame de Pompadour was sealing a
"Catholic" alliance with Austria. Moreover, in the memoir noted
above which the government attempted to track down without success, he apparently drafted the specific plans for how the rebellion
was to take place. The prince's demand that Rabaut develop an apologia for the "antiquity and unity of synods" seemed to reflect either
Conti's commitment to Le Paige's conciliar theory or his awareness
that Reformed synods as far back as the sixteenth century had on
occasion opposed royal despotism. Protestants could serve the prince
well in the present circumstances.

Rabaut was genuinely shaken by the prince's *volte-face*. Conti's disarming interest in improving the plight of suffering Protestants had
suddenly been transformed into plans for an armed rebellion against
the king. Rabaut understood only too well that there were Protestants in the south who were from his point of view foolhardy enough
to follow the prince de Conti down the irreversible slide into sedition. Rabaut wrote to Antoine Court and Court de Gébelin on
March 17, 1756, about what had transpired.[27] The Courts' response,
dated March 30, 1756, exhibits both relief and consternation:

> We have just received your letter of the seventeenth of the current
> month. It has relieved us of the very great pain occasioned by your
> silence which made us fear the worst for you in these unfortunate cir-
> cumstances. We enter tenderly into all that you have traversed and
> against which you have resisted with so much generosity and intrepid-
> ity. You will be no doubt disconcerted by the new plans of an enemy
> which is always the same and which in order to persecute the innocent
> continuously takes on new forms and sets in motion the blackest tac-
> tics. What a terrible scheme [it is] that it just designed and whose
> results could have been deadly if you had not been so cherished and
> esteemed as you are. We are even yet trembling: and we shudder that
> there were persons so weak to fall into the trap. May you be able to

bring them back to better principles, to have them open their eyes
regarding their true interests, and to have them retain you with a zeal
and ardor above that which they evidenced when they tried to have
you yield to the Torrent. Thereby, men seduced by the present, and little affirmed in the principles which make them act, let themselves be
lured into extreme actions of which they would never have believed
themselves capable. Happy are they when they have at their head persons who think for them and who, above the capriciousness of events,
never abandon the system which appears to them to be true and the
only natural one. May you soon experience the happy results of your
conduct which is worthy of the greatest praise and which fills us with
admiration.[28]

An important group of Protestants had fallen into the prince de
Conti's "trap," to use the Courts' expression. In addition, they had
apparently attempted to persuade Rabaut to accede to Conti's radical
proposals. Rabaut had rejected their seditious appeal, but now he had
to win these dissidents back to his own "moderate" political stance
and at the same time soothe the potentially wounded pride of a prince
of the realm.

After receiving the prince de Conti's proposals, Rabaut had them
sent to influential Protestants in the merchant cities of Bordeaux and
La Rochelle. According to a later report by Herrenschwand, a spy for
Madame de Pompadour and Louis XV, the Protestants at La Rochelle,
greatly disturbed by their contents, threw the proposals into the fire.
The Bordelais also responded negatively. A group of "notables"
warned that Protestants should cease all commerce with the prince.[29]

With this counsel from La Rochelle and Bordeaux, Rabaut prepared the National Synod (or, in his disguised language, the "Grand
Fair"). Tucked away in the Cévennes, the synod met from May 4 to
May 10, 1756. A reading of the synod's formal statements does not
pierce the tension shrouding its meetings. There is a simple reason:
Rabaut did not take Conti's proposals before the entire synod. But
after the official sessions, he called a private meeting of the pastors
(without their *anciens,* or elders) to debate the prince's proposals. In a
report to Madame de Pompadour, the spy Herrenschwand stated:

> A small number of ministers desired absolutely to give a carte blanche
> to the Prince, and they were willing to be led blindly by him, whatever

were his intentions. Gibert of Saintonge and Roux [the] Minister of Alais with several others were of this opinion; a greater number, at the head of which was Paul Rabaut, were of the opinion that they should follow the ideas of the prince to a certain point, but remain resolved never to contravene the principles of fidelity by which all good citizens ought to be animated for the service of His Majesty and impede the plans of the prince, if they went too far. Finally, the greater number of the pastors decided that the Protestants should break absolutely all direct commerce with the Prince.[30]

It appeared that the radical pastors, ready to follow the prince's directives, had been soundly defeated. Jean-Louis Gibert, a Conti partisan, and Paul Rabaut, the two leaders of the Reformed churches in the south, were once again on opposite sides of a critical issue.

The ministers attending the private session drew up twelve secret articles to summarize their sentiments. Article 1 reads: "We declare . . . that our intention is not, nor ever will be to take up arms, to revolt, or to resist in any manner whatever the will or the laws of our sovereign Louis XV." Article 2 declares: "We promise never to listen to the seditious propositions of the enemies of the state, and if we are able to discover the network of their emissaries, we declare that we will report them to the government." Although most pastors were unprepared to enter fully into the conspiracy of the prince de Conti and were willing to report foreign agents, even the "moderate" pastors would recommend emigration: "But if our supplications and our tears are not able to obtain the revocation of the irksome penal laws against us and a situation which we never deserved, we beg His Majesty to leave us no longer in the cruel necessity of disobeying him despite ourselves and to allow us to go to new climates and to leave our country which we will never have abandoned except to have obtained the liberty to obey the laws of God and to live there, moreover, faithful to those of Louis le bien aimé. Made and given at the National Synod assembled in the Cévennes in the month of May 1756 (Article 12)."[31]

Once again, the ambiguity of the "moderate" Protestants' stance emerges. Whereas they affirmed their desire not to break any of Louis XV's laws, they recognized that they were obliged to do so, given their religious convictions. Moreover, they understood that emigration was "illegal."

Pastor Paul Rabaut was satisfied with what took place at the National Synod—from his point of view, things could have hardly gone better. The "moderate" parties had triumphed at the national level. The temptation to rebellion, so beguilingly proffered by the prince de Conti, had been apparently resisted by the majority. Nonetheless, Rabaut believed that the prince might still serve the Protestant cause if he could be persuaded to pursue a more cautious tactic. On August 23, 1756, Pastor "Chaloux" wrote to Rabaut, thanking him for the news that the prince de Conti had not given up on his plans to help the French Protestants, despite his recent setbacks. "Chaloux" asked if Rabaut would return to Paris with Le Cointe for further negotiations with the prince; "there would be no one in a better situation than you to accomplish this commission."[32] Rabaut had apparently discussed plans for renewed negotiations with the prince in an earlier letter to "Chaloux." Thus Rabaut wanted to continue contacts with the prince but on the pastor's more moderate terms, if that were possible.

The Government and Protestant Activities

Rabaut believed that the majority of his colleagues had thoroughly rejected Conti's plans for a Protestant revolt; governmental officials, however, were not convinced, even as late as the fall of 1757, that the prince had forsaken conspiratorial relations with Protestant pastors.[33] They viewed many French Reformed pastors in the south as promoters of rebellion, entirely capable of aligning themselves with the conniving prince.

The correspondence between the comte de Saint-Florentin, the secretary responsible for the affairs of the "Religion Prétendue Réformée," and governmental officials in the south reflects this perception of the Reformed pastors. It also highlights the ad hoc nature of the policies the government put together when faced by a restive Protestant population.

In January 1756, the duc de Mirepoix replaced the duc de Richelieu as the commander in chief of Languedoc. Mirepoix had just returned from serving as ambassador to England. He attempted to follow a policy of moderation without letting Protestants assume that they enjoyed outright toleration. Religious assemblies began to multiply, but on occasion were suppressed harshly. More generally, Mirepoix wanted to use fines and consultation rather than violence to keep the Protestants in line.[34]

During his first months in the Languedoc, Mirepoix pondered the explosive Protestant question. "Disorders" were becoming more and more numerous. In a letter of February 1, 1756, Saint-Florentin concurred with him that the Protestant pastors were the authors of the "disorders." The secretary suggested that if Mirepoix could gain assurance that Rabaut would leave the kingdom "toujours," the king might be willing to make an agreement with the Protestants.[35] On February 2, 1756, Mirepoix indicated to Saint-Florentin that he had received intelligence reports from Paris regarding the activities of the English in his province and their projects against the city of Cette (AN, TT 441, doc. 187). On February 23, Mirepoix wrote to Saint-Florentin that he had intelligence reports from a Monsieur Boyer, the son of a Reformed minister. The informant described the messenger system linking French Protestants and their correspondents in Switzerland and in England (doc. 194). Boyer indicated that the French contact in England was M. du Cayla, a gentleman from Villeneuve de Berg who had sought refuge in London; in Switzerland, the contact was Antoine Court at Lausanne (doc. 192). Boyer suggested arresting both individuals. For his part, Mirepoix asked Saint-Florentin to acquire an order from the king so that the local Director of the Post at Nîmes could open Protestants' mail (doc. 193). Mirepoix apparently on his own ordered this mail intercepted, thereby eliciting Saint-Florentin's anger.

One of the most alarming reports that made its way to Saint-Florentin in February 1756 came from the spy Lagarde. According to Lagarde, the chevalier de Beauteville at Nîmes had indicated that two English emissaries were traveling from time to time in the Cévennes. The spy reported on his own conversations with the Reformed ministers Cambon, Puech, Latour, and Algre. The first two he characterized as "much more violent than the others, but they are all generally badly intentioned" (doc. 191). Lagarde had seen a letter dated January 17, 1756, in the hands of Algre. In this letter Jean-Louis Gibert observed that all the Protestants to whom he preaches are armed for defense and that he exhorts them to do this to "profit from the circumstances that the war is able to furnish for them to procure the liberty of conscience after which they have been aspiring for so long."

Lagarde indicated that great ferment existed in several quarters of the Cévennes. It was fueled by the pastors Jean Roux, Gabriac, Cambon, Dugas, Merton, Latour and others (ibid.).

The group of Protestants who tried to pressure Paul Rabaut to accede to Conti's seditious proposals early in 1756 probably included the pastors Lagarde named in this report. In fact, Herrenschwand's analysis of the special meeting at the National Synod in May 1756 cited Jean-Louis Gibert and Jean Roux as individuals who were ready to follow the prince de Conti's directives wherever they might lead.[36] On certain important particulars, the reports of the two governmental spies, Lagarde and Herrenschwand, dovetailed.

Although Rabaut rejoiced that the National Synod had been a success, the basic problems confronting the Protestant communities persisted. The patience of the "people" was wearing thin. Both spies and governmental officials reported to Saint-Florentin that many Reformed communities were restive during the summer and early fall of 1756. On June 12, 1756, Saint-Florentin advised Moncan at Montpellier that Louis XV was not at all inclined to tolerate the assemblies of the religionnaires, whose spirit he viewed as seditious. The secretary also stated that undermanned detachments of soldiers should not be used against them. These troops might become "witnesses" to the contravention of the king's laws without the capacity to stop the violations. This sorry happenstance would further embolden the Protestants.[37] Moreover, the subdelegate to the Vivarais received a letter dated July 6, 1756, from a pastor who declared that the Protestants would resist troops who attempted to break up their assemblies.[38]

In early August, one of the worst outbreaks of violence took place when troops did attack a religious assembly at Brissac near Nîmes. The Protestants treated the event as no less than a massacre. Rabaut described it in his diary: "August 8, 1756, an assembly having been convoked between St-Cosme and Marvejol in the Vanage, the detachment from Fond surprised it and fired upon it such that several Protestants were wounded, some of them mortally so."[39] The violence was so severe, it evoked a pained lament from the Protestants: "They [the soldiers] acted towards them [the Protestants] as one would towards ferocious beasts which should be purged from the earth. . . . If they [Protestants] continue to be treated as beasts, can anyone blame them if they look for climates where they will be treated as men?"[40] Once again, the threat of emigration appeared in the context of Protestant desperation.

Saint-Florentin understood that the spirit of revolt among Protestants in the Midi had reached serious proportions. Nonetheless, on October 29, 1756, he wrote Mirepoix about the king's reaction to the events at Brissac: "His Majesty regards it as an essential component of his service, and for the maintenance of good order that you make the effort to go to those places where you know that there will be ferment and a disposition to revolt." Saint-Florentin also indicated that Mirepoix should watch out for emissaries from Frederick II or other foreign powers who might be introduced into the countryside; further, he should chart the maneuvers of English fleets.[41]

Saint-Florentin's worst fears about a potential Protestant rebellion linked to an English invasion were realized when he received a letter from Nîmes:

> The members of the R.P.R., aided by the counsel of proposants and elders of this religion, inform you that the King of England, who has the resolution to favor and uphold the rights of said religion and to render its worship practices public if we wish to join our forces to his own, has determined us to give you a warning, hoping for the clemency of the king that he should treat us as advantageously as possible. Should he not do so, we are determined to favor his [the king of England's] intention, break the bonds of our captivity and uphold our liberty and that of our religion, even at the cost of our lives.
>
> Thus unanimously deliberated
Signed Paul Rabot

The addendum to the letter reads: "If the intentions of the king to not respond to our desires which [response] we hope to see soon, we will take the necessary steps for the defense of our common liberty."[42] Unfortunately, the letter with its patent threat of revolt bears the simple date, 1756, with no month or day given.

Was this piece a forgery rather than an authentic letter? Did crafty conspirators create it to incriminate Protestants in plots they would have never really contemplated? Upon first glance, this explanation of the letter's provenance seems compelling. Paul Rabaut, the alleged signatory, had repudiated the use of violence to bring about the liberation of Protestants as recently as the National Synod in May.

But other issues make the letter's provenance more complex. In August 1756, French governmental officials intercepted another alarming letter. It spoke of a potential English invasion, which seemed to give credence to the threat found in Rabaut's letter. The alleged author was a Catholic prior, Thibaut, prieur d'Auriac de Boursan; its recipient, the duke of Cumberland, George II's son, in London. The contents were unsettling:

> I have received the honor of your letters. I have here one of my colleagues with two gentlemen who ought to leave on the morrow for La Rochelle and Rochefort. We meet every day to discuss the way they might set on fire the military depots of these two cities. I hope that they will have all the success that ought to be hoped for them with the help of the Lord. I am able to assure you that if you are able to disembark two thousand men in the Médoc, we will find fifty thousand Protestants who are ready to take up arms for you and for the dear country. I receive news every two weeks from my colleagues Gilbert and Cousain, who still reside among them in the Cévennes. They keep them under their orders in having them hope that you will soon be in the country. Send as many arms as you are able to send. Here I only fear Messieurs Ferrand et Lavergne, whom I am going to try to get rid of as much as is possible. . . . Henceforth I will sign as Lavergne in case my letters are intercepted, that he might perish. I will be for all my life with respect, your faithful servant,
>
> Signed, Thibaut Prieur D'Auriac de Boursan
>
> I will join you as soon as you arrive. In this area, I only have confidence in the Fauches, who will be able to give us grain if we need it.
>
> To Monseigneur de Cumberland
> at his Louvre in London.[43]

The revelation of this letter caused a sensation in Bordeaux, and the echoes reached the duc de Luynes and others in Paris.[44]

Monsieur de Tourny, intendant of the generality of Bordeaux, and other officials attempted to ascertain whether this letter was a forgery or an authentic communication. On August 23, 1756, Sr. Barret Prévôt was ordered to arrest the prior in Périgord. Barret's instructions included this warning: "It is especially important to observe that being in a countryside inhabited by Protestants who are armed and frequented by the Minister Gibert, one should be continually on his guard, so that the prisoner will not be kidnapped, and that in case one is attacked, no hesitancy should occur in the use of arms by his troops and by his escort."[45] Governmental officers were wary of tangling with Gibert's "armed" Protestants, whom they regarded as a real threat.

Thibaut, prieur d'Auriac, was duly arrested and put into prison in Bordeaux. Lengthy legal proceedings ensued. Eventually, the prior was exculpated of any wrongdoing: handwriting experts concluded that the contested letter to the duke of Cumberland was not written in the prior's own hand. The prior was set free, but the author of the letter was never found. French officials apparently believed that an enemy had tried to incriminate the prior.[46]

Another interpretation of what the letter represented, however, commends itself. The writer noted that he would henceforth use the name Lavergne, apparently another cycle in his informing the duke of Cumberland what name he would use in his next letter. Thus, in the letter before the intercepted one, he probably indicated that he would use the name of the prieur d'Auriac next. The author chose the names of individuals about whose fate he cared little and whose reputations he wanted to compromise. And in fact a suspect named Lavergne was arrested.

In brief, this letter may well have been authentic, partisans of the English in France planning the English invasion of La Rochelle and Rochefort. Two agents, possibly French Protestant émigrés, apparently had a portion of the Huguenot population in the Cévennes under their control, because they stressed their direct contact with potential English liberators. In fact, the spy Lagarde had informed governmental officials earlier in the year that two English emissaries were in the Cévennes.[47]

This perspective gains further credibility from the correspondence of Horace Walpole. His letter of October 14, 1756, to George Montagu contains some fascinating references: "The King of Prussia has sent us over a victory, which is very kind, as we are not likely to get any of our own—not even the secret expedition, which you apprehend, and which I believe still less than I did the invasion—perhaps indeed there may be another port on the coast of France, which we hope to discover, as we did one in the last war. By degrees, and somehow or other, I believe, we shall be fully acquainted with France."[48] Interestingly enough, in 1757 the English chose Rochefort as the site for a descent; it, too, was called the "Secret Expedition." Jean-Louis Ligonier, one of the duke of Cumberland's associates and himself a Huguenot, planned the military operation, which had as one of its goals bringing French Protestants out of France.

If this interpretation is correct, then the letter attributed to Rabaut may not have been a forgery. He may have made the threat to Saint-Florentin, and the English government was indeed planning to invade southern France and to join with French Protestant forces. Whatever the real status of this letter, however, jottings on it afford no indication that Saint-Florentin or others deemed it a forgery: "Written on the propositions that the King of England made to the Protestants to favor the exercise of their Religion."[49] This may explain why the government's interest in monitoring Rabaut's activities became more intense in the last months of the year.

It may also explain why several governmental officials attempted to placate Protestant pastors in the late months of 1756. The same intendant, Jean Baillon, who had earlier ordered Pastor Gibert hanged if captured, proposed to his elusive quarry that if the minister would allow two houses of worship to be destroyed, he, Baillon, would allow others to exist. In a letter of November 8, 1756, Court de Gébelin described this offer to Pastor Jean Royer in La Haye. Gébelin noted that Gibert would "in no wise listen to such a proposal" and that in the meantime the Saintongeois were going in large numbers to their assemblies, which constituted a "phénomène bien surprenant."[50]

The Prince de Conti at Court, Summer 1756

As to the prince de Conti, his influence at court seemed curtailed in the summer of 1756. With the help of his Jansenist advisor, Adrien Le Paige, he gave strategic counsel to members of the Parlement of Paris, encouraging them to resist wartime taxes.[51] More generally, his activities were shadowy. He crafted his letters by pinpricks so that their author would not be recognized. According to an August 5, 1756, report of the Prussian minister plenipotentiary at Paris, Baron Knyphausen, to Frederick II, Conti's political stock at court had sunk low indeed:

Since his arrival here, the Prince de Conti has had several conferences with the King and with the comte d'Argenson which according to rumors have concerned an observation camp which Conti has had the idea of assembling on the Meuse. I have, however, had no reason to believe this conjecture. All indications I have found to the present lead me to believe that the visit of the Prince here has to do with different small affairs which concern the Parlements of the Kingdom and which have to the present passed through the Prince's hands. It is also possible that the Prince, who finds himself extremely forsaken for some time, has spread this rumor expressly with the hope of once again stirring up his courtesans and conserving those who remain faithful but whose number is very small.[52]

Knyphausen believed that Conti felt trapped in a weakened political situation.

Knyphausen's estimation is fairly accurate as an assessment of the prince's actual political power at court. But the prince still enjoyed a sizable following. The duc de Luynes noted that Conti continued to have conferences with Louis XV in September 1756 and that his own audiences attracted "beaucoup de monde, gens de robe, militaires": "Everyone had something going on with him."[53]

The duc de Luynes also observed: "But what ought to be noted are the principles which he entertains and which are the same as those of the Parlement: that the authority of a sovereign ought to be restricted by the laws of the Kingdom, and that it is the Parlement of Paris which is the depository of these laws."[54] De Luynes suspected the prince de Conti, a hero to the Parlement of Paris and to the people of Paris, propounded ideas that were potentially subversive.

Although Madame de Pompadour undoubtedly suspected the same thing, a specific worry gripped her mind: the prince de Conti's dealings with Paul Rabaut and other French Protestant pastors. She wanted Rabaut captured and questioned about his exchanges with the prince. And Madame de Pompadour was used to getting her way.

In September 1756 the duc de Mirepoix in the Languedoc wrestled with a command from Paris to arrest Pastor Rabaut. Mirepoix, who prided himself on having established good relations with the Protestants, balked at the idea. He was engaged in delicate negotiations with Pastor Jean Pradel and several other pastors. He was prepared to refrain from interrupting the meetings of Protestants as frequently, if the pastors would hold them with less noticeable public commotion.[55] These talks were proceeding after Mirepoix had demanded the pastors keep them an "inviolable secret." Mirepoix informed Saint-Florentin that Rabaut was the most respected pastor among the *religionnaires* and that he could not predict what would happen if the minister were seized. Mirepoix was certain, however, that this act would destroy his own credibility with the Protestants. Nonetheless, he would await new orders from Saint-Florentin and from Madame de Pompadour. He declared: "However, if madame de Pompadour persists in wanting it [Rabaut's arrest], I would do all that is feasible to bring it about" (AN, TT 441, doc. 181).

Mirepoix set about to discover what contacts Paul Rabaut had established with the prince de Conti. In a letter of December 13, 1756, he explained to Saint-Florentin how he had proceeded in this sensitive research. Mirepoix had asked M. Caveirac, who was esteemed by the Protestants, to talk with Pastor Rabaut. Caveirac was to inquire if Rabaut had made a trip to Paris and for what reasons, but Caveirac was not informed by Mirepoix about the government's particular interest here. Mirepoix explained this safeguard: "I had observed not to name the person [the prince de Conti] to M. Caveirac with whom it was suspected that Paul Rabaut had communication." Caveirac was simply to report what Rabaut had told him (doc. 190). Caveirac did as directed and sent the résumé of his conversation with Rabaut to Mirepoix on December 8, 1756 (doc. 189).

According to the report, Caveirac inquired if Rabaut had ever made a trip to Paris. The pastor replied that he had done so about eighteen months ago and that his only motivation was his curiosity to see the capital. Rabaut acknowledged that he spent time with Protestants in the city and that he had tried to gain protection for his wife, who was being harassed at their home. Caveirac summarized Rabaut's explanation: "That his trip had no other kind of motivation, and that he protested before God and with an oath that he had made no engagements with anyone during the trip concerning issues that interested the religionnaires in general" (ibid.). In his cover letter for this report, Mirepoix assured Saint-Florentin that Rabaut had not been in Paris recently, as Madame de Pompadour had suspected, and that the pastor's account was open and honest (doc. 190).

The duc de Mirepoix's agent and the duc himself had been misled by the Protestant pastor. Rabaut had been in Paris in July and August 1755 specifically to speak with the prince de Conti. Later, a correspondent who had carefully observed Mirepoix's interactions with the Protestant pastors suggested to Saint-Florentin that Mirepoix had been too trusting and was duped by them (doc. 268).[56]

Not so Madame de Pompadour and Louis XV. So worrisome had rumors become about French Protestants entering into seditious compacts with English and Prussian agents and with the prince de Conti that Louis XV, in mid-December 1756, issued the following order to the lieutenant of police, Berryer:

> Monsieur Berryer, I order you to see M. Herrenschwand, Grand Judge of the Swiss, as often as it will be necessary in order to be instructed as much as possible concerning the Protestants of my Kingdom, and to report to me alone what you find out.
>
> A Versailles December 11, 1756.
>
> Louis[57]

Berryer's assignment was a carefully guarded secret. Saint-Florentin and other governmental figures (including Mirepoix) apparently had no inkling of what amounted to the lieutenant of police's parallel instructions to gather intelligence about the Protestants. Madame de Pompadour, who saw the specter of the prince de Conti lurking behind even the semblance of Protestant unrest, in all likelihood had a hand in setting up this apparatus. She had little confidence in Saint-Florentin, whom she later described as "without consequence at the Court"; he fulfilled his charge with all the dignity of a "minister who only had to sign [documents]."[58] By contrast, she esteemed Berryer as one of her closest confidants, and she had earlier furnished Herrenschwand political protection.[59]

The Political Crisis of December 1756

In December 1756, one wave of the political crisis in France swelled towards its zenith with the king's *lit de justice*. But Conti, who had served Louis XV as a counselor, was no longer available. Indeed, the antagonism between them had been further exacerbated a month earlier. When the prince had sought to be named the head of the Army of the Rhine, Louis XV, who had "promised" Conti the post, refused to give it to him at the behest of Madame de Pompadour.[60] Conti fumed. He complained with rancor about the evil (*mal*) the king was doing to him. Through Nicolas Monin, a confidant, Conti turned over most of his dossiers regarding the "king's secret" to Jean-Pierre Tercier at Fontainebleau. On November 9, 1756, an angry Louis XV wrote to Tercier: "Because I did not give to him the command of the army which will probably assemble on the Rhine, he said that he had been dishonored. It is a strange word that people presently are putting forward and which infinitely shocks me. Perhaps he will draw in his horns; what is certain is that I will receive him, but that I will not go ahead of him especially after the letters he has written. These are his affairs, and he will only bring trouble back on himself, if God be pleased."[61] Moreover, in early December the prince de Conti moved out of his apartment at Versailles, declaring that he would never return. The rumor circulated that the king had given all Conti's memoirs back to him.[62] Then again, Louis XV and Madame de Pompadour suspected him of outright betrayal and had set up a secret intelligence-gathering operation to determine what the nature of his treachery might be.

The papers of Adrien Le Paige provide additional insights into what the "dishonored" prince was thinking and experiencing during the critical month. On December 9, 1756, Le Paige begged, flattered, and cajoled the prince de Conti in an attempt to have him forget the "unjust" wrongs he had suffered and to come to the aid of his besieged cousin and "to save the country." Le Paige viewed the political crisis of late 1756 as similar to the one that troubled Henry III's reign. He urged the prince to swallow his bitterness. Did the prince not recall the pathetic words of Louis XV: "If you abandon me, M. the Prince de Conti! If you do, I will carry on, even though understanding that I will act in desperation and that I go from bad to worse."[63] Here we can sense how much the king depended upon the prince's counsel.

Conti did not accede to Louis XV's anguished appeals. D'Argenson tells us of Louis XV's promulgation of the *lit de justice* of December 13, 1756: "They say that at the *lit de justice* M. the Prince de Conti complained bitterly when the chancellor asked him about it, and that the King heard him, and looked at him with eyes of anger. Here we are, then, completely at loggerheads with the King, and a chief completely ready to participate in the movement of resistance and revolt which could follow."[64] D'Argenson did not fully grasp the extent to which Conti had been ready to launch a revolt earlier in the year. The prince had turned his intervention on behalf of civil rights for French Protestants into an appeal for an armed rebellion against his cousin, Louis XV.

But would the prince de Conti's traumatic break with Louis XV give him fresh resolve to resurrect those plans? And what role were French Protestants in the south playing in any new schemes dreamed up by this daring prince? These questions apparently churned in the minds of the lieutenant of police, Berryer, and Madame de Pompadour as the dark days of December 1756 finally ebbed away.

The next month, on January 5, 1757, a servant named Damiens, well known to many of the prince de Conti's associates, stabbed Louis XV.

The Prince de Conti
"Embroiled" in Damiens' Attempt
on the Life of Louis XV

✣ ✣ ✣

Concerning news from Paris having to do with an alleged insurrec-
tion by the people led by the prince de Conti, I am persuaded that
the rumor is absolutely false and destitute of any foundation.

From a letter by Frederick II, January 25, 1757

A deep darkness had already settled, shrouding the countryside
on that late afternoon. The cold was bitter sharp, the kind that
penetrates to the bone. At 5:45 P.M., Louis XV was just about to board
his coach after he had visited his daughter, Madame Victoire, when
a cloaked figure somehow pushed his way through the king's guards.
He grabbed Louis XV by the shoulder with one arm, and then with
his free hand he proceeded to drive a knife into the side of his royal
victim. In stabbing the king of France, Robert-François Damiens, a
domestic servant whose motives seemed perfidiously obscure, suddenly gained forced entry into the ranks of the Ravaillacs and the
Cléments as one of France's most infamous assassins.

Reckoned as a "monstrous" deed by contemporaries, Damiens'
stabbing of Louis XV on January 5, 1757, occurred at a somber moment
for the monarchy. Sinister rumors about an uprising of the people
of Paris circulated in December 1756 and January 1757. In his memoirs
for December 23, 1756, the marquis d'Argenson commented: "In fact,
all this announces to us some kind of revolt. . . . All the people have
become partisans of the Parlements: they see in them the only remedy for their vexations; they have a hatred for priests. Thus it is feared
that at Paris Jesuits and priests will be massacred one of these days."

Lamented the barrister Edmond Barbier, "[We] are in very critical circumstances."[1]

Sensational rumors specifically pinpointed the prince de Conti as an agitator fomenting rebellion among the people of Paris and Protestants in the Languedoc. One of these rumors made a fleet and sinuous passage across foreign borders to Frederick II in Germany. Frederick II categorically rejected the news that the prince de Conti had attempted to provoke an insurrection in Paris.[2] At Paris itself, a *mauvais discours* reported to the police on March 1, 1757, indicated that Sieur Le Blanc, who lived at rue de la Croix des Petits Champs, had declaimed before and after the king's *lit de justice* of December 13, 1756, that the king had acted poorly by "not following the counsels of the prince de Conti"; rumor had it, rather, that he had exiled the prince. The prince would do well to wait in the Languedoc, where there were malcontents ready to take his side.[3] Damiens' fateful blow fell when conspiratorial gossip was rife. Not insignificantly, strands of this gossip conveyed ominous information about the seditious intentions of the prince de Conti.

Louis XV's wound was not mortal. Although there was not the same surge of emotion and prayers expended for the king when he was ill at Metz in 1744, a wave of sympathy did affect segments of the populace. "The consternation was general in Paris," wrote Barbier. "Few there were who did not shed tears."[4] Even Louis' most severe critics recognized that spewing invective against the king, common before the assassination attempt, might not be prudent when Damiens' potential coconspirators were being sought. Nonetheless, in early 1757 numerous placards bearing sinister complaints against the king adorned Paris. In late January, a man was arrested in the capital for having posted an *affiche* that blandished this grim triplet:

> lit de justice a Paris
> lit de justice a Versailles.
> lit de justice a St-Denis.[5]

The *affiche* implied that Louis XV might yet be dispatched to a tomb owing to his oppressive actions against the Parlement de Paris.

On January 19, 1757, Saint-Priest wrote to Saint-Florentin that the day before, M. de Mirepoix had received an anonymous letter in which each government official, M. de Mirepoix, M. de Moncan, and Saint-Priest, was threatened with assassination. Saint-Priest took the threat seriously and linked it to the attempt on the king's life. He also worried about the restlessness of certain Protestants.

Few contemporaries could believe that Damiens acted alone in his attempt to "touch" Louis XV on January 5, 1757. The supposition that had currency was that a "domestique" could not have conceived a plan for regicide.[6] Thus, the trial of Damiens was directed not so much at determining his guilt, that being assumed by his judges; rather, it centered on the perplexing task of ferreting out his accomplices. This assignment was largely frustrated because the suspect obstinately refused to admit that any coconspirators existed.[7] Moreover, promising leads in the case almost inevitably turned out to be hearsay and rumor. To complicate matters further, the judges seemed determined to hobble the inquiry: when leads pointed in their own direction or towards their friends, they quashed the investigation.

For Damiens' judges, Louis XV had appointed "loyal" presidents and councillors of what remained of the Grand' Chambre, several honorary councillors, and the princes and peers. Given this selection, Conti, a prince, found himself included.

Conti played the part of a sincere and untiring judge to the hilt. For example, on February 19, 1757, he urged his colleagues to investigate Damiens' potential contacts with Jesuits in Flanders: "Remember that the judges would have terrible remorse if the criminal, at the point of death or during torture, reproached their inaction by indicating accomplices in an area where reason alone was saying to look for them. I would succumb to deep grief into which another assassination would take me, born of a principle I would have left unrevealed and still existing."[8] By a vote of 45 to 21, the judges decided not to seek information in Flanders. Stung by this defeat, Conti declared that his attachment to the person of the king and his concern for the tranquillity of the state had prompted him to make the proposal. Moreover, he still believed that his opinion had been right.

In other instances the prince demonstrated his willingness to follow evidence where it might lead. He acted as a gadfly, often irritating other judges by his pesky and time-consuming motions. Charles Collé cited Conti's disputes with several colleagues as a sign that three judges at least, Messieurs Maupeou, Severt, and Pasquier, were "slaves of the court"; they allegedly allowed only evidence approved by the king to become public. Collé also indicated that people were irritated that the judges did not approve Conti's suggestion about Flanders.[9] On February 25, 1757, Conti declared that if a single doubt remained, he would inherit "a most bitter life in the constant terror of witnessing another offshoot of a conspiracy which could be real."[10]

Nonetheless, Conti's magnificent histrionics during the trial earned him mixed reviews. Pasquier, who had received criticism from the prince, reportedly complained that Conti "spread trouble all around" during the proceedings and that his Jansenist lawyers had "stoked the fire" in his "loins."[11] More generally, however, Conti garnered plaudits from an appreciative public. As the trial drew to an end, the *Gazette d'Amsterdam* (March 25, 1757) offered this fulsome praise for the prince:

> Never has a law case merited more attention than this one of the miserable Damiens. Thus it should be investigated and pursued with all possible exactitude and activity. The prince de Conti, whose superior talents in war are so well known, evidences in this affair the greatest knowledge of the laws, applying them with the greatest justice, concerns himself with the smallest details, and neglects no circumstance which might help discover the accomplices. Nothing escapes his sagacity. In all the meetings he has spoken with this noble and vigorous eloquence which the Roman Senate admired in Caesar . . . , he rendered with the greatest force the sentiments of love of all French hearts for their Monarch; and it is in his own heart that he finds these tender sentiments.[12]

If anyone had shown his devotion to the king during the trial, if anyone had been zealous to discover Damiens' coconspirators, it was the prince de Conti—or so a current of public opinion firmly believed.

Conti's zeal, of course, had an ironic underside, one not visible to many of his contemporaries. In the previous year, he had conspired against his cousin, the king: he attempted to raise the French Protestants in armed revolt. Late in the year (November 1756) he declared that the king had dishonored him by not giving him a military command. In the same month he surrendered much of his control of the "secret du roi." By the critical month of December 1756, the prince was at loggerheads with the king over his *lit de justice* directed at the

Parlement of Paris. According to d'Argenson, he seemed "ready to participate in the movement of resistance and revolt which could follow."

For his part, the month before the assassination attempt Louis XV secretly ordered the lieutenant of police, Berryer, to monitor the prince de Conti's relations with French Protestants. Moreover, on December 24, 1756, he indicated to the comte de Broglie that "it is he [Conti] who spurns me because I said to him that I had not put him in command of an army which is assembling on the Rhine. I believed that I am the master of my own choice; too bad for him [*tant pis pour lui*]."[13] The powerful cousins, Louis XV and the prince de Conti, then, had experienced a severe falling-out just before the assassination took place. The irony, if not the hypocrisy, of Conti's professions of loyalty to the king and concern for the state's tranquillity at Damiens' trial is conspicuous.

Dale Van Kley observed that those judges who wanted to see the conspiracy emanate from Jesuit sources faced a particular difficulty: "For no matter how far they cast their bait in a Jesuitical and devout direction, the bobbers floated perversely back toward the parlementary-Jansenist boat." Indeed, the captain of this boat was the prince. Van Kley notes that Marc-René, the marquis de Montalembert, for a time considered a suspect as a potential conspirator with Damiens, had been a protégé of the prince and captain of his guards. Only Conti's intervention in a session on February 12, 1757, helped the parlementary lawyer Jean-Baptiste Le Gouvé escape arrest. Le Gouvé, also a member of Conti's entourage, was reported to have said that France was in need of a "bloodletting" and that the race of the Bourbons should be "entirely destroyed."[14] Under torture Damiens was asked "who had induced him to commit his crime." He cried out, "C'est Gautier."[15] Dominique Gautier, "intendant" of the marquis Le Maistre de Ferrières, had allegedly proposed to Damiens back in 1753 the idea of "touching" or "hitting" the king. Gautier, who also had connections with the prince de Conti, spent a year in prison. Conti arranged that M. Zalusky, "grand référendaire de Pologne" and a family friend, would not have to make a formal deposition regarding the "conspiracies" against the life of the king revealed to him by an elderly priest named La Chapelle. Under questioning, the priest claimed that he had heard about these conspiracies eleven years earlier and that they compromised foreign powers. Upon Conti's urging, the judges did not pursue the matter.[16]

One of the persons the investigators quite reasonably should have questioned, but did not, was the Jesuit Simon de La Tour. A former principal of the *collège* Louis-le-Grand, de La Tour had known Damiens for years and had communicated with him as recently as 1755 or 1756.[17] An intimate friend of the prince's and his preceptor, de La Tour served as one of his most trusted advisors. Not only did he act as the procureur général des missions étrangères of the Jesuits, but with the prince he had directed the "secret du roi."[18] Whether by pure chance or by a genuinely incriminating pattern, many of Conti's associates seemed to know Damiens or to have heard rumors about conspiracies against the king's life.

At the same time the trial was unfolding, police in Paris collected *mauvais discours* from the people of the streets. These Parisians had scooped up their fair share of tantalizing tidbits about conspiracies. Several of these rumors, like the one that reached the ears of Frederick II, directly implicated Conti as instigating a potential insurrection at Paris and identified Protestants in the south as rebellious subjects. A certain Sieur Le Blanc, as noted earlier, reportedly said that the prince should wait in the Languedoc, where discontented people would not fail to take his side. A certain Chaumont reportedly declared that "His Majesty was the usurper of a crown . . . that the Protestants take arms and join enemies to dethrone the King and that if such a project had taken place the people would be then a thousand times more happy."[19] This latter discourse hinted at a missed coup in which French Protestants would have toppled Louis XV from the throne with the help of the nation's enemies.

Did the prince de Conti actually try to provoke an insurrection of the people of Paris and discontented Protestants of the Languedoc in December 1756 and January 1757? Did Conti have any part in planning the assassination of Louis XV? Had not the archbishop of Paris, Christophe de Beaumont, bluntly attributed Damiens' attack to "treason and a premeditated design in the palace"? Among the major figures of the king's household, the voraciously ambitious prince de Conti did embody a choice candidate who could imagine the unimaginable: angry and hurt, he plunged into a rebellious state of mind; disgraced and yet self-righteous, he had an ideology that could conceivably justify a dramatic act. He regarded Louis XV as a tyrant who had trampled the "fundamental laws" of the kingdom. The prince grandiosely deemed himself the savior of the people of Paris and a hero to the Parlement of Paris. Moreover, he had entertained aspirations to be a king (the throne of Poland). He knew that if Louis XV were removed, Madame de Pompadour, whom he roundly detested, would instantly lose all political power. What could generate more delicious satisfaction than that? No piece of evidence, however, has emerged to demonstrate conclusively that Damiens was in fact hired by the prince de Conti to assassinate the king.

And yet, and yet. Suspicions about his involvement with Damiens ran deep among the king's closest intimates. Conti knew this. He specifically complained to Le Cointe that the king regarded his name as blackened and that he had been "embroiled" in the Damiens affair.[20] On the eve of the trial, Madame de Pompadour and Berryer already suspected him of open sedition with French Protestants. There is good reason to suppose that they also thought him the potential mastermind behind the assassination attempt.

The suspicions Madame de Pompadour, Berryer, and the king maintained about Conti even during Damiens' trial may explain why they did not press the judges to find out who the "scélérat's" accomplices were. Louis XV could not risk allowing the judges to discover that the suspected conspiracy may have issued from the palace. Damiens at one time had claimed this was the conspiracy's place of origin. Several contemporaries observed that the Crown used Berryer to pursue its own investigation, whereas it rushed the judges in the more formal trial to come to their verdict.[21] By the rules of the game, the judges apparently could not conclude that someone of high station had orchestrated the plot. Damiens had to be a loner, even if one whose ferocious and stubborn mindset few could grasp. By a priori definition, he could not be an agent of either a faction of nobles or a foreign power. If it were proven that a noble like the prince de Conti, for example, had tried to kill Louis XV, this could only showcase the frailty of the king's rule.

In his *Mémoires historiques*, Soulavie remarked on the court's fettering of the judges' inquiry: "The more one studies the documents of the trial of the parricide of Damiens, which the government has allowed to be published, the more one finds that the court of France bound the hands of the judges and did not permit them to have the necessary formalities to punish this attack and to uncover its sources."[22] Other Frenchmen came to the same conclusion. On March 10, 1757, the duc de Luynes indicated that Conti himself had impeded the inquiry by causing useless multiplication of sessions; nonetheless, wrote the duc, the king was evidencing "the same disposition to keep his distance from the prince de Conti, but the prince is no less occupied with the project for which he is duly under suspicion."[23]

The trial ended with the predictable judgment: Damiens should be put to death. With his horrific execution on March 28, 1757, the only sure source of information about potential conspirators was ushered into eternity.[24]

Intelligence Reports on Conti and French Protestants

Lieutenant of police Berryer and Madame de Pompadour apparently could not establish with certitude Conti's involvement in the assassination attempt, although they suspected this. On February 7, 1757, the duc de Luynes claimed that Madame de Pompadour understood that the king now "feared and hated" the prince. In addition, the abbé de Bernis, one of her confidants, undoubtedly echoed her sentiments when he declared the next year that the prince de Conti's reputation would probably never heal owing to a "violent suspicion."[25]

Berryer and Madame de Pompadour, however, did not give up their attempt to monitor Conti's dealings with French Protestants. In December 1756, Louis XV had secretly ordered Berryer to consult Herrenschwand, Grand Juge des Suisses, to whatever extent necessary to be informed of "everything" regarding the activities of French Protestants. As the king put it, Berryer was to report "à moi seul." Madame de Pompadour in all probability approved, if not suggested, this measure because she was convinced that the prince de Conti and Protestants were engaged in sedition. Berryer did her bidding, spying equally upon both her friends and her enemies—as the abbé de Bernis, one of her "creatures," complained. As for Herrenschwand, he benefited from her political protection.

Berryer and Herrenschwand pursued their covert assignments with due diligence. In the early months of 1757, Herrenschwand scored a coup. With his own military and Protestant credentials to flaunt, the spy ingratiated himself with Jean-Louis Le Cointe, the Protestant representative in Paris. It was Le Cointe, the organizer, who had arranged for meetings between Pastor Paul Rabaut and the prince de Conti in July 1755. It was Le Cointe, the reckless soldier, whom the socially secure Parisian Protestants had feared as a person given to seditious plots in the last months of 1755. It was Le Cointe, the prince's confidant, who, if plied well, might speak too freely about Conti's suspected machinations. Whatever his stealthy methods, Herrenschwand persuaded the voluble Le Cointe to talk.

Once the informer had elicited conversations from Le Cointe, he relayed their contents to Berryer, who recorded them in a meticulous hand in a small private notebook. The contents of his notebook, then, reflect either Herrenschwand's accounts of conversations between the prince de Conti and Le Cointe as retold by Le Cointe or accounts of Le Cointe's own conversations with Herrenschwand. Although disjointedly presented, Berryer's notes crack open an extraordinary aperture into the thoughts of the prince de Conti about French Protestants and the monarchy.[26]

On April 4, 1757, Berryer received this information from Herrenschwand. Three weeks earlier the prince de Conti had told Le Cointe that he intended to interest the Parlement of Paris in the Protestants' cause when its session began—an effort known to Paul Rabaut and for which the pastor rejoiced (BN, F.F. 10,628, fol. 75r). Le Cointe met with the prince de Conti almost daily. They continued to entertain "relations" with the Protestants of the Languedoc but did not keep other Protestants informed of their projects. Herrenschwand wanted authorization to make a trip into the Languedoc to uncover the exact nature of the relations between the Protestants and Conti.

On April 26, 1757, Berryer entered another report from Herrenschwand. Both the prince and Le Cointe complained that their mail was being opened (fol. 72r). They determined to use couriers as well as a code. The Protestants participating in their correspondence were from the Haut- and Bas-Languedoc and from Hautes- and Basses-Cévennes. The prince was intent upon enlisting the Rochellois in this correspondence, but these Protestants had so far refused. At the beginning of 1757, English agents had been in the Cévennes, but the Protestants would not listen to them or deal with them.

The informer Herrenschwand had tried to tell Le Cointe that there were not enough Protestants in France to make others fear them. Le Cointe responded that before four or five years, fifty thousand young men would be ready to bear arms for the Protestant cause. These young persons understood that they had no civil rights because they were the issue of Protestant marriages contracted in the "Desert." Without much difficulty, these Huguenots could be stirred to revolt (fols. 72r–72v). Le Cointe wanted to establish a council in the Languedoc of five or six well-known persons who would watch over matters and communicate with him by means of couriers (fol. 73r).

Berryer's harvest of notes for April 30, 1757, is especially revelatory regarding the prince de Conti's troubled state of mind. Le Cointe asked Herrenschwand: "If the prince de Conti would retire from the Court, and in retiring makes a manifesto to complain about all that had been done to blacken him in the mind of the King and to embroil him in the Damiens affair, what do you think would happen?" (ibid.). Le Cointe would not comment further about this ominous question, but his remarks make plain how worried the prince de Conti had become about being a suspect in the assassination attempt.

Le Cointe indicated that the prince de Conti had said that he would not return to the court as long as Madame de Pompadour remained there (fol. 73v). In addition, the prince had written to Louis XV, observing that he would not come back to the court if the king continued to think Conti had given His Majesty bad counsel.

Le Cointe said he knew a way to thwart all the Protestants' schemes.

And then Berryer recorded an account of this shocking conversation. One day Le Cointe had said to Conti that the people of Paris loved him and regarded him as a defender of the laws. The prince bluntly responded: "It is not uniquely for the people that I act, but also for myself. For the moment that there are no longer any laws, the throne would be for the first occupant, and I have interest that the rights of my family are conserved in their entirety, and that it does not happen as in Turkey where they squeeze out the eyes of those who belong to the royal family" (fol. 73v). The date of this observation is not specified. Conti may have uttered it before Damiens' assassination attempt, because the statement seems to refer to the same political context noted in a remark allegedly made by a domestic (December 31, 1756) regarding the "entire destruction of the Bourbon household."[27] Incredibly enough, Conti envisioned such turmoil in Paris that it might prompt the suspension of laws and precipitate the vacancy of the throne of France. As for the prince, he was planning to act decisively in these events (to assert his dynastic rights as king?). In any case, Conti did not want his family to suffer for "despotic" acts allegedly perpetrated by his cousin, Louis XV.[28]

Berryer's remarkable account continues. Le Cointe indicated that eleven-twelfths of the population of the comté d'Alais and other lands under the jurisdiction of the prince were Protestants. They could revolt under the pretext that the parlements were too weak, and they would demand four deputies in each parlement to determine the privileges that should be given them.[29]

As to the possibility of incriminating Conti in a conspiracy, Le Cointe informed Herrenschwand that the prince did not possess a shred of paper that indicated his bad intentions. Obviously, Conti had destroyed all compromising materials. Le Cointe said that he had often told the prince, "Monseigneur, I know that Your Altesse could think about forming a faction. I would be the first to declare myself against it." Le Cointe may have given this advice after Damiens' attempt and to profess — for Herrenschwand's hearing, at least — his own loyalty to the king.

Conti had confessed to Le Cointe that it would be a chimerical design to form a faction in the kingdom in these circumstances (post-Damiens' assassination attempt?). The prince also said that Louis XV had ordered him to make an extract of the memoirs concerning the Protestants and that His Majesty had very much liked the digest.

Berryer's handwritten account, with its swiftly shifting focus, projects a prince de Conti scheming to regain his political power base. He did not eschew the possibility that a French Protestant revolt might benefit him. Moreover, he was intent on protecting his family's rights, should Louis XV's throne suddenly become vacant. He was still attempting to help French Protestants win their liberties through the parlements. Madame de Pompadour's worst fears, that Conti was continuing to conspire against Louis XV, seemed amply confirmed by Berryer's notes.

Herrenschwand furnished Berryer and Madame de Pompadour with more information about the prince. In this memoir, noted earlier, he detailed the prince de Conti's specific dealings with the Protestants (BN, NAF 1799, fol. 9r).[30] Where it is possible to corroborate his account, from Protestant sources and the reports of other governmental spies, the report is quite reliable.

Herrenschwand noted that the prince de Conti and Pastor Paul Rabaut had held secret meetings in August 1755 and that the prince had later sent a memoir to Rabaut, asking for an assessment of the Protestants' military capacity. In the same memoir Conti had instructed Rabaut about addressing the National Synod so the delegates would follow the prince's plans for rebellion (fols. 10r–10v). The spy indicated that Rabaut was "effrayé" by the idea and forwarded the memoir to Protestants at La Rochelle and Bordeaux who promptly threw it into the fire (fol. 11r). At the National Synod in May 1756, only a few pastors (Gibert, Roux, and others) were prepared to give carte blanche to the prince in his seditious proposals (fols. 11v–12r). Herrenschwand observed that when he was writing his report, three ministers were still corresponding with the prince: two were from the Bas-Languedoc and one from the Hautes-Cévennes (fol. 12r).

Herrenschwand decided to try to track down a copy of the seditious memoir outlining the prince de Conti's specific plans for revolt. If this material evidence were acquired, then Berryer and Madame de Pompadour, the spy's patrons, would have proof in hand to demonstrate the prince's culpability.

On April 11, 1757, Herrenschwand proposed to Berryer that he, Herrenschwand, travel to the south of France and try to ingratiate himself with the Protestants. He asked Berryer to arrange for the liberation of two Protestant galley-slaves. If he could refer to his decisive role in securing this release and if he touted his own credentials as a Protestant, Herrenschwand, Grand Juge des Suisses, hoped that he might win the confidence of the French Protestants in the south and thereafter be made privy to their secrets (fol. 8r).

Berryer forwarded Herrenschwand's request to Madame de Pompadour. She approved it, and remitted 3,500 louis to cover the costs of the spy's voyage (ibid.). And in May 1757, Herrenschwand set off on his espionage mission. On May 24 he reported to Berryer, in a letter written at La Rochelle, that there was hardly any doubt that Conti's memoir was characterized by "mauvaises intentions." He continued: "This Memoir, filled with tricks and suspect information, made on the Religionnaires of this province an impression opposite

to that which had been intended" (fol. 17r). These Protestants did not
hesitate to throw it into the fire.

Herrenschwand reiterated how important it would be to obtain a
copy of the memoir. Moreover, he was quite concerned that the Rochellois described the Protestants of the Saintonge as a "dangerous
people" and indicated that "a blind and misinformed zeal could easily
lead them to forsake their duties; they guard the greater part of the
coasts of this province" (fol. 17v). According to the spy, the Protestants of La Rochelle did not want to have anything to do with them.
The sharp division within the Protestant community was obvious.

The spy then traveled through the Saintonge itself. On June 8,
1757, he recounted his experiences to Berryer in a letter written from
Montauban after he had left the province. In the Saintonge he had
witnessed Protestants meeting regularly on Sunday, marrying, and
baptizing their children. Several of their recently constructed houses
of worship could hold as many as twelve hundred persons (fol. 19r).
Moreover, he had held four conversations with none other than Pastor Jean-Louis Gibert. One had lasted an entire evening. The spy
excoriated the Huguenot as "the author of all these contraventions
against the King's ordinances." Then taking rhetorical flight, Herrenschwand labeled the pastor "the most dangerous and violent man
in the world" (ibid.).

Despite mustering his best arguments, Herrenschwand could not
persuade Pastor Gibert to forsake his rebellious ways—what the spy
called his "pernicious system"—and "agree to imitate the wise submission of the Rochellois." Herrenschwand continued: "I found him resolved and unshakable in his ideas." The spy was disheartened: "This
miserable person even dared to tell me that he would defend them
[houses of worship] and that he was in a position to do so, having
about four thousand well-drilled men who lacked neither chiefs nor
arms; that if, however, against everything he was not successful in his
design, then he would decide to leave the Kingdom with about fifteen thousand religionnaires, that all the arrangements for this departure had been taken beginning at the present [by June 1757] and that
he defied whoever it might be to stop it given the measure by which
it was assured" (fol. 19v). According to Herrenschwand's report, not
only were French Protestants well-prepared to defend their houses of

worship, but there were fallback plans for a massive Protestant emigration from France.

Herrenschwand cajoled Gibert this way and that, attempting to find out about his relationship with Conti and his knowledge of the seditious memoir Conti had sent to Paul Rabaut. Gibert would not admit that he was corresponding with Conti. Finally, he did at least acknowledge that he knew that Monsieur Dugas (a Reformed pastor and a close associate of both Gibert and Rabaut) had received Conti's controversial memoir in Nîmes and had sent copies of it to La Rochelle and to Bordeaux. Herrenschwand later learned from Huguenots in the Saintonge, especially at Cognac, Jarnac, and Jonsac, that "Gibert boasted that he was protected by a powerful prince, without giving his name" (fol. 20r). Obviously, this protector was the prince de Conti. These Huguenot testimonies further convinced Herrenschwand that Pastor Gibert and the prince de Conti had together become traitors.

Other letters from Herrenschwand made their way back to Berryer in Paris. In one, dated June 16, 1757, Herrenschwand explained that he had talked to a minister from Haut-Quercy about the twelve articles approved in the secret session held after the National Synod in 1756 (fol. 22r). In another, dated July 4, 1757, the spy spoke of having met with Paul Rabaut and fourteen ministers and having learned details about Conti's involvement with the Protestants in 1755 and about the way many Protestants had rejected the proposals of the seditious memoir (fols. 23v–24r).

This, however, was the past; Herrenschwand was especially worried about the immediate future. He observed that Pastor Gibert and other dangerous ministers in the Cévennes and in the Saintonge might provide the prince de Conti with a large contingent of armed men:

> If these two men enter into the views of the person in question [Conti], they would be able to furnish him with at least twenty thousand men all provided with arms; foreign help, which it would not be difficult to bring in, would be able to double this number and it would take no more to put all in combustion; I hardly dare say what I think, but there is every reason to believe, that the person in question has

already made attempts on the exterior as he has made in the interior; many reasons make me suspect this; [I hope] God wills that I am mistaken, but it is of the greatest consequence not to lose sight of this affair; of all the objects which should occupy the Government, this one seems to me to merit the most attention. (Fol. 25r)

In one sense, Herrenschwand wrote better than he knew. At the very same time (early July 1757) that he was tracking the prince de Conti's conspiratorial relations with Pastor Gibert in the interior and was suspecting that the prince had also contacted France's foes on the exterior, William Pitt began to make final plans for an English military descent on the city of Rochefort. It was projected that English forces would raze the naval stores there. Pitt also had in mind that the eight thousand troops aboard the huge armada of eighty ships would help spark a Huguenot rebellion. If the rebellion failed, it would go back to England with French Protestants, who if they remained in France would be at great risk.

By July 29, 1757, Herrenschwand had returned to Paris and was asking Berryer for authorization from Louis XV to pursue his mission and for assurances that the galley-slaves would be released (fols. 26r–26v). Moreover, he emphasized that Berryer should not explain to Mirepoix why he had been in Nîmes recently. On August 27, 1757, the spy got at least one of his wishes: Louis XV ordered Berryer to continue (through Herrenschwand) to survey the activities of Protestants in the kingdom and to pay "a particular attention to Paul Rabot and Gibert" (fol. 3r).

In his investigations Herrenschwand thought he had uncovered what several Protestant pastors hoped to gain from their dealings with the prince. The spy asked a minister from the Bas-Languedoc if the prince risked anything in treating with the Protestants. The pastor responded brusquely:

> The Prince risked nothing, that no one could ever prove anything against him, that he had everything in order as much at home as abroad; surprised by the term abroad, [I] wished to pursue the matter further and asked him for explanations regarding this subject, but he evidenced much embarrassment and sensed his imprudence and wished to say nothing more; other ministers seemed to take pride in the fact that sooner or later the prince was going to change religions and in conse-

quence unite all Protestants; finally, there were those who believed that the Prince was working to interest the Parlements in the cause of the Religionnaires and they hoped he would succeed; it also appeared that several ministers in both the Bas-Languedoc and in the Hautes- and Basses-Cévennes flattered themselves in thinking that the Prince would be coming to see them in accordance with the promise which he had made to Paul Rabaut. (Fol. 12v)

What interpretation seems capable of cobbling these diverse accounts into a meaningful perspective on Conti's designs? Conti had persuaded some Protestant ministers that not only would he convert to Protestantism, he would unite Huguenots and create a "Protestant" state within a state, one again encompassing nobles like himself, the middle classes, and peasants. His own lands were densely populated with Protestants. Moreover, he had led some pastors to suppose that he had already secretly allied himself with foreign powers who might provide him with military aid. He was also seeking support from the parlements of France. Conti's "dream" seemed strikingly similar to those of earlier "conspirators" who, like the comte de Linange, had envisioned an English landing between La Rochelle and Rochefort, the creation of a Protestant republic, and a rebellion against the king, who would be replaced by a noble.

Conti's schemes in 1757 had not changed much from what they had been in 1756. He knew well that the Protestants were armed. Their men might serve as troops to support his daring stratagems as he attempted to bolster his own flagging political fortunes.

Herrenschwand could testify firsthand about the extent to which the prince de Conti's partisans were armed: "Moreover, in nearly all the Provinces and especially in the Hautes- and Basses-Cévennes, in the Haut- and Bas-Languedoc and in the Saintonge each Protestant has his arms and in the last Province all the Religionnaires are, according to Pastor Gibert's own words, regimented and in a state to defend themselves" (fol. 12v). As we have seen, Herrenschwand feared that an English invasion could add twenty thousand troops in the field to twenty thousand troops from the French Protestant side; joining these contingents would "put all in combustion." The spy speculated that the tinder was already in place for a conflagration; it lacked only a spark.

And if the rebellion failed and it was impossible for the Huguenots to defend "our re-built churches," Pastor Gibert had a back-up plan. He was going to extricate thousands of Protestants from France. The only possible means to accomplish this daunting task would have been the returning English ships.

The threat of an invasion issuing from a triangular conspiracy of the prince de Conti, French Protestants, and the English, as Herrenschwand's letters and memoirs portended, set the French government on edge in the summer of 1757. Members of the government knew the threat was a real one. Rumors about a huge expedition being assembled in the ports of England made their way to the French court. Where was the expedition headed? What measures could be taken to thwart it? Was it linked to a conspiracy hatched in the fertile mind of the prince de Conti? Would French Protestants welcome invading English soldiers? These questions greatly disturbed the government.

Herrenschwand believed he could foresee where any English armada might proceed: the coastline of the province of Saintonge. He feared that Protestants there had entered into a "criminal" conspiracy. On September 26, 1757, he described his willingness to try to counter these "designs": "The interests which the enemies of the State seem to entertain for this portion of the coasts of the Ocean which touch a Province, whose fidelity I have never dared to confirm with positive assurances, redouble my zeal for the service of the King; I burn with impatience to give proofs of it and I would have believed myself to have failed the most essential duty if I had neglected to inform you of how I am ready to use my best efforts to turn away the criminal designs with which one may have inspired the Protestants of Saintonge" (fol. 39r).

By the time he wrote, however, the huge expedition from England already sailed menacingly off the coast near Rochefort. Herrenschwand's offer "to turn away the criminal designs" he believed foreign powers and the prince de Conti had inspired in the Protestants of Saintonge had come too late. William Pitt had put his own plans in motion. From Pitt's point of view, they were not criminal but shrewd and liberating.

Conti's Potential Agents

Was there in fact a prince de Conti — French Huguenot–English government conspiratorial triangle? Compelling evidence exists that the prince de Conti entered into seditious relations with certain Protestants, especially the firebrand Pastor Gibert. Various Protestants informed Herrenschwand that Gibert had boasted of being protected by a powerful prince at court. Moreover, as we shall see, sworn interrogatories, taken by a lawyer for the French government, indicated that French Huguenots had sent directives to the English government about how a military descent should proceed. A former Huguenot had described the communication system. So the prince did have the capacity to communicate with Holdernesse or Pitt through Pastor Gibert. But was he also in a position to contact these English cabinet ministers more directly? Who would have been his messengers?

To identify and unravel the strands of communication networks in the murky world of secret agents and counteragents is often an elusive quest. Those who knew their way through this particular maze were generally circumspect in covering their tracks. And so also the prince de Conti, master of the spy trade. For years he had used agents and double agents to do his bidding. As chief overseer of the "secret du roi," Conti had set up a parallel network of secret agents which operated independently of the official French diplomatic corps. Although he had remitted the papers of the "secret du roi" to Tercier in November 1756, he knew well how to communicate with those agents who remained loyal to him.[31] As late as the fall of 1757, he had limited access to the system.

Three individuals stand out as potential agents for the prince de Conti in carrying communications to the English government. The first, Louis Dutens, had been born into a French Protestant family in Tours. He decided to emigrate to England as a young man because he saw little future for a Protestant in Catholic France. With the recommendation of the sister of William Pitt, he quickly advanced socially and politically, becoming a diplomat for his adopted country.

In his memoirs, Dutens explained what drove him, a French Protestant, to emigrate: "People often said to me that I am French because I was born in France, but I always contend that being born of French parents who raised me in their religion, I was not able to regard France as my country, because the government itself of this kingdom had for a maxim that there were no Protestants in France, and that is what a minister of internal affairs told me."[32] Dutens said that every man needs a country and thus at the age of fifteen he had decided to emigrate. In conversations with Frederick II and the prince de Conti, both of whom he knew, Dutens found that they agreed that he had been right to do what he did.[33] Conti could well understand why French Protestants would want to leave their native land.

Dutens greatly admired the prince de Conti and extolled him as a dominant personage of his day. He described Conti as "one of the most amiable and greatest men of his age; his figure was perfectly handsome, his air noble and majestic, his features fine and regular. . . . His dignity of mind, the firmness of his character, his courage, and his abilities were so well known throughout all Europe, that it is unnecessary for me to speak of them." On familiar terms with both Conti and Pitt, Dutens could have served as a conduit for messages between them. In his memoirs, he accurately named several of Conti's agents who were involved in the "secret du roi" network.[34] To have been privy to this kind of knowledge, he was in all likelihood an agent himself. In the 1770s, Dutens' name was put forward by Protestants as their choice for the Huguenot community's chief secret representative. They cited among other qualifications the fact that Dutens was on "familiar" terms with the prince de Conti.[35]

A more likely candidate for messenger is an unsavory character named Theobald Taaffe.[36] A native of Dublin and a former member of Parliament in England, Taaffe was undoubtedly one of Conti's agents. Thrown in jail in 1751 for a dispute he had with an English Jew in Paris, Taaffe was quickly released because of his powerful connections. He was not permitted, however, to reassume his post in Parliament. A London police report targeted him as a potential spy for the French. On the other hand, French police suspected he might be a spy for the English. Taaffe, then, had all the trappings of a double agent. He also enjoyed the close friendship and protection of the prince de Conti.

During an interrogatory of November 22, 1758, Taaffe was asked by French police if he had knowledge that the king of England gave, in time of peace, considerable pensions in France. He responded that in time of war pensions dispensed amounted to 600,000 livres, and he reportedly provided specific instructions for identifying English spies at Toulon, Brest, Dunquerque, and Rochefort.[37]

What makes Taaffe even more attractive as a messenger for Conti is this notice from the archives of the Bastille: "When war was declared against the English, he [Taaffe] had been ordered to leave the kingdom, no longer having the permission to remain there. He hid with the prince de Conti. Finally, forced to depart, this prince lent to him his *chaise de poste* for leaving his hôtel and conducted him out of Paris."[38]

But in fact Taaffe gained a reprieve: he was allowed to stay in France. According to another interrogatory, of December 14, 1758, Taaffe claimed that the prince de Conti could attest to his loyalty in France. In the same interrogatory, Taaffe revealed he was receiving intelligence in code from a M. Clevland and a M. Cole in London who had close contacts with the military and the government. These individuals sent letters to the Lammens in Ghent, and the businessmen forwarded the letters to a John Edwards, who in turn sent them to Taaffe's address. Taaffe also revealed that a Mr. Healy of London sent his letters to Taaffe via Holland and signed them simply "W." Taaffe assumed the posture of a loyal citizen by averring that he passed this intelligence on to the maréchal de Belle-Isle.[39]

In the early years of the war, then, Conti could with relative ease have used Taaffe, his own agent, to convey seditious messages to the English government. It would have been relatively simple. Taaffe could send Conti's coded communications back down the same circuit through which he was receiving intelligence from individuals close to the English government and military.

In fact, Taaffe identified Mr. Clevland as the Admiralty secretary. From Taaffe to Clevland, then, Conti would have had a direct line of access to the English government. A member of Parliament, John Clevland reported to Lord George Anson, first Lord of the Admiralty, who in turn reported to William Pitt, a key actor in our story. From time to time, Clevland also attended ministerial meetings. As for Mr. Cole, he was privy to messages sent in code by the English government regarding France.

A third possible contact in England was M. du Cayla. This gentle-

man was specifically named as a French Protestant agent by the informer Boyer.[40] The prince de Conti may have had contact through
M. du Cayla with the English government.

The identification of these three individuals suggests that Conti
had at his disposal agents who could have facilitated direct communication with the English government. Certainly, Herrenschwand
had spoken with a Reformed pastor who was convinced that Conti
had entered into contacts on the exterior. Moreover, we know that
the English secret service received direct intelligence from spies in
the French court. Pitt spoke of having received such a report in July
1757 from one of Holdernesse's "most confidential correspondents"
planted at court.[41]

Was Conti's agent Taaffe weaving tall tales when he claimed that the
English government had dispensed large sums of money to "friendly"
parties in France and had set spies in the countryside during the first
years of the Seven Years' War? Apparently not. English emissaries did
travel through the south from time to time, as French intelligence
sources reported and French Protestant pastors confirmed.

English intentions may have been more hard-fisted than surreptitiously planting agents to gather intelligence. During Damiens' trial
an unnerving tale of an English plot surfaced. Fifteen days after the
assassination attempt, two French captains of the ships *Imbert* and
Duperier presented themselves at the Ministry of Foreign Affairs,
claiming they had information about what had prompted that attempt. They declared that, taken prisoner by the English, they had
escaped and returned to Paris with an Englishman associated with
the central post service in London. According to what they learned
from him, English emissaries and Frenchmen in their pay were pur-
posefully stoking the troubles between Jansenists and Molinists in
the clergy, between the clergy and the Parlement, and between the
party of the king's favorite and the party of the dauphin. According
to the plan, when dissension reached a fever pitch especially in the
royal family, the king was to be assassinated; the dauphin replacing
Louis XV would be inclined to seek peace and would leave a threatened England and Prussia alone.[42] In a strange way the captains' scenario shadowed several recent events.

Soulavie, who reported this testimony, claimed he had acquired it
from the notes of a judge at Damiens' trial. As a group, the judges did

not follow up the French captains' report because they felt there was no way to ascertain its accuracy. If the account were correct, then an English faction may have masterminded the assassination attempt and had a number of Frenchmen in its employ. But the captains' account could have as easily been devoid of any foundation.

Whatever the ultimate goals of Lord Holdernesse's agents in France, Herrenschwand suspected that the prince de Conti had created direct contacts with the exterior—the enemies of France. This perception was relayed to Berryer, who undoubtedly communicated it to Louis XV as he was commanded to do. When a huge English fleet appeared off the coast of Rochefort in September 1757, Herrenschwand's alarmist predictions about a possible military conflagration in the south seemed on the brink of fulfillment. Would there be any way to impede French Protestant forces from welcoming the invading English soldiers?

A few months earlier, William Pitt, the English southern secretary, had made the fateful decision to send this expedition on its way. The planning for it occupied Pitt for several months during the summer of 1757. To its success he was willing to hitch his political star. The secretary launched these sensitive operations at least in part because he, like the prince de Conti, felt genuine compassion for suffering French Protestants. The fallout from Pitt's involvement with the expedition would almost cost Pitt his political career. Now the reach of the Conti conspiracy apparently extended beyond the shores of France to embrace certain members of the English government.

FIVE

William Pitt
and the Secret Expedition

✤ ✤ ✤

*Whoever is in, or whoever is out, I am sure we are undone, both
at home and abroad; at home, by our increasing debt and expenses;
abroad by our ill-luck and incapacity. The King of Prussia, the
only ally we had in the world, is now, I fear, <u>hors de combat</u>. Hanover I look upon to be, by this time, in the same situation with Saxony; the fatal consequence of which is but too obvious. The French
are masters to do what they please in America. <u>We are no longer
a nation. I never saw so dreadful a prospect</u>.*

A letter from the earl of Chesterfield
to Mr. Dayrolles, in the early summer of 1757

On June 29, 1757, William Pitt the Elder once again came to
power. He entered what became one of the most celebrated
ministries in English history: a coalition including the powerful duke
of Newcastle, first Lord of the Treasury and responsible for parliamentary matters; Mr. Legge, Chancellor of the Exchequer; Lord Holdernesse, northern secretary; Pitt, southern secretary; Sir Robert Henley,
Lord Keeper; Lord George Anson, first Lord of the Admiralty; Mr.
Fox, paymaster of the forces; Barrington, at the War Office; Lord Temple, holding the position of Lord Privy Seal and advised by the ever-
astute Lord Hardwicke.

The English domestic and foreign situation was far from auspi-
cious at Pitt's accession to power. A general paralysis gripped the
government. The duke of Newcastle, who had obtained the post of
first Lord of the Treasury in 1754, had watched Fox leave his ministry
and had himself resigned in October 1756. Thereafter followed the

Devonshire administration, which was incapable of handling the crisis of the war effort.[1] In these circumstances, George II asked a recalcitrant Newcastle if he would form a fresh government. Newcastle hesitated to do so unless he could have greater latitude in making appointments. Angered by this stubborn stance, George II declared: "I shall see which is King of this Country, the Duke of Newcastle or myself."[2] Ultimately, a compromise of sorts was worked out with Newcastle. It included the headstrong but popular Pitt in a coalition. Only slightly chastened and certainly unbowed, Newcastle agreed to work with Pitt, his former political opponent, for whom he had a certain awe. Despite his personal distaste for Pitt, George II was especially pleased by Pitt's presence in the coalition. The king realized how badly the nation needed Pitt's singular leadership.

The war effort was not going at all well. The loss of Minorca to the French in 1756 had led to scapegoating and the court-martial of Admiral Byng, who was blamed for the military setback. Although Pitt had spoken on Byng's behalf, the admiral was found guilty of dereliction of duty and executed on March 14, 1757.[3] In North America, military action continued. On the continent of Europe, not only were the 45,000 men of the duke of Cumberland ominously outnumbered by the 100,000 in d'Estrées' army in Germany, but Frederick II was pleading with his English ally for military aid of some kind. Badly defeated on June 18, 1757, at Kolin in Bohemia, the king of Prussia had lost his aura of invincibility.[4] Under pressure from the Swedes and the Russians, Frederick II implied that, failing English aid, he might sue for a separate peace with the French. Then again, George II's electorate of Hanover seemed a plum ripe for the plucking by French armies.[5] If it fell, the French government could demand in exchange for Hanover's welfare the restoration of several of its territories lost to English armies.

English public opinion was ravenous in its hunger for a clear-cut military victory. Hardly insensitive to public opinion and understanding the desperate situation in which Frederick II found himself, Pitt knew he had to act. But what to do? He moved decisively, as was his habit, but whether he moved well has remained a debating point for students of his illustrious career.[6]

In early July 1757, Pitt determined that the launching of a sea and land expedition against the French coasts would constitute the best means to bring relief to Frederick II while at the same time shielding England from any potential invasion by French armies. If such an expedition alarmed the French coast, the French court would be obliged to withdraw forces from Germany to protect exposed ports on the Atlantic Ocean. Because a naval expedition could move more swiftly than an encumbered army on foot and wheel, the French government would be forced to disperse large numbers of stationary troops up and down the coast. This defensive obligation would entail a reduction of offensive troop strength in Germany, thereby slackening military pressure on a beleaguered Frederick II and the duke of Cumberland.

The idea of an English invasion of the French coastline was, of course, by no means novel. Precedents could be culled from as far back as the Middle Ages. During the War of the Spanish Succession the self-styled comte de Linange had proposed a project to the allied military command which eerily resembled the one that Pitt envisioned, including the same landing spot and the involvement of French Huguenots. John O'Connor has described the plan in some detail:

> It included a landing on the western coast of France, between La Rochelle and Rochefort, by English and Dutch troops with Huguenot exiles. The grand scheme involved the creation of a republic in France made up of Normandy, Guyenne, Languedoc, Provence, Dauphiné and Brittany. The republic would be protected by the allies and would be organized in the same fashion as the Dutch Republic. Representatives from *parlements* and the nobility would be treated as ambassadors by the allies. Grain and arms would be sent to the provinces at Dutch expense; refugee French officers would put themselves in command of those who joined the rebellion. The plot's culmination would be the deposition of Louis XIV who would be replaced by the Duke of Lorraine.[7]

Linange spoke with the duke of Marlborough about this scheme and made other contacts with Huguenots. But the conspiracy collapsed. Linange ultimately died in a jail in Vienna.

During the War of the Austrian Succession, an abortive expedition had been sent to L'Orient in 1746.[8] In the very recent past (1756), George II had possibly offered to send troops to liberate French Protestants, as correspondence purportedly written by an English agent in France implied. In 1756, Saint-Florentin was the recipient of a letter allegedly from Pastor Paul Rabaut. It offered potential military assistance from George II. Whatever the authenticity of these communications, Frederick II's military memorial of December 9, 1756, included a suggestion of a diversion along the French coast: "1. Make a diversion by threatening the coasts of Normandy or Britanny; 2. Take Corsica as a set off to Minorca; 3. Move an army . . . towards the Rhine early in the spring; 4. Stir up the Turks to make a diversion against Russia or Austria."[9] Andrew Mitchell, the English emissary to Frederick II, communicated this memorial to Holdernesse.

The French had issued their own threats about invading English soil in 1756 and 1757. Newcastle learned about the invasion plans through intercepted diplomatic correspondence and from Frederick II. As early as January and February 1756, the French government marched troops to the coast as if they were intended to participate in an invasion of England. This maneuver turned out to be a feint, but concern about a potential invasion created panic among a portion of the English populace. This concern shrouded politicians' minds throughout 1756. On December 9, 1756, Andrew Mitchell wrote to Holdernesse that he had discussed the matter with one of Frederick II's principal emissaries, Baron Knyphausen in Dresden.[10] Knyphausen indicated that the project of the maréchal de Belle-Isle, sending fifty thousand soldiers to invade England, could not be mounted without the English having sufficient time to counter it. On April 26, 1757, Mr. Symmer wrote to Mitchell that the House of Commons was still discussing intelligence reports about a potential invasion of Great Britain and Ireland.[11] One of the reasons Pitt hesitated to send a Baltic fleet to help both the duke of Cumberland, George II's son, and Frederick II was that he sensed the pressing need to have a fleet close by to head off any French armada bearing down upon the homeland.

By July 7, 1757, Pitt had formalized his plan of action. He would send an expedition to the French coast, and the naval-stores port of Rochefort would be its destination. To the implementation of this stratagem Pitt devoted unstinting energies and political capital.

Jean-Louis Ligonier, a Huguenot who was one of England's most decorated generals, played a critical role in shaping Pitt's thinking in this regard.[12] Raised in a French Protestant home, Ligonier had emigrated from Castres, France, to England as a young man. With a lengthy record of distinguished service in the armies of his adopted nation, Ligonier was greatly respected. He had served for many years with the duke of Cumberland and enjoyed the friendship of politicians including Pitt and Newcastle. The king, George II, appreciated his military counsel. During the year 1756, Ligonier attempted to bolster the defenses along the English coastline against the much-feared potential invasion by the French.

Disturbed by baleful news regarding the English military situation in Canada, Ligonier, lieutenant general of the ordnance, began to contemplate what offensive strokes might boost English morale. On August 15, 1756, Ligonier indicated that there must be "some attempt on France in consequence of my paper" and noted other targets besides the coasts of France that would constitute worthy military objectives.[13] Ligonier, then, was probably the proximate originator of what became known as the "Secret Expedition." It was he who convinced Pitt by July 1757 that an invasion of the French coast was feasible.

Ligonier had recently received important military intelligence from a young officer named Robert Clerk, to the effect that the defenses around Rochefort were woefully insufficient. In 1754, Clerk had made a chance visit to the city and had been obligingly shown the defenses by a French officer. Clerk took no notes, but he later recounted to Ligonier what he had seen. Upon Ligonier's request, Clerk wrote a report, dated July 15, 1757, to confirm his conversation with Ligonier. He noted: "There were parts of a rampart in existence around the town but it was incomplete and about 25' high at most."[14] Horace Walpole, who disliked Clerk (Clarke) and described him as "ill-favoured in his person," indicated that the Scot had persuaded himself (and probably Ligonier) that the countryside around Rochefort, cut through with dikes and appropriately called "Little Holland," could be traversed by troops.[15]

In addition, Joseph Thierry, a French pilot who had served for twenty years along the coasts of France, had told Ligonier that ships could draw sufficiently close to shore that the landing of troops near Rochefort was feasible. Thierry, like Ligonier a Huguenot, assumed that he could guide a naval expedition to the coast opposite Aix or to a location near Chalet-Aillon. Once ashore, troops could move the five miles from either spot to Rochefort, one of France's principal military ports, possibly surprise the garrison there, and then proceed to raze the military stores and set fire to the docks and the ships under construction or in the harbor. Not only could a strategic coup of this magnitude gravely cripple the French navy, it might force the French court to recall troops to fortify the entire Atlantic coastline against any other potential English invasion. An intelligence report from France, "Mémoire sur la Force actuelle de la France, et les Services, auxquels Elle est employée dans l'Année 1757," indicated that only ten thousand troops were scattered along the western coast in July 1757.[16] This report figured as an important factor in decision making about an invasion of French soil.

Lieutenant General Ligonier and Lord Holdernesse had other designs beyond razing military stores and burning French ships, however. They envisioned the possibility that the expedition could help spark a rebellion among the Huguenots in southern France. Ligonier informed the expedition's chief land officer, General John Mordaunt, that there would be Protestants in the area around Rochefort who would wish the English expedition well. According to one source, Holdernesse, who directed the English secret service, had provided the ministry this counsel: "An English expedition would be able to transport at least fifteen thousand men to the coasts, without counting the soldiers of the marine and with this mass one would be able to aid the discontented [in France] and favor a sudden revolt of the Huguenots." Holdernesse was convinced that an "expedition well conducted could incite the people and particularly the Huguenot party in the Cévennes to rebellion."[17]

Ligonier and Holdernesse had apparently received word from Pastor Jean-Louis Gibert in the Saintonge about his force of four thousand Protestant men, which lacked "neither leaders nor arms." We recall that Pastor Gibert had boasted to Herrenschwand in late June or early July 1757, the same time-frame, that his troops were ready to defend their newly acquired church buildings and, if this project failed, that he was prepared to take thousands of Huguenots out of France. Gibert let it be known that plans for the emigration had already been made. He believed that there was no way to thwart the enterprise. The pastor also boasted to his Huguenot compatriots that he was acting under the protection of a powerful prince. Herrenschwand assumed that this person was none other than the prince de Conti.

From Pitt's point of view, the diversionary effect of the expedition to Rochefort had undoubted military merit. But the vision of inciting a Huguenot rebellion, which might give birth to an independent Protestant state within a state, converted the Rochefort expedition into something far more compelling than a strategic military operation: it became a mission laced with religious sentiments. In 1757 both King George II's rhetoric and Pitt's own portrayed the conflict between France and England as a struggle between Catholicism and Protestantism. Moreover, in parliamentary addresses, George II declared that one of the great objects he had at heart was "the preservation of the Protestant religion, and the liberties of Europe."[18] Heightening the ministry's sensitivities about the religious stakes in the contest was an English spy's intelligence report from Paris, dated July 6, 1757: "The Protestant Religion will subsist no longer than it may be Policy in the Two Courts [Versailles and Vienna] to tolerate it; the Republic of Holland will become first, dependent, and then subject to France; and England will be the last ruined. These are some of the sentiments of those in Power."[19] Aware of the officious anti–Protestant aims of its foes, the English government required action, not mere rhetoric, to preserve Protestantism.

For Pitt, it was imperative that this additional motivation for the expedition remain unannounced and cloaked in the strictest secrecy. Only a select number of trusted officers and ministers were made privy to it. Pitt feared that a revelation of this design could bring the full wrath of the French monarchy down upon French Protestants, who had already suffered enough. If the plans were uncovered, the Huguenots would be deemed traitors for having treated with the English. Therein lay the justification for such secrecy.

In early July 1757, Pitt and Ligonier energetically attempted to convince George II and leading members of the ministry that the newly devised strategy should be pursued with all possible dispatch. On July 7, 1757, Pitt ordered that the Admiralty arrange to transport "ten battalions of infantry, 160 horses, ordnance and hospital equipment," with food for two months, to the Isle of Wight.[20] On July 9, 1757, Ligonier wrote to Pitt about a critically important interview with George II:

Dear Sir,

I have been to receive His Majesty's Commands, in relation to what you know and found him after I had related what passed at our conference, extremely pleased with the Project, and he was pleased at my request to name the Generals and Regiments himself: Mordaunt, Conway, Cornwallis.

I thought this would be extremely agreeable and L. Holdernesse sends me a messenger. I am with great Respects . . . J. Ligonier[21]

Not only was George II persuaded to back the plan, but he chose the commanding officers for the expedition.

In his postscript, the comment about the messenger could simply signify that Holdernesse was sending a courier who could take his message to Pitt. But another interpretation obtains as well: the minister responsible for intelligence gathering for the cabinet was sending someone who could take the expedition plans to those in France who would welcome this news. It seems most unlikely that Ligonier would have had to wait for a courier to take a message to Pitt or another cabinet minister.

With the king favorably disposed to the project, Pitt then turned his attention to members of the ministry and the military. Several of them offered genuinely frustrating opposition.

Earlier, on June 26, 1757, the duke of Newcastle had written to Lord Hardwicke that the sending of a Baltic squadron seems "almost absolutely necessary" (BM, Add. MSS 32,871, fol. 407r). Frederick II was calling for such an expedition. But Pitt, who had consistently bucked attempts to protect Hanover through subsidies to Continental powers or other means, strenuously resisted this idea. Nonetheless, Newcastle declared that Pitt "must seriously think of Foreign Affairs in a different Manner, from what he has hitherto done, or the King of Prussia will make His separate Peace; and we shall lose the Electorate [Hanover] this year, and God knows what the next" (ibid.). In a "most secret" letter, dated June 29, 1757, Mitchell, the English emissary to Frederick II, lent credence to Newcastle's analysis. "[If] England will not endeavor to save Him [the King of Prussia], He must save himself, as well as He can" (fol. 438r). In another "most secret" letter, dated July 9, 1757, Mitchell reported that Frederick II wanted troops (six thousand foot-soldiers and three thousand cavalry) to reinforce the duke of Cumberland; this would be "one of the effectual means to support the Common cause, and to restore everything" (BM, Add. MSS 32,872, fol. 324v).

To receive backing from Newcastle and others for the expedition to Rochefort, Pitt would have to persuade them to ignore the strong appeals of the king of Prussia for a Baltic expedition. This was no paltry task.

So secret were the plans for the French expedition which George II had initially approved, he directed that the written record be made more general, "for fear of discovery" (fol. 204r). Thus Lord Holdernesse altered the topics or the headings of the project. In consequence, later drafts of the plans that were ultimately released to the public omitted several sensitive directives. But Lord Hardwicke, Lord Holdernesse, the duke of Newcastle, and Lord Anson had all approved the original draft.

Several ministers feared how Frederick II would react to these plans. In mid-July, Mitchell was instructed to inform the king of the English government's decision about the "Intended Expedition to the Coasts of France." Nearly eight thousand land forces, besides marines, with "almost the whole Fleet at home," were to participate in this "powerful diversion." Mitchell was to say to the king of Prussia that "Nothing but an absolute impossibility . . . would have prevented the King [George II] from sending a squadron into the Baltick; which impossibility appears from the whole Fleet being employed upon this Expedition to the Coasts of France; which may be done, safely, as the Fleet will always be at hand in the Channel, in case of any unexpected attempt upon His Majesty's Dominions here" (fol. 206r). The fear of the French invading England served as a major hindrance to the Baltic expedition.

Governmental officials were kept busy sorting out these sensitive matters. In a letter dated July 16, 1757, Newcastle commented to Mitchell that as much business had been accomplished in the last ten days as in many months before (fol. 214r). Newcastle claimed that he alone was responsible for the message in the letter that he was certain would please Frederick II. The next day, in a "most secret" letter, Lord Holdernesse instructed Mitchell to reiterate to Frederick II that the secrecy of this expedition should be guarded and that the king could expect "more relief from these operations" than from "the precarious Efforts of a Baltick Squadron" (fols. 238r–38v). The die had been cast.

Or had it? Several ministers began to harbor serious second thoughts, as did the king himself. These thoughts were apparently reinforced by the doubts various military officers had regarding the practicality of the expedition. On July 21, Newcastle wrote to Hardwicke that Mordaunt and Conway, commanders of the land forces, were full of apprehension because they thought the expedition might be extremely hazardous (fol. 286r). Ligonier reviewed the pros and cons of the expedition in a meeting of the war cabinet on July 24, 1757.

Newcastle was wavering badly in his commitment to the French expedition. On July 25, he again wrote to Hardwicke that he had been informed by Admiral Anson that the generals believed the expedition to be "Hazardous, and almost impracticable" and that George II had been "very severe with Mr. Pitt, both with regard to his abilities, and his intentions" (fol. 321r). On July 26, Newcastle and Pitt politely debated Frederick II's demand that nine thousand troops be sent to reinforce the hard-pressed duke of Cumberland (fol. 358r). Now Hardwicke and Newcastle favored sending the troops to Germany and putting aside the expedition to France. From Newcastle's point of view, there would be great use and little hazard in acceding to the king of Prussia's demand; in the French expedition, perhaps a "very uncertain advantage, and a good deal of risk" (fol. 358v).

But if Newcastle was pleased with the irenic character of his first exchange with Pitt ("Pitt and I, are equally pleas'd with each other," said Newcastle), he was not at all happy with the next ones (ibid.). On July 30, 1757, Newcastle wrote to Lord Ashburnham: "I am sorry I can't confirm to you the good Account I sent in my last [July 27, 1757]. Since then we have had great Altercations, and I am afraid Nothing will be done for the King's Assistance—which indeed gives Him very just Uneasiness" (fol. 397r). The English government was in a state of turmoil.

Pitt acted swiftly. He arranged for a meeting of Captain Clerk, the Huguenot pilot Thierry, and the sea and land officers who would lead the expedition. The officers interrogated Clerk and Thierry regarding their intelligence reports about Rochefort and the surrounding areas. The officers' doubts were temporarily allayed by the responses of the two men. With the officers satisfied about the plans, several of the vacillating ministers began to fall into line with Pitt once again.

On the first day of August, Holdernesse wrote to Newcastle about the meeting: "I cannot go to bed without letting your Grace have the satisfaction of knowing that after a very full examination of the French Pilot and Capt. Clarke all the former difficulties both of the sea and land officers have vanished, and both the admirals and generals have declared their opinions in favour of the expedition, which now seems to have a most favourable aspect" (fol. 413r). On August 2, Newcastle indicated to Lord Dupplin that George II felt abandoned by those who now were willing to proceed with the French expedition. The king thought that the ministers would do nothing to help him save Hanover. Moreover, his son, the duke of Cumberland, found himself locked in a deteriorating military situation in Germany. On August 3, 1757, news reached the government that Cumberland had been defeated a week earlier. But, on the matter of the French expedition, Pitt would not be budged.

Also on August 3, Newcastle wrote to Hardwicke that the military officers had obtained "entire satisfaction" from their meeting with Thierry and Clerk; "the Expedition is now going on" (fol. 429r). On August 4, 1757, Hardwicke replied to Newcastle that he was pleased that the officers were satisfied, but he personally was "so heartbroken" that he did not hold out any great hope for the expedition (fol. 442v).

The same day, August 4, a larger meeting of the cabinet convened at Lord Holdernesse's house on Arlington Street. There, cabinet ministers had the opportunity to question Thierry and Clerk. The land and sea officers, the dukes of Bedford and Devonshire, General Ligonier, and others attended. The minutes of this important consultation indicate unanimity of opinion was reached:

> Lord Holdernesse and Mr. Secretary Pitt laid before their Lordships the several steps that have been taken, in relation to a Secret Expedition, as also the several Informations they had received of the present Disposition of French Forces upon their Coasts, and of the State and Situation of the Place intended to be attacked; their Lordships were likewise attended by Sir John Ligonier, Sir John Mordaunt, Sir Edward Hawke, Major General Conway, and Admiral Knowles, and having

heard their sentiment, are humbly of the opinion, that it is advisable
for His Majesty, to direct the Expedition to be forthwith undertaken.
Mr. Secretary Pitt laid before their Lordships a Draft of Instructions
for Sir Edward Hawke, and Sir John Mordaunt, which was unanimously approved. (Fols. 241r–41v).

The "several Informations"—intelligence reports from the Huguenot
pilot Thierry, Clerk, and sources in France—had played a major role
in consolidating support for the expedition.

On August 5, George II drew up orders for the commanding
officers. The king's orders included, among other objectives for the
expedition, a cryptic allusion to adding "Life and Strength to the
Common Cause"—possibly code for abetting the "preservation of
the Protestant religion, and liberties of Europe" as represented by the
French Huguenots. The next day, Newcastle, a former skeptic himself, acknowledged to a doubting Hardwicke that "we were all unanimous for the expedition" (fol. 468v). Still a holdout, Hardwicke
graciously observed that he was pleased that a larger meeting had been
held to discuss it. But he personally saw little hope for the expedition's
success.

Pitt and Ligonier had won the day. Now they faced the problem
of getting the huge expedition launched without the secret of its destination being pilfered by French spies. Pitt was in no mood to brook
excuses from his subordinates. Time was of the essence. In all likelihood he had agreed for the expedition to make a rendezvous with
French Protestants on fixed dates. Moreover, Frederick II's situation
was so dire that he needed immediate relief. Even Newcastle expressed to Pitt concern about the unfortunate passage of time: "I
am very sorry to hear, that the transports are not yet out of the
River. The King mention'd it to me with concern on Wednesday last.
I heartily wish we may not lose the most favourable wind for our
operations that can blow. Am sure I need not recommend to *you*
expedition."[22]

In early August, George II took desperate steps to protect his interests in Germany. On August 9, 1757, he gave this directive to the duke
of Cumberland: "Therefore you will receive powers to get me and
my country out of these difficulties at the best rate you can by a separate peace as Elector, including my allies the Duke of Wolfenbüttel,

and the Landgrave [of Hesse-Cassel]." Then on August 11, the king sent a specific authorization to his son to negotiate a separate peace "for me as Elector, that the several dominions may be relieved and the troops saved."[23] As elector of Hanover, George II thereby promised that he would no longer take part indirectly or directly in the war in Germany, if Cumberland's army would be preserved and Hanover spared.[24] Cumberland was apparently free to sue for peace with the French if that measure would permit the electoral army to be kept intact.

Unexpected delays for the expedition's departure mounted, and Pitt began to realize that chances of a rendezvous with French Protestant forces were vanishing. Despair engulfed the secretary, even before the expedition set sail.

Any talk of delay made Pitt extremely irritable. Admiral Anson discovered this, to his personal chagrin. When Anson indicated that he could not comply with Pitt's order that the fleet be equipped and reach the rendezvous for departure on the appointed day, Pitt resorted to outright menace. If Anson failed to comply with orders, Pitt would take the matter before the king and flatly impeach the admiral in the House of Commons.[25] Admiral Anson fulfilled his obligation. Because of the efforts of Admirals Anson and Hawke, seldom was an armada in the eighteenth century better equipped than that of the Secret Expedition.

Whereas Admiral Anson and others felt it necessary to yield to Pitt's autocratic demands, capricious winds could not be so intimidated. On August 30, Mitchell wrote to Frederick II that the fleet had been held back by stormy and contrary winds that had blown for three weeks.[26] The various delays played on the already jangled nerves of Generals Mordaunt, Conway, and Cornwallis, who began to question once again the practicality of the venture. On September 3, Newcastle wrote to a correspondent: "It is now the 3rd of September. They were to be at Home by the End of the month and Lord Anson also told us, that Dr. Hay, and Mr. Elliot, who had been at Portsmouth, said, that both Land and Sea Officers talked down the Expedition. But Pitt is deaf; and in our present circumstance, especially after what has been insinuated with Relations to Hanover; I don't know who dares take upon Him, To stop it's going."[27]

On September 5, a peevish Pitt sent a stiff letter to Sir John Mordaunt in which he ordered the vacillating officer to proceed "without the Loss of a Moment" in the execution of his orders.[28] Moreover, Pitt nullified a secret order from Hardwicke that the armada return within a month. George II was informed that ten battalions, under Sir John Ligonier, were all completely embarked at Willemstadt.

Frederick II, who had his own wishes for a Baltic expedition rebuffed, was not at all pleased by the delays for the French expedition. On August 30, he wrote Mitchell that French land forces remained on his back.[29]

Finally, on September 8, 1757, after what seemed interminable delays to Pitt, the huge fleet—eighteen ships of the line, six frigates, several warships, two hospital ships, forty-four transports, and six cruisers—moved out to sea. The *Royal George* boasted one hundred canon; the *Ramilies,* the *Neptune* and the *Namur,* ninety; and other ships, a lesser number. Approximately eight thousand land troops were aboard. Much discussed in the English press, the Secret Expedition sailed for parts known only to a trusted few. A young volunteer aboard ship later recounted his impressions of the fleet's departure. He was awed by the military might of what he saw: "With this noble fleet consisting of eighty sails, we headed out to sea, on September 8, full of expectation and confidence. Every individual seemed transported by the sight of our invincible armament. Indeed, it was the most formidable and impressive that I had ever seen. The ships were the most powerful and the best conditioned in the entire navy. The regiments, although they were only ten, were second to none in the service; and we viewed our commanders as people of recognized ability, whose talents and courage could never be doubted."[30] At least initially, the soldiers aboard ship were proud to participate in this formidable expedition. They had confidence in their officers. Who could doubt that they would triumph, no matter what their mission?

On shore many Englishmen, especially those who were Pitt's friends, wished the armada Godspeed. They sensed that Pitt had, in the public's mind, become identified with the expedition. Beckford prophesied: "Whatever it is, Mr Pitt will either have the glory or the disgrace of it, for every one calls it his scheme."[31]

But would the expedition reach its destination too late? This question still haunted Pitt. The secretary suspected that the fleet had been deliberately delayed by parties associated with the government itself.

On September 7, 1757, the day before the expedition set sail, Newcastle made these cryptic notes about a conversation he had with Pitt: "My Discourse with Mr P. about the Expedition. His strong answer. He would defend it with His Head. Whoever stopt it, should answer for it. That he saw it would not go, but that he would send the King's Orders to Sir Edward Hawke. His suspicion of the Land, and Sea Officers."[32] Pitt caught the stench of treason at the highest level; he especially suspected some of the expedition's officers. He fretted and became even more downcast. He feared the worst even before the fleet had set sail for its foray along the French coasts.

Compounding Pitt's worries were the flagging fortunes of the English in North America and Cumberland's critical military situation in Germany. On September 5, 1757, Pitt, Newcastle, Anson, Ligonier, and others determined to send a squadron of ships to the Weser and the Elbe and to furnish Cumberland more ordnance for the defense of Stade. On September 8, the day the Secret Expedition set sail, Ligonier wrote a revealing letter to the duke: "The King continues, thank God, in good health and he bears the terrible situation of your R. H. and His unhappy Country like a man. He also feels like a father and as the father of his people and my heart bleeds for him."[33] Thinking that the various measures taken by his government might prop Cumberland up, the king wrote the duke, on September 15, and directed him not to enter into a separate peace with the French.

These steps to save Cumberland had come too late. The shocking news that he had surrendered in Germany arrived in London on September 17. He had been trapped in Stade with his troops, and on September 8, 9, and 10, he had agreed to and signed the Convention of Kloster-Zeven. According to its terms, "Half of the Hannoverian contingent was to be interned at Stade and the rest to return east of the Elbe, while the Hessians and Brunswickers were to go home and be disbanded." And Hanover was to be occupied, as security.[34]

George II was both stunned and infuriated by the news: "Never have I felt like this." It was bad enough that Cumberland had been humiliated militarily. It was unpardonable that his son had not negotiated an article guaranteeing the neutrality of Hanover. The city still dangled helplessly in harm's way. On September 21, the king wrote to Cumberland: "You have seen fit to make a convention . . . by which not the least thing has been stipulated in favour of my states and those of my allies, but which soon gives the enemy possession of the posts and countries. . . . All this was done without writing for ratification . . . a convention shameful and pernicious. . . . Come back at once by a warship and explain."[35] The king called Cumberland, his own son, a coward. Cumberland was disgraced. Along with other ministers, Pitt had earlier repudiated the Convention of Kloster-Zeven, claiming that the English government had never approved it.[36]

Pitt believed that his own political situation nevertheless remained bleak. On September 12, Newcastle described Pitt's state of mind to Lord Mansfield: "He [Pitt] continues to despair; or seems or would have me think, He could not continue in service; as nothing now could be found to give the least possibility of getting out of our present difficulties."[37] Not only did the chief strategist of the Secret Expedition apparently know that the armada could not arrive in time for the agreed-upon rendezvous with French Protestants, but he could also speculate that his decision not to send more troops to support Cumberland might be charged to his political account.

Although Pitt wrestled with these worries, others pondered a different set of questions. Once the expedition set sail, the French court and the press in various lands sought to map exactly where the huge fleet was headed. An international guessing-game opened in Paris, in London, and in La Haye. Incredibly enough, the destination had remained a genuine secret. Even the soldiers aboard the ships did not know where they were headed until the armada was well out to sea.

Countermeasures by the French Court

If the English soldiers were initially uninformed about the ultimate mission of the huge expedition, so was the French court. Despite attempts to put a bold face on the matter, French ministers began to fear that the news issuing from the Atlantic coastline might be disastrous. The court decided to take several precautionary measures even before the Secret Expedition left port. According to a report from France that reached La Haye by August 16, 1757, the court at Versailles had already dispatched some Swiss Guards to the coasts of Brittany and two battalions to the Isle of Rhé and to Belle-Isle.[38]

Only too aware of potential complicity of French Protestants, the

English, and the prince de Conti, Louis XV chose to pay particular
attention to the activities of the members of the Reformed churches
in the Saintonge and in Aunis. These were the Protestants to whom
Jean-Louis Gibert ministered. The pastor had helped reestablish the
Reformed church on the Isle of Rhé and pastored several others along
the coast. Herrenschwand's reports to Berryer had further fed these
suspicions about the Protestants in the area.

And yet Louis XV and his ministers did not know with assurance
that the Secret Expedition was headed towards the coasts around La
Rochelle and Rochefort. In the early evening of September 20, 1757,
the fleet was observed from the Tour des Baleines on the Isle of Rhé.
The governor of the island, Monsieur de Prince, immediately sent a
sloop to La Rochelle to warn the maréchal de Sennecterre, commander of the province. On September 24, the king received a dispatch from Sennecterre, who was in Poitou, to the effect that the
English fleet, estimated at 135 sails, had appeared on September 21 off
the Isle of Rhé. Sennecterre thought that the fleet might be bound for
La Rochelle. On September 25, an English spy sent an intelligence
report to England from Fontainebleau, and he indicated that three
couriers from the maréchal de Sennecterre had arrived at the French
court on the previous day. According to one of the messages, the fleet
had anchored near the little Isle of Aix between Oléron and Rhé,
close to the mouth of the Charente, about five leagues from Rochefort. The intelligence report then described the reaction at court:
"People therefore naturally guess, that the English will make themselves Masters of the above mentioned Islands, and attempt something against Rochefort, or at least try to destroy the Harbour."[39]
Louis XV had previously ordered that the *Gardes Côte* assemble,
along with different battalions in the area. Now, he directed four battalions of French Guards and two of Swiss Guards to set out from
Orléans for Rochefort. A report of September 26 noted the rumor in
Paris that another message from Sennecterre said that the English
had landed without much resistance at Chalet-Aillon. The fear gained
credence that the English wanted first to destroy Rochefort to ruin
the navy; then they would make incursions into the interior. The same
report continued: "We have only 4,000 men in this area to put up
against them. This was a weak spot. Moreover, we fear the Religionnaires [Protestants] of the area of which the countryside is full."[40]

The French court suspected that many Protestants of Saintonge and Aunis would in fact welcome an English invasion.

The unsettling possibility that English troops might join up with Protestant troops had actually been on the minds of several members of the French government since at least 1755. In that year a governmental official drew up the "Mémoire sur les Costes de l'Aunis et du Poitou depuis la Rochelle jusqu'à l'embouchure de la Loire," in which he addressed this contingency. He astutely observed that Protestants engaged in commerce along the coast would not encourage an English invasion because it could interrupt trade. He claimed that the Protestants lacked disciplined troops, artillery, and a chief, and could cause no sizable difficulty for the government unless they received support from an English military descent. To counter that maneuver, he recommended that forts be established along the coast and that the *Gardes-Côte*, overpopulated by Protestants, be manned by mixed contingents of Catholics and Protestants to keep the Protestants on tether. To his mind, the forts would close off access routes for French Protestants to the coastline and therefore to an invading English army. This strategy would destroy once and for all Protestants' hopes of receiving military help from the English government.[41]

What was discussed with relative calm in 1755 became patently alarming in 1756. The interception of correspondence allegedly between the duke of Cumberland and the prieur of Auriac and Herrenschwand's warnings increased fears that the Protestants were armed and the English might launch an invasion to coincide with a Protestant revolt.

Governmental officials were nervous and taut when the sails of a large English fleet ominously appeared off the French coast in September 1757. Could the available troops along the coast withstand an invasion? Would French Protestants join the English in their foray? These questions troubled officials in Paris and in regions along the western coast.

Besides the steps taken by Louis XV, probably the most energetic measures to counter the expedition focused on disarming suspected Protestants. On September 24, 1757, in the same time-frame the expedition was spotted off the coast of La Rochelle and Rochefort, the maréchal de Thomond, commander of Guyenne, and M. de Tourny, the intendant of Guyenne, promulgated an ordinance (followed by a

second, on October 8) that obliged all inhabitants of the towns and
the countryside, except royal officers and military officers, to give up
their arms.[42] Several days later, Thomond forbade all assemblies.
Tourny then urged consuls and syndics to have the soldiers responsible for enforcing the ordinances actually lodge in the homes of "suspect Protestants."[43] The dreaded days of the *dragonnades* were returning to haunt the Huguenots.

As the Protestants of Bergerac observed, people complied with
the weapons ordinance, sometimes creating a pathetic farce: they had
to buy arms to be able to surrender them. If they did not submit to
the ordinance, they faced fines or prison. Those Protestants who criticized this measure argued that it was based on "unjust suspicions
and calumnies" imputed to "all the Protestants of Guyenne and of
Saintonge."[44] The officials who drew up these policies simply doubted
Protestant professions of loyalty, especially when a large English
fleet was menacingly plying the waters off the French coast. Interestingly enough, a later governmental inquiry received testimony that
an English agent had visited Bergerac before the fleet's arrival. The
agent was to help arrange a Protestant uprising that would coincide
with the English invasion.

In early October 1757, Saint-Florentin ordered troops sent to
Libourne, La Roche-Chalais, and Coutras, considered to be Protestant trouble spots.[45] Speaking of the year 1757, Pastor "Nogaret" later
claimed that the "disarmament had been general."[46] The possibility
of a sizable contingent of armed French Huguenots making their way
to a rendezvous with invading English troops on the coast had been
largely quashed by the disparate hard-nosed measures of the French
government. Then again, the English armada had been delayed for
several weeks, thereby upsetting the timing of a potential rendezvous. Pitt was prescient when he suspected that the Rochefort expedition would falter badly.

A sense of expectancy ran through the ranks of the English soldiers
when they received their first orders, on September 14, 1757, as the
fleet entered the Bay of Biscay. They had been well drilled before the
expedition, simulating combats, attacks, and retreats. The right brigade consisted of the Regiments of Old Buff, King, Kingsley, Hume,
and Hodgson; the left brigade was made up of the Regiments of

Brudenal, Loudon, Cornwallis, Amhurst, and Betinck. The soldiers viewed themselves as the finest in His Majesty's armies. They were at last going to invade enemy territory. They were anxious to prove their mettle in combat once again.

Such was not to be. As reported in one French account of the expedition's activities, the fleet did relatively little damage to French military installations. There was a startling reason for this: the bulk of the soldiers of the right and left brigades never landed on the mainland.

On September 20th, an English fleet of 80 to 100 sails was spotted after dinner from the Tour des Baleines, on the Isle of Rhé. Towards six o'clock it entered the Pertuis d'Antioche and anchored on the coast of the Plantin d'Ars. This fleet stayed at anchor during the 21st. The evening of the 22nd, one portion went and anchored in the Basques and the other in the Pertuis. On the 23rd, about eight o'clock in the morning, eight vessels left the fleet and moved toward the Isle of Aix. At noon, two of the ships advanced within the range of the small fort of the island whose fortifications were even yet imperfectly in place. They began to fire strongly. The fort responded with fire for three-quarters of an hour before it surrendered. Three hundred men from the battalion of Poitiers, which made up the garrison, were taken prisoner. The launches of the fleet were used on the 24th, 25th, 26th, and 27th to tear down the waterfront. . . . The 30th, the English, after having fired several bombs on Fort Fouras and the Isle of Madame, and having blown up the fortifications of the Isle of Aix, set on fire the caserns of the fort. . . . Finally, on October 1, the fleet weighed anchor at nine o'clock in the morning, passed immediately through the Pertuis d'Antioche, and at five o'clock in the afternoon completely disappeared from view.[47]

Despite the troops' willingness to fight and the careful preparations of Pitt and Ligonier, no invasion of the French mainland and no razing of the military stores at Rochefort had taken place. All that the commanding officers of the Secret Expedition could report was that they had captured the small fort on the Isle of Rhé, done heavy damage to it, but then abandoned it.

One French commentator compared the Secret Expedition to the famous elephant that had labored long, only to give birth to a mouse.

The comparison was apt. Not only had the expedition faltered, it had failed.

What had provoked the failure? And who should be blamed for it? These questions began to churn in the agitated minds of many Englishmen as the news from the French coasts began to reach the general public. The outrage quickly surpassed that associated with the loss of Minorca. Seldom would William Pitt face a more excruciating personal crisis than the one after the fiasco of the Secret Expedition. It seemed he had not only brought disrepute on the English nation by his alleged "chimerical" designs, but he had inadvertently offered his own head on a platter to his political foes. The nation wanted a thorough accounting of what had taken place in the planning of the Secret Expedition, what its true objectives had been, why it had failed, and who should bear responsibility. Moreover, the nation was not in a mood to draw back from finding out if the failure stemmed from the highest echelons of government. Many suspected that William Pitt should receive full blame for this expedition that had compounded the nation's sense of deep frustration about the war effort.

During the fall of 1757 and the winter of 1758, in pubs and Parliament alike, Englishmen tried to recreate the planning and the activities of the Secret Expedition. Their task was a difficult one. The expedition had indeed been cloaked in strictest secrecy, as one author pointed out: "As the eyes of all Europe, as well as those of our nation have been intent upon an expedition conducted with such profound secrecy and caution, that scarce an officer (except Admirals and Generals) were acquainted with its destination, at least ten days after we embarked."[48] Just as Louis XV and Madame de Pompadour could not afford that the public learn about the prince de Conti's dangerous seditious activity, so several members of the English government had too much to lose if the basic components of the Rochefort expedition's planning and pursuit ever came to light. As Pitt acknowledged later, "Several causes were attributed for the failure of this expedition, but the true one was perhaps never publicly known."[49]

And what was this carefully hidden secret to which Pitt alluded? French Huguenots, under the direction of Pastor Gibert, the prince de Conti's firebrand partisan, did not await General Mordaunt's forces on the beaches, either as armed soldiers or as emigrants. They had been thwarted from joining their English "liberators."[50]

SIX

The Failure
of the Secret Expedition

✤ ✤ ✤

I feel more and more I shall never get Rochefort off my heart. Nor
do I believe England (which is the misery) will cease to feel, per-
haps for an age, the fatal consequences of this foul miscarriage.

William Pitt to Thomas Potter, in the fall of 1757

The disappearance of English sails from the Atlantic horizon on
October 1, 1757, represented a solemn moment for many French
Protestants in the provinces along the coast, even if few of them observed the passage. With the vanishing sails faded their own hopes
for direct military assistance in their attempt to win freedom of conscience, or, that goal eluding them, to escape France as emigrants on
the returning ships. Moreover, governmental officials now harbored
deep-seated suspicions about their complicity with France's foreign
foes. In the fall of 1757, many Huguenot communities in the Guyenne
and the Saintonge feared the possibility of retribution.

By no means had all French Protestants along the coast welcomed
the impending invasion or viewed the English as liberators. Protestants in the merchant community in La Rochelle had joined in the
defense of the city, when the English fleet approached the coast.[1]
Four of the city's five batteries were commanded by Huguenots. So
pleased was Louis XV by this demonstration of Protestant loyalty
that, on November 1, 1757, he ordered the removal from a city gate of
plaques that celebrated the fall of the city in 1628 as a Huguenot
enclave.[2] Henceforth, the king wanted to remember only the proofs
the inhabitants had given, "even before this epoch, of their inviolable

attachment to the interests of the State."[3] As Pastor Paul Rabaut observed in a letter, the maréchal de Sennecterre, commander of the province, had informed the court that a "quantité" of Protestants had volunteered to help in the defense of the coastline. "Enchanted" by the reassuring news, Louis XV said "he would remember this."[4] How large the number of volunteers actually was is difficult to estimate.

Retribution

Whereas the Protestant Rochellois were the recipients of a gesture of appreciation from a grateful and relieved king, their brethren elsewhere in the Saintonge, Aunis, and Guyenne were suspected of having participated in a frightful conspiracy against the French government. Officials believed that these Protestants from the countryside and smaller towns had fallen under the seditious sway of Pastor Jean-Louis Gibert and other rebellious ministers. For that matter, many of the more socially secure Protestants in La Rochelle shared that conviction. It was the Rochellois who had disdainfully thrown into the fire the prince de Conti's invitation to rebellion. They suspected that even after the National Synod in 1756, Pastor Gibert and his "fanatical" partisans in the Saintonge had continued to follow the dangerous schemes of the headstrong prince.

Governmental officials believed that one of the more effective ways to stymie rebel Protestants was to disarm them. When the English fleet was sighted, the maréchal de Thomond and M. de Tourny issued ordinances requiring all Protestants of Guyenne to remit their arms. Moreover, M. de Tourny also sent brigades to lodge with the townspeople of Libourne and La Roche-Chalais. As he explained to Saint-Florentin, he did so "to contain the Religionnaires."[5] This was a strong preemptive move against any revolt.

A period of retribution set in, making the lives of many Protestants in the Saintonge and Guyenne miserable. In a letter dated February 19, 1758, Antoine Court described to Jaques Serces in England their terrible fate: "M. de Sennecterre had three of the temples of the Saintongeois demolished in December . . . and M. de Tourny, Intendant of Bordeaux, sent soldiers through all the parishes where there are Protestants, lodging with them at discretion, committing a thousand ravages and a thousand infamies, obliging all those who had their children baptized in the Desert to have them rebaptized by priests, demanding fines from them."[6]

The Protestants of the Saintonge complained bitterly about this new wave of fines, forced contributions, and other harassments. In writing to Louis XV, they described what they were experiencing as nothing less than a "general desolation": "Fathers and mothers and children are in flight, all seeking to avoid prison, exile, the convent or some other even worse penalty, perhaps the galleys or the gallows. Caves and the forests have become the retreats of these innocent victims."[7]

The Huguenots also feared that Louis XV might suspect them of having consorted with the English to launch a rebellion:

> Perhaps, Sire, (and this is our principal fear) the enemies of our peace have painted us to Your Majesty under false colors and as rebel subjects. . . . . When the enemies came near Rochefort . . . , with what willingness did we present ourselves to the Commanders at Bordeaux and at La Rochelle. They view our actions with satisfaction. Finally one should not forget that we have offered hostages recently in the Saintonge as proof of our constant disposition to consecrate ourselves to your service and to dissipate the injurious and insulting suspicions which have been maliciously charged to us.[8]

Despite these pathetic professions of Protestant loyalty, a number of governmental officials remained convinced that many Protestants in the Guyenne and the Saintonge had participated in traitorous relations with France's enemies.

Once the immediate danger of an English invasion had passed, these officials attempted to winnow out more systematically who among the Protestants was involved in the alleged conspiracy. This was no easy task: tight familial and religious bonds knit together the smaller Reformed communities. Moreover, as a governmental officer observed, many suspects had already fled for their lives. As late as March and April 1758, several officials were still seeking to identify suspects and taking interrogatories. For example, the aforementioned Tourny sent a lawyer, Antoine Bulle *fils*, the son of the *subdélégué* Léonard Bulle, to Libourne to gather information about possibly conspiratorial activities of Protestants.

On March 21, 1758, Michel Leboeuf from La Roche appeared

before Bulle for an interrogatory. He identified himself as a Roman Catholic. He was asked if, during the time the English fleet was off the coast of La Rochelle and Rochefort, he had not learned from the Protestants of La Roche "something . . . that was against the interest of the state." He replied that on one occasion during that period, he had been in a shop and heard a voice coming from outside. Speaking of the English, the voice declared that "they have finally arrived with a fleet of one hundred and twenty sails." Leboeuf decided to go outside the shop to draw nearer to the person who was talking this way. There he saw the Protestant François Aubie *fils*, talking with Sr. Trigant Prévot, his first cousin, also a Protestant. The latter then said, "They did not let us know in advance." The cousins continued their conversation, walking farther away from Leboeuf, who heard nothing more.[9]

On March 22, 1758, Michel Frappier appeared before Bulle and provided startling testimony. He indicated in an interrogatory that several individuals at Léparon, while felicitating each other on the arrival of the fleet, were disturbed that the English had not followed the directives they had received from the province.[10] These directives had been given to the English by the Huguenots before the expedition set sail.

On March 22, 1758, a servant girl of thirteen or fourteen named Isabeau Frégère also came before the lawyer to be questioned. She, too, was a Roman Catholic, but she had worked for a Protestant family, the Thévenins, for five or six months. She was asked if towards October 1757, an "inconnu" had paid a visit to her masters' house, been greeted warmly, and been obliged to drink some liquor. She responded that a stranger had come, but he had not been served liquor. She had been washing dishes during his visit. She was asked if the stranger had not said to her masters that "their minds should be put at ease, that they would soon see things take on a new look, that the English were going to land in France, that the religionnaires should give them a hand, that Saint-Foy and Bergerac had agreed to this, and that he, the stranger, was going into the Saintonge to prepare the way."[11] Isabeau Frégère concurred with this account and added that the wife of Matthieu Thévenin said to the stranger to take care not to be caught, and that the man was about thirty to thirty-five years old.

In a letter of March 24, 1758, Bulle informed the intendant Tourny that the suspect Aubie was no longer at La Roche: "Thus, in this spot, [there is] one less enemy, but very likely, he will augment the number elsewhere." Bulle thought that the Thévenins, however, could be arrested. Moreover, in a letter of April 28, he pointed out that he had received testimony that the Protestants kept abreast of the intendant's directives for their area: regular access to the intendant's mail was provided by a Protestant postal worker.[12]

In his correspondence with Tourny, Bulle noted that the Thévenins ran a cabaret. He suggested that they be summoned to Bordeaux, where they could be arrested more easily. He recommended that the local postmaster, a Protestant, be deprived of his functions and replaced by a Catholic. The lawyer also observed that a witness was worried about recriminations, once he gave testimony against the Protestants.[13] Bulle, then, did his best to track down those whom he suspected of conspiratorial activity with the English.

Bulle's diligent research penetrated a segment of the Protestants' network of communication with their English "liberators" and military allies. This network had existed before the Secret Expedition. Little reason exists to doubt the accuracy of the testimony he had received. Bulle's own correspondence with Tourny gives no hint that he believed that any of it had been concocted or had been motivated by spite.

If we use these interrogatories, we can reconstruct what took place before and during the Secret Expedition, along the following storyline. At least one English agent who spoke French (perhaps a French Protestant émigré) had traveled through the Guyenne and Saintonge before the expedition. His purpose was to enlist Protestants to abet the invading English forces. Protestants in several towns, such as Bergerac and Saint-Foy, had committed themselves to provide military help. The agent was on his way to the Saintonge. Also before the expedition, the French Protestants themselves had sent the English directives about how to pursue the descent. The plans had gone awry because the fleet had been delayed. Moreover, many French Protestants had been disarmed, and governmental troops had been lodged in the homes of "suspects."

This interpretation has much to commend it. Pastor Jean-Louis Gibert had boasted in June and July 1757 that he and his well-armed

Protestants were prepared to defend their newly built houses of worship. If they were not successful, plans were in place which would permit thousands of French Protestants to emigrate. He indicated that nothing could impede their exit. Gibert's claim meshes with General Ligonier's advice to General Mordaunt, commanding officer of the expedition's land forces, that there were Protestants in the provinces around Rochefort who wished the English well and who would want to board the English ships. It also accords with Lord Holdernesse's counsel that the arrival of English troops on French shores could spark a Huguenot revolt. Gibert was the pastor for several of the Reformed churches along the coast near Rochefort, and possibly for Protestants on the Isle of Rhé.[14] Le Cointe had informed Herrenschwand that large numbers of Protestants were armed and did not lack for leaders. Pastor Gibert had related the same thing to Herrenschwand. The timetable for the Secret Expedition had been thrown off by at least three weeks, precipitating Pitt's "violent" anger. The fleet apparently missed the date of its rendezvous with French Protestant forces in the Rochefort area. Moreover, the systematic disarming of the Huguenots had dramatically reduced their military capacity.

The lawyer Bulle may never have realized how successful he had been in piercing the secrecy surrounding the English government's planning with French Protestants. His sleuthing permitted him to know far more about the ultimate plans behind the expedition than did several of the most enterprising of Pitt's political enemies and gossipmongers back in England, where speculation about the expedition's objectives had begun to build to a fever pitch in the days following the fleet's return. What assessment Bulle's superiors made of the lawyer's precious harvest of information is not known.

Reaction in England

In England, the public waited with great anticipation for any scrap of news about the Secret Expedition's activities along the French coast. But news merely dribbled in. On September 17, 1757, Newcastle wrote to the duke of Devonshire that the Admiralty had heard little from Sir Edward Hawke, who had sailed a week before. Newcastle was glad that the fleet had finally departed because "the King of Prussia took the delay, as a design to lay aside the Expedition, on account of some supposed overtures for the Neutrality of Hanover."[15]

With no hard data to contradict them, intoxicating rumors about English successes spun the heads of even the dispassionate. On September 23, Symmer in London wrote to Mitchell in Berlin that the destination of the fleet still remained a secret. The "generality of People" thought it was headed for Brest, the largest anchorage of the French navy. But a ship had met the fleet south of Brest, ruining that hypothesis. No "probable conjecture" concerning another destination had taken its place. On October 4, Symmer wrote Mitchell that an express had arrived that day from Sir Edward Hawke with the news that the Isle of Rhé had been taken and La Rochelle was in the process of capitulating.[16] This was Symmer's last letter containing vain illusions about the success of the expedition. On October 6, Symmer again wrote to Mitchell that the news he had earlier reported, which was "believed by all," had not been based on accurate intelligence. In addition, an express from the fleet had not arrived, as he had been led to think.[17]

William Pitt, too, believed the recently received "authentic" account of English victories on the French coast. On Wednesday, October 5, Pitt wrote to Lord Bute that English troops had landed at Chalet-Aillon between La Rochelle and Rochefort and that the Isle of Aix had been captured. Pitt leaped to quick conclusions. He claimed that "consternation at Paris is great" and rejoiced that Germany is "redeem'd *si l'on veut*."[18] Unfortunately, Pitt had based his enthused assessment on the illusory intelligence report from France.

The next day, Thursday, October 6, Pitt's political and personal heavens came crashing down onto the hard ground of reality. He received a brief communiqué that proved to be only too accurate. At two o'clock in the afternoon, he wrote to Lord Bute once again: "I just received the afflicting news that our Fleet and troops resolved the 30th past not to attempt Rochefort. The road was found spacious and safe riding for the whole fleet of England. The *Magnanime* silenced the batterys on L'Isle d'Aix in 35 minutes of incessant firing and the fort surrender'd. This is all the short extract of this sad dispatch, which alone has been sent me here, contains. My heart is too full to write more."[19] From Pitt's point of view, a tragedy of the greatest magnitude had taken place. In a private letter (made public in the

Bath Journal) to his friend Potter, he lamented his disappointment, "which had broken his heart."[20] Later, he wrote: "I feel more and more I shall never get Rochefort off my heart."[21] Pitt was convinced that the English commanders had not only bungled a feasible military mission—to raze the stores at an important French naval port and to incite a Huguenot revolt—but they had abandoned Huguenot emigrants to a horrible fate. Whether England's status as a moral nation could survive this disgrace in the immediate future, he did not presume to know. Pitt's moral outrage overwhelmed him. He wanted to send the fleet back to Rochefort, but in the cabinet only Holdernesse would back him as he grasped for this slender straw.[22]

If Pitt had Rochefort on his heart, he soon had an enraged public on his back. As the magnitude of the fiasco began to wear on an already chafed public opinion, an explosion of uncontrolled anger fueled by pent-up frustration rocked London and other cities. It quickly surpassed the uproar caused by the loss of Minorca and the trial of Byng. From Bristol, Thomas Potter wrote to Pitt on October 11, 1757: "I am sorry to tell you that at Bristol, and all this country, the discontent at the sudden return of the fleet rises to a degree, and points to a place which makes me tremble." On October 13, Horace Walpole wrote to Harry Conway, one of the land commanders of the expedition: "The city of London talk very treason, and connecting the suspension at Stade with this disappointment, cry out that the general [Mordaunt] had positive orders to do nothing, in order to obtain gentler treatment of Hanover. They intend in a violent manner to demand redress, and are too enraged to let any part of this affair remain a mystery."[23] On October 15, a worried Newcastle wrote to Hardwicke, "It is certain that even Port Mahon [the loss of Minorca], did not occasion a greater run than this miscarriage has done."[24] Lord Shelburne noted later that everyone with whom he spoke thought the nation undone. Some believed that the military setbacks signaled God's displeasure with the sins of the English people.

The uproar was enormous. London was buzzing with accusations and counteraccusations. On October 26, Lord Chesterfield wrote to his son: "The whole talk of London, of this place, and of every place in the whole kingdom is of our great, expensive, and yet fruitless expedition."[25] A volley of charges was aimed directly at William Pitt and General John Mordaunt. The memories of Byng's recent court-martial and execution gave these charges particular velocity.

The fleet had anchored, on October 8, 1757, at Spithead. But an ugly spirit of recrimination had already begun to grow two days earlier, the black Thursday when news of the fleet's failure reached England. On that day, Admiral Anson wrote to his father-in-law, Lord Hardwicke: "I wish I could send your Lordship any agreeable news, but there seems to be a fatality in everything we undertake and that nothing succeeds. I shall not reason upon the enclosed papers. The Fleet having done well and all in their power gives me satisfaction, but why Hawke put his name to any council of war, when I warned him so strongly against it, astonishes and hurts me."[26] On October 9, Anson dined with Hawke in London. Early on, Anson surmised that his sea officers might escape blame, but not the land officers.

Initially Admiral Hawke seemed to skirt any major difficulty, as Anson had guessed he would. General Mordaunt was less fortunate. As Charles Jenkinson told George Grenville: "I hear that the King gave Sir Edward Hawke a good reception and Sir John Mordaunt an indifferent one."[27] Indifferent was too mild a word. In a letter of October 12, 1757, Henry Fox observed to the duke of Bedford: "Sir John Mordaunt is in an ugly scrape; his Majesty and his ministers are equally and excessively angry with him."[28] Even though Mordaunt had been George II's choice to lead the land forces, the king treated the returning general with cold contempt.

As for Pitt, he could hardly curb his rage. More important, despite George II's reproachful reception of Mordaunt, Pitt initially suspected that Mordaunt's inactivity was based upon the general's alleged belief that George II did not want the Secret Expedition to succeed. This was a politically dangerous interpretation for Pitt to enunciate; it would obviously offend the king. At first, however, Pitt was ready to accept that risk, and he discussed the scenario with the duke of Newcastle. On October 8, Newcastle explained to Hardwicke what he perceived was going on in Pitt's febrile state of mind:

Your Lordship has had a full account of the most extraordinary and unintelligible and absurd proceedings of the land officers upon our expedition. Mr. Pitt is outrageous upon it; is not angry with the officers, but imputes it to a prevailing opinion that neither the King nor the Duke wished success to this expedition, treated it as a chimera of Mr. Pitt's, which must miscarry, in order to show that the only practicable thing to be done was to employ our whole force in a German war, and this he combines with Lord Loudoun's conduct in North America. He talked high and passionately to us. He did not see how he could go on, and that in these circumstances he did know whether he should enter at all into the affairs of Germany, as he should otherwise have done; but your Lordship will see that he altered his mind as to that."[29]

According to this evaluation by Pitt, Mordaunt had kept the troops from landing in Rochefort, because he believed that George II feared what would happen to Hanover (under the control of the French) if the military stores in Rochefort were razed. The French might take horrible vengeance upon George II's Hanover. On November 4, 1757, Lord Chesterfield summarized Pitt's assessment: "In all these complicated machines, there are so many wheels within wheels, that it is always difficult, and sometimes impossible, to guess which of them gives direction to the whole. Mr. Pitt is convinced that the principal wheel, of if you will, *spoke* in the wheel, came from Stade."[30] Pitt's hypothesis implied that George II had ordered Mordaunt not to send the land troops against French forces in the area around Rochefort.

Pitt's interpretation corresponded with what many Englishmen suspected. The rumor circulated that there had been secret articles in the Convention of Kloster-Zeven which provided that no landing would be attempted if Hanover would be spared. In his letter to Pitt (referred to earlier), Potter clearly outlined how one segment of the public in Bristol viewed the matter: "It is to no purpose to talk of the misconduct of the officers concerned. The people carry their resentments higher. They will not be persuaded, that this pacific disposition was not a preliminary for the convention of Stade. They have been told, that an express was sent out after Hawke, that it arrived when the boats were prepared to land the soldiers, and that immediately in consequence of it, orders were given to re-embark. They say this has been done without your knowledge."[31] Ironically, it was Pitt himself who had dispatched the only known set of orders sent to Hawke after the fleet had sailed.[32]

Not wanting to be politically impaled owing to this false rumor,

Pitt decided to publish the directives of September 15, 1757. He did not much fancy being suspected of serving as a conduit for a pro-Hanoverian conspiracy. On October 13, the *Gazette* published George II's instructions that Pitt had relayed to Hawke.[33] The essential directive noted that the fleet did not need to return to England before the end of September, as earlier instructions had stipulated.

Whereas the *Gazette* publication allayed suspicions that Pitt had directly countermanded the invasion, it did not answer a second charge that also circulated. In a letter of October 15, Newcastle described it thus: "The other Insinuation which is propagated with great industry" is that the expedition had been "chimerical," "impracticable," and "the production of a hot-headed minister." According to Newcastle, this charge "levell'd directly at Mr. Pitt, affects him most. And here Mr. Pitt stands His Ground."[34] Pitt attempted to deflect this criticism by claiming that the planning for the expedition had been thorough and thoughtful, but that the military officers, especially General Mordaunt, did not follow their orders.

In trying to make this argument stick, Pitt confronted a serious dilemma. If he drubbed Mordaunt's failure too strongly, the cornered general might reveal a major secret: Ligonier had told Mordaunt that Protestants awaited the fleet in France and wanted to go aboard the ships. If Pitt criticized Mordaunt's activities too lightly, then the public might think that Mordaunt and he were accomplices. If he did not criticize Mordaunt at all, then he as the minister who planned the mission might receive full blame for its failure. By mid–October 1757, another political obstacle-course beckoned the minister, for a demonstration of his renowned dexterity.

The nation's fixation on this affair was intensified by a flood of newspaper articles, tracts, odes, and "true accounts" of the expedition. Released in mid–October, *A Genuine Account of the Late Grand Expedition to the Coast of France* promptly sold out three editions.[35] As Marie Peters notes, the *Herald*, the *London Evening Post*, and the *Monitor* were inclined to blame the commanders of the expedition and not Pitt, but even these newspapers wanted a detailed explanation. The *Monitor* warned Pitt that as the minister who had helped plan the expedition, he should "search this matter to the bottom."[36] As the different versions of what took place along the coasts of France multiplied, it became clear to many politicians that an official investigation into the Secret Expedition would have to occur. The public's interest was not abating, its anger was not cooling.

On October 14, 1757, Pitt told Newcastle that either he, Pitt, would have to be tried, or Mordaunt, or the two of them together. Obviously, Pitt, a proud man, had no real intention of putting his own head on a plate. That left Mordaunt's. Pitt reckoned that his own popularity would increase if he could convince public opinion that the expedition, to use Newcastle's summation of his sentiments, "failed purely from the behaviour of the Land officers."[37] Pitt operated from a position of strength on this point. After their return, Pitt had received assurances from the sea officers, Sir Edward Hawke and Admiral Anson, that they thought that the expedition had been feasible and of "infinite consequences."[38]

Apparently suspecting what Pitt's strategy might be, Sir John Mordaunt appealed to George II that there be an "examination of the whole, meaning the conduct of the land and sea officers."[39] The general's request fell on deaf ears.

The City of London made its own demands: an inquiry before Parliament. The ministry headed off this move, fearful that it might bring serious embarrassment to the government. At Pitt's behest, Mr. Blair of the secretary's office went to the Lord Mayor of London to tell him that an inquiry was being established. On November 1, 1757, the ministry appointed a Commission of Enquiry to "enquire into the Causes of the Failure of the late Expedition to the Coasts of France."[40]

Composed of the Duke of Marlborough, Lord George Sackville, and General Waldegrave, the Commission of Enquiry began its sessions on November 12, 1757. It was particularly concerned with the failure of the expedition to capture Fort Fouras and with the decisions made by the commanding officers at a council of war on September 25, 1757, to terminate their mission and return to England. The commission also considered specific elements of the orders that Sir John Mordaunt had received for the expedition and the quality of the intelligence reports he possessed at the time he decided whether or not to land the troops near Rochefort. The commission wanted to determine if Mordaunt should be court-martialed.

In these circumstances, General Mordaunt attempted to defend himself by insisting that Ligonier's directives for the mission be read before the commission. Mordaunt hoped to prove that his superiors had not planned the expedition sufficiently well and that the intelligence reports upon which they had relied were not adequate. In a word, Mordaunt sought to convince the commission that the expedition was not "practicable." Mordaunt's defense flew directly into the teeth of Pitt's own apologetic about the expedition's feasibility.

As if to demonstrate that General Ligonier, his superior, had given him inadequate directives and intelligence reports for his mission, Mordaunt read a paper containing Ligonier's own words, in which the role of the French Protestants in the affair briefly surfaced. Ligonier had described to Mordaunt the principal design of the mission: "If I am rightly informed, the great Point His Majesty has in View of this Expedition, and the alarming of the Coasts of *France* is the Hope of making a powerful Diversion in Favour of H. R. H. the Duke, as well as the King of *Prussia* who desires and presses much the very measure. In the Execution of this general Plan, a Project of giving a mortal Blow to the naval Power of *France*, is in his Majesty's Thoughts, by attacking and destroying, if possible, the Dock, Shipping, and naval Stores at Rochefort."[41] This seemed a reasonable set of military objectives.

But then Ligonier made these cryptic remarks about what Mordaunt should do, once the landing had been made: "I would advise to procure Guides upon the Spot, and paying them greatly; there are Numbers of Protestants in that Province, that wish you well, and would be glad to go on board with you."[42] Mordaunt could expect guides at the landing location to lead his troops to Rochefort. Most important, "Numbers" of French Protestants hoped the English descent upon the coast was successful. They also would want to return with the fleet to England. In shockingly brief compass, Mordaunt had hinted at one of the most sensitive secrets of the Secret Expedition: English leaders and Huguenots had conspired in planning the English descent. Somehow the import of Mordaunt's comments had to be quashed.

Ligonier attempted to do just that. He sent William Phillips to the Commission of Enquiry with the original of the paper Mordaunt had cited. Phillips also delivered the message that Ligonier had not intended that his remarks to Mordaunt be considered instructions. They were, rather, "Hints, which he had put upon Paper and read to

Sir *John Mordaunt* who thereupon desired a Copy." Mordaunt responded that "those Hints proceeded from his pressing Sir John Ligonier to give him a positive order; which, he [Ligonier] said, he could not do, but would give him thoughts."[43] General Conway supported Mordaunt's contention, testifying that he had witnessed Mordaunt, albeit unsuccessfully, press Ligonier for definite orders. Mordaunt apparently wanted to leave the impression that his derelicton of duty was not possible if in fact his directives were unclear. The mysterious "hint" about the French Protestants served as an excellent if ill-advised illustration to bolster his argument.

To demonstrate further that the expedition was not feasible, Mordaunt produced evidence suggesting that the French had fortified the coast before the armada arrived. Mr. John Eiser, an engineer, offered the commission a letter he had found in a priest's room on the Isle of Aix after the fort was taken. It was dated "At Rochefort, this eighteenth" and included the observation that, although the season was too advanced for enemies to attack the coasts, the "precaution of Monsieur le Gouverneur was none the less worthwhile." Mordaunt argued that it was the better part of wisdom not to attack an enemy whose numbers were unknown owing to poor intelligence.[44]

According to Horace Walpole, Mordaunt had "defended himself weakly" before the commission. Even if Walpole's assessment was too harsh, Mordaunt had not successfully extricated himself from his difficult position. On November 21, 1757, the commission reported to the king that "there were not then, or at any time afterwards either a Body of Troops or Batteries on the shore sufficient to have prevented the attempting of a descent."[45] On November 30, George II ordered that Sir John Mordaunt alone be court-martialed.

The king's decision had been a delicate one. Newcastle's private notes for November 28, 1757, point to the choices George II had: "Would the King break the Commander in chief in order to prevent the enquiry in the House of Commons?" Newcastle also wrote about the king's apprehension: "A Court Martial *for all*. Some secret Reason. Some connection with the Neutrality. Fear lest the Officers should speak out. He must think so." According to Newcastle, "These Gentlemen about Behind the King's Chair at the Opera — Sees Everything look ill. Suspicions . . . King will not take it upon Himself — Suspects Ligonier to be Pitt's Man — His Project."[46] Unfortunately,

Newcastle did not explain further what his notes meant. Nonetheless, they leave the impression that Newcastle, along with Pitt and many people, now suspected a possible link between Mordaunt's failure to prosecute his mission and the king's concern for the well-being of Hanover. Moreover, George II apparently attributed the whole scheme to Ligonier, his Huguenot general. The wheels within wheels concerning the Secret Expedition seemed to be spinning more rapidly.

Between December 14 and 18, 1757, the court-martial of Sir John Mordaunt unfolded; it reopened for another day, December 20, for the testimony of Sir Edward Hawke. Pitt tried to take advantage of the occasion by arguing in no uncertain terms that the mission was feasible. No partisan of Pitt, but devoted to Commander Harry Conway, Walpole described the minister's intervention:

> Mr. Pitt appeared before them, as he said, to authenticate his own orders, but took the opportunity of making an imperious speech, and defended Clarke and Thierri, the pilot; who, he affirmed, had supported their information, though sifted in so extraordinary a manner. General Cholmondeley interrupted him reminding him that he only came thither to authenticate. Pitt replied with haughtiness; and being asked, who had sifted Clarke and the pilot, he said, the military men; and often spoke of Mordaunt and Conway by name. There have been times when a Minister, in less odour of popularity, would have been impeached for presuming to awe a legal Court of Justice; but as it did Mr. Pitt no harm, neither did it produce any good to the cause he favoured. The whole Court treated the expedition as rash and childish; and acquitted the General with honour. Sir Edward Hawke reflecting on Thierri as an ignorant *Fanfaron*, General Cholmondeley asked if there were two Thierris? Surely, he said, this ignorant *Fanfaron* could not be the one so applauded by Mr. Pitt![47]

Despite Walpole's bias against Pitt, he described quite accurately the attitude of those who sat in judgment of Mordaunt and, in one sense, of Pitt. They scored Pitt's planning of the Secret Expedition and absolved Mordaunt of wrongdoing regarding any specific charge. Pitt's strategy of attributing the expedition's failure to Sir John Mordaunt had itself failed.

George II had also been foiled. The king was said to have fumed for several days about the commission's decision but he finally gave his approval of the general's acquittal.

Regardless of what face Pitt might attempt to put on it, the acquittal of General Mordaunt represented a personal rebuke for the secretary. The general's defense was that the expedition had been planned poorly and was not feasible. How could Pitt escape the conclusion that whatever their personal assessments of Mordaunt's bravery or lack thereof, the members of the commission agreed with Mordaunt's argument and disdained that of the secretary? Perhaps Pitt took some solace in his knowing more about the expedition's objectives than he could ever relate to the judges.

Pitt was troubled by another matter: the potential duplicity of the king. Had George II actually ordered General Mordaunt not to attack Rochefort, as cartoonists and others had speculated? Had not Admiral Hawke reported that Mordaunt and Conway were talking down an invasion even before the ships reached Rochefort and the shoreline had been reconnoitered? Did not those facts signal Mordaunt's treacherous designs?

They appeared to do so. But George II's own attitude towards Mordaunt does not reinforce the thesis that he and the general were collaborators in a subversive scheme. The king gave Mordaunt an icy reception when the general returned to England, and he was apparently genuinely angered when the commission acquitted Mordaunt. He removed Mordaunt from his private staff.

There appears to be no conclusive evidence that George II subverted the Secret Expedition in an effort to win less harsh treatment for Hanover by the French. The king was severe with the duke of Cumberland when, on October 12, 1757, his son came to him to explain why he had accepted an armistice. Newcastle described this meeting to Hardwicke: "His Majesty gave me an account of the whole. The King told His Royal Highness that he had ruined his country and his army and had spoiled everything, and hurt, or lost his own reputation." Even before this meeting, the king had described Cumberland as "His rascally son" or had lamented that "his blood is tainted."[48]

But the duke of Cumberland seems innocent of the charge of treachery as well. Even after his own personal reversals, Cumberland did not grumble about the launching of the Secret Expedition. Writing from Stade, on September 30, 1757, to Mitchell, Cumberland declared: "Lord Holdernesse mentions also his Majesty's plan (which I find is now carried into execution) of employing no inconsiderable part of both his sea and land forces to cause a diversion of those of the enemy, which, I hope will be productive of some immediate advantage to his Majesty's affairs, as well as of a favourable influence for those of his Prussian Majesty."[49] Neither father nor son apparently attempted to halt the expedition at the last moment.

More likely, a combination of other factors undid the expedition. At the controversial council of war, held aboard the *Neptune,* anchored off the Isle of Aix on September 25, 1757, the land and sea officers drew up a statement of five specific reasons why they had decided not to land their troops: "The French had been for some time in expectation of a Descent from the English in these parts; the long detention of the troops on the Isle of Wight; our meeting with contrary winds, fogs and calms upon passage; the several Informations received of troops assembled in the neighborhood; the great improbability of finding the Place unprovided, or of surprizing it, or consequently succeeding in an Enterprise founded on the Plan of assault in Escalade merely, & the uncertainty of a secure Retreat, for the troops, if landed; the Council are unanimously of opinion, that such an attempt is neither advisable nor practicable."[50] This statement was signed by both Hawke and Mordaunt, but for differing reasons.

Mordaunt and other officers aboard ship did not give credence to intelligence reports that their troops outnumbered French soldiers in the area of Rochefort. They thought it likely that they were facing superior numbers of French troops — from fifteen thousand to twenty-five thousand. A French commander had skillfully paraded his own small contingent of soldiers within sight of the English. The soldiers reversed their uniforms periodically so that the English would think that more French soldiers were stationed in the area than there actually were. The ruse worked splendidly, much to the relief of the townspeople who, assuming that all was lost, were preparing to surrender to the English troops.[51] In addition, Mordaunt was worried about how his troops could extricate themselves from the shore if they encountered stiff resistance from French troops. What would happen if adverse winds made impossible the troops' quick escape to the ships? Would his troops be trapped on the beaches and subject to the withering fire of superior enemy forces? In this larger context, Mordaunt's decision not to land his troops becomes at least somewhat understandable.

Another concern apparently troubled General Mordaunt. No Protestant soldiers or Protestant emigrants presumably met his scout parties on land, as General Ligonier had intimated they would. Was it not Thierry, the Huguenot pilot, in whom Ligonier and Pitt had such confidence, who had chosen the specific place where the English troops would land? At his court-martial, Mordaunt testified that "the only Place for landing the Forces which had ever been mentioned, or come under consideration in England, was a spot near Fort *Fouras* that was the place mentioned by the *French* Pilot. His was the only Information of any Place to land at, at all: With the view of landing there, we set out; but when we came there, we found a Fort erected upon the very spot, of which he appeared to have no knowledge."[52] Had not Ligonier implied that there would be guides at the point of landing and Protestants who would want to go aboard his ships? Mordaunt had ostensibly expected to receive military help from Pastor Gibert's vaunted Protestant troops.

Even if denied in the same article, the story was boldly trumpeted in print that so certain were the English of joining up with Huguenot forces, they had brought uniforms to dispense to the friendly Protestants. These uniforms would distinguish Protestants from regular French soldiers. This rumor, so importunate from a Protestant perspective, circulated rapidly.[53] It was in all likelihood true, denials notwithstanding.

Rather than encountering welcoming Protestant forces, Mordaunt's troops spotted loyal French soldiers in the very area where the English forces had planned to disembark. Symmer described this unsettling turn of events to Mitchell: "Our Friend Black had a good reflecting telescope on board with him, it was the only one in the Fleet; and of consequence he saw better than any of our Generals with their refracting Glasses. He discovered two different camps upon the higher ground, and saw several bodies of Horse moving about on the shore."[54] The French Protestants were nowhere to be found.

Admiral Hawke, on the other hand, could not understand why

Mordaunt had delayed sending in the troops. Rather, the land general called interminable meetings during the critical days the fleet was off the coast. Certainly, as Clerk reported later, the weather was favorable for a landing: "There is seldom finer or more moderate weather in the Bay at any time of the year than the ten days we were upon the French coast. The wind blew off shore, so we had no swell. At night, it commonly freshened up a little, but never so much, not even the 28th, as to prevent us going ashore in boats." Hawke's frustration and puzzlement with Mordaunt seemed eminently justified. And yet Hawke signed off on the document that permitted the return of the mission to England. He realized that he had no discretionary power to oblige the senior land officers to do what they obviously did not want to do.[55]

Despite the bravery and the yearning for battle of the soldiers on board the ships of the Secret Expedition, they did not engage in a *coup de main* on French soil. The French government's disarming the Protestants and lodging soldiers in their homes, combined with the arrival of the English ships at a time when the French Protestants did not fully expect them, create a context that helps explain the dismal failure of the Secret Expedition. Mordaunt's unwillingness to innovate new plans and land his soldiers, even though armed Protestants were nowhere to be seen, also contributed to the debacle.

For Pitt, the expedition was nothing less than an appalling disaster. It grievously affected him. Few Englishmen were in a position to fathom the depth of Pitt's despair. He could not unburden his heart to the public about the hidden objectives of the Secret Expedition—the sparking of a Huguenot revolt or, if that failed, the taking of thousands of Huguenots out of Catholic France. To do so would have risked equipping the French government with a rationale for exacting even harsher retribution from a suffering people.

Indeed, it was this specific fear that induced one commentator to note the "infinite pain" he experienced when he observed the publication of General Ligonier's "hint" to General Mordaunt: "This hint was doubtless purely intended as a private one, and never for publication, so that no blame can in that light fall upon it. But is it not unhappily published? All who know the nature of the French government, especially its constant disposition to oppress the Protestants must easily allow that such a paragraph cannot come unwelcome to it, as it may give it a handle, at least for a great vigilance, over a set of people thus marked out to them." The commentator quickly tried to dismiss this "hint" about French Protestants who would welcome the English armada and want to go aboard its ships as having "nothing to the purpose of the Enquiry."[56] In reality, Ligonier's "hint" referred to a significant factor with which to reckon, if the inquiry were to reveal one of the principal objectives of the Secret Expedition. The "hint" also pointed, albeit unknowingly, in the direction of a carefully camouflaged conspiracy gone desperately astray.

SEVEN

The Conspiracy of the Prince de Conti against Louis XV: The Aftermath

✤ ✤ ✤

Lately, He [Louis XV] has frequently burst into tears; and, at times, discovered an Inclination to resign the Crown.

Coded message of an English spy
to Lord Holdernesse, August 1757

On August 5, 1757, a spy at the French court wrote in code a remarkable message to Lord Holdernesse, who directed the English secret service: "Ever since the attempt on the King's life by Damiens, His Majesty has been daily, growing more uneasy and melancholy. Lately, He has frequently burst into tears; and, at times, discovered an Inclination to resign the Crown. At first, this was only regarded as an Effect of His melancholy; and it was hoped, it would pass with it. But having lately, persisted in so extraordinary a resolution, the whole Court were alarmed. The Queen, the Dauphin, Madame de Pompadour, the Nuncio, the Confessor, and several of the Court, who were honored with his Majesty's Confidence, were employed to prevent the accomplishment of so ill-timed a design."[1] If the spy is believed, Louis XV had become so "melancholic" that on several occasions he had contemplated resigning the throne.

Whatever the veracity of the communication, its contents leaked to persons outside the English cabinet. In his memoirs for 1757, Horace Walpole alluded to this revelation about Louis XV's desire to resign the crown of France: "Their King threw a damp on all operations: melancholic, apprehensive of assassination, desirous of resigning the crown, averse to the war from principles of humanity, perplexed by factions, and still resigned to the influence of his mistress, every measure was confirmed by him with reluctance or obtained by intrigue."[2] Obliquely lending credence to aspects of the spy's report, the well-placed Choiseul commented about Louis XV's difficulties in recovering from Damiens' attempt upon his life: "The fear of an imaginary danger lasts as long in the weak mind as that of a real danger."[3]

In August 1757, Louis XV did have "real" worries weighing on his mind, besides the assassination attempt. Engendering deep anguish was the king's suspicion that the prince de Conti, his own cousin, upon whom he had depended so much, had been a party to Damiens' treachery and had promoted outright rebellion among French Protestants. Intelligence reports warned the king that an English Secret Expedition of huge dimensions was preparing for a descent somewhere upon his poorly defended western coastline. Herrenschwand had surmised that "foreign help" might join Conti-led French Protestant forces and thereafter put "all in combustion" in the south. A disgruntled noble fomenting sedition, restive Protestants presumably impatient to follow him, English ships poised to send in troops to reinforce armed Protestants — these elements took on the horrendous allure of an eighteenth-century Fronde.[4] Not surprisingly, on August 27, 1757, Louis XV issued this secret order: "M. Berryer will continue to have M. Herrenschwand follow the correspondence of the affairs of the Protestants of my kingdom, and will pay a particular attention to Paul Rabot and Gibert."[5]

Undoubtedly, Louis XV's melancholy was partially the result of unresolved personal tensions. Madame de Pompadour allegedly believed that the king was constitutionally the "unhappiest man in his realm" because he could not reconcile his religious beliefs with his sexual mores.[6] As Michel Antoine observes, Louis XV's education had inculcated in him an "inveterate habit of submission to the church and a special respect for the episcopacy." His faith in Catholicism was authentic; his fascination for his mistresses was genuine as well.[7] The story was recounted that the king would sometimes teach his partners to pray before he bedded them. And yet even this singular form of devotion did not still his stricken conscience. He experienced bouts of remorse and rounds of renewed religious devotion.[8]

Melded together, these concerns were eminently suited to pull the king down into the morass of melancholy. In this unsettled state of mind, he "discovered an Inclination to resign the Crown," or so said the English spy, in an otherwise unconfirmed coded message.

The Prince de Conti in "Exile"

Although the Secret Expedition failed miserably and the Protestant revolt fizzled out, Louis XV could not thereafter embrace his wayward cousin, as if all were either forgiven or forgotten. The king now feared and hated the prince. Moreover, the subversive quality of the prince de Conti's "frondish" intrigues had placed him beyond the pale of usefulness and reliability and generally into the "opposition." In the following years the king's correspondence is adorned with polite comments about the prince de Conti, but they do not carry sentiments of acceptance. For example, Louis XV indicated that if the Poles were to choose the prince de Conti as their king, he would be "charmed."[9] But if they chose someone else, that would be agreeable also. In September 1757, Louis XV informed Tercier that he would allow the prince de Conti to become the commander of the armies of the empress of Russia, who might give him the Principality of Courlande; at the same time, however, Louis XV arranged that the prince be deprived of any access to the network of the secret du roi."[10] Indeed, Conti regretfully surrendered to Tercier the ciphers for decoding secret messages. He claimed that he did not want "the Service of the King to suffer on account of 'mon mal.'"[11] The chevalier d'Eon, one of Conti's agents, later explained to the comte de Vergennes how and why Louis XV excluded Conti from the "secret": "This book also contained my cipher with the King and M. Tercier, and another with the Prince de Conti, M. Tercier, and M. Monin. But the Prince de Conti having quarrelled with the King and Madame Pompadour, I was ordered to proceed only slowly with the secret negotiations of that Prince. I received a new cipher for corresponding only with the King, M. Tercier and the comte de Broglie at Versailles."[12] The exile from court which the prince de Conti had initiated in late November and early December 1756 became, for all practical purposes, definitive. The prince rarely appeared at court, and then only when his presence was indispensable. The king would not permit Conti to reassume the close working relationship they had enjoyed until the fall of 1755. As was noted, in a letter of May 13,

1758, the abbé de Bernis, Madame de Pompadour's advisor, asserted that the prince de Conti sowed "suspicions everywhere" and that Conti's reputation would probably never heal on account of a "violent" suspicion. It was this suspicion, too ominous to be disregarded, that disquieted the king.

Although an "exile" in the king's eyes, the prince continued to enjoy certain privileges associated with his station. At either the Temple or the Isle Adam he lavishly entertained his friends from high society with resplendent banquets, fashioning to a certain degree his own oppositional court.[13] He had contact with Beaumarchais, Diderot, and Voltaire. At various times the prince tried to help and protect Jean-Jacques Rousseau when the furor over his publications or person seemed ready to engulf him. Conti encouraged Rousseau to flee Paris after *Emile* was condemned.[14] The friendship between the two was apparently based on mutual fascination; Rousseau indicated in his *Confessions* that one of the greatest honors he had received was to be visited by the prince de Conti. But when the prince de Conti threw himself into the Maupeou revolution (1770–74), once again on the side of the parlements of France, he did so adhering to the basic political premises of his old advisor Adrien Le Paige, less obviously as a partisan of Rousseau.[15]

Protestant pastors continued to regard the prince as favorably disposed to their continuing struggle for toleration. In 1758, the spy Herrenschwand claimed that Protestants in Poitou still had "relations" with Conti. Moreover, the spy asserted that the prince was engaged in providing them military counsel: "M. Le Cointe is putting together under the guidance of the prince a work which has for its only object to spell out how to defend well the bourgs, villages, and other small posts and to make what one calls *la petite guerre* with the greatest possible advantages."[16] Few pastors, however, had the heart for enlisting in any grandiose schemes for revolt the prince might concoct.

Nonetheless, the prince remained a potential ally. A letter of September 4, 1775, by Pastor Betrine of La Rochelle, reviewed the prince's earlier involvement with the king on behalf of the Reformed community: "We know without doubt that Monseigneur the prince de Conti and the archbishop of Toulouse were charged by the deceased King to create a plan to help improve our lot: a thousand difficulties have suspended their operations and when they took them up again under the new reign, they were held back by a thousand other obstacles. However, it would be easy to facilitate them in looking for a person of confidence who could solicit the help of these Lords and of Monsieur Malesherbes, the Minister of Religion."[17] Pastor Betrine went on to suggest the name of Louis Dutens as this person, noting Dutens' familiarity with the prince de Conti. As was proposed earlier, Dutens may have been one of Conti's agents. If Betrine's version of the prince de Conti's involvement with the Protestants fails to specify the nature of the prince's intrigues in 1756–57, it does demonstrate that Protestants in the 1770s still believed he was interested in their welfare.

After 1756–57, the prince de Conti, then, by no means retreated from a public role in French politics, religion, and letters, but he never regained his status as the preeminent power broker. Louis XV had lost one of his most trusted confidants and talented though tempestuous leaders at a critical conjuncture, the beginning of the Seven Years' War. What this signified for France's military and political fortunes during the war is difficult to assess, as are all such hypothetical queries. The loss, however, was in all likelihood consequential. Even in the last years of Louis XV's reign, Conti remained a beacon for the "opposition." When other "oppositional" leaders, such as the duc d'Orléans and the Condés, sought reconciliation with the king in 1772, the prince de Conti would not join them. Louis XV coyly remarked: "My cousin the lawyer had not yet quarreled enough."[18] The king knew whereof he spoke.

William Pitt: A Political Survivor

In the late summer of 1757, Louis XV did not have a monopoly on bouts of depression. In September 1757, it will be remembered, William Pitt became so downcast about the Secret Expedition and other aspects of the English war effort that he told Newcastle he could not "continue in service." He sensed that events were rapidly slipping out of his control. A few months later, General Mordaunt, upon whom he had tried to fix the blame for the expedition's failure, was court-martialed, only to be found not guilty of dereliction of duty. Mordaunt was acquitted with honor. Pitt, who had in some people's minds harangued the court when he argued for the practicality of the mission, had his plea rudely dismissed. This turn of events did not augur well for the secretary. It placed him on the cusp of public humiliation.

After the debacle of the Secret Expedition, the prince de Conti drifted into relative obscurity, but William Pitt regained his political balance and pursued a career that, as judged by his countrymen, made him one of the greatest secretaries in the history of the English government.

The suggestion that Pitt's prodigious skills as a politician sheltered him from the massive firestorm after the expedition's failure is an attractive one. Early on, the *Citizen* "spared only the Vowel of Mr Pitt's Name" when it asked for "an Account of the Late Expence and Disgrace." Other weeklies and the newspapers amplified the charges against Pitt, who was pilloried as a "hot-headed Minister." In January 1758, an exposé entitled *Candid Reflections on the Report . . . of the General Officers* questioned the feasibility of the expedition and touched off a new round of debate.[19]

A lesser politician, one without Pitt's cunning, would have fallen, crippled by the harsh criticism and by the circumstances in which the government was immured. On November 1, 1757, Mitchell wrote to Holdernesse: "The English 'til now were envied and hated upon the Continent. At present they are despised." The Rochefort descent made them look like "triflers incapable of acting for themselves or of assisting their allies."[20] On November 20, Horace Walpole offered this gloomy appraisal: "Our fleet dispersed by a tempest in America, where, into the bargain, we had done nothing, the uneasiness on the convention at Stade, which, by this time, I believe we have broken, and on the disappointment about Rochefort, added to the wretched state of our internal affairs; all this has reduced us to a most contemptible figure. The people are dissatisfied, mutinous, and ripe for insurrections, which indeed have already appeared on the militia and on the dearness of corn."[21] Pitt had reason to be dejected, as did other members of the Newcastle administration. A spirit of revolt seemed to be brewing within England itself.

But during the fall and winter of 1757–58, a number of other writers for the newspapers and periodicals gave Pitt some relief. They urged the government to find out why the expedition failed; the public had a right to know. But they also generally accepted Pitt's argument that the expedition had been "practicable." The first comments by the

Gentleman's Magazine (October 1757) affirmed that the plan was not only feasible but astute. In November 1757, the *London Magazine* published a letter that encouraged Pitt not to become despondent.[22] This kind of support for Pitt played well with a segment of the public that still held the minister in high esteem and thought he had been betrayed by men of lesser stature and daring.

Indeed, Pitt's durable popularity, a corollary of his political skills, can not be ignored: it was a critical factor that helped secure his survival. As we saw, Horace Walpole, who disliked Pitt, argued that a secretary "in less odour of popularity" would have been impeached for the way he spoke at the court-martial of Mordaunt. Pitt's savvy and popularity served him well in the politically turbulent months after the Secret Expedition.

Even if one does not discount Pitt's catlike ability to land on his political feet, it should be emphasized that Frederick II's military victory at Rossbach, on November 5, 1757 (followed the next month by the victory at Leuthen), graced Pitt with undreamed-of help. Gerhard Ritter describes well how unexpected the victory was: "The extreme tension of the last months of 1757 was suddenly relieved by a near miracle: the triumph of the Prussian cavalry at Rossbach on the afternoon of 5 November. . . . In one hour the enemy was scattered and Frederick had won the most popular of his victories, the first triumph gained by German arms over the French in generations. From this day on the French leaders never again dared to engage a force led by the king in person."[23]

The fact that Frederick II did not succumb militarily but actually achieved a major battlefield victory without having been the beneficiary of a Baltic expedition, which had been shelved in favor of the Secret Expedition, represented a political boon for Pitt. If Frederick II had been ruined by not receiving sufficient support from England, then Pitt's enemies could have skewered and turned the secretary like a roast on a spit. Had he not committed a strategic blunder when he dismissed the counsel of Newcastle and Hardwicke to send aid to Frederick II in exchange for what his critics called a "chimerical" scheme, the descent upon the French coasts? On October 22, 1757, William Beckford advised Pitt that there were those already turning this political spit: "I wish I could say as much of some of your associates, who are constantly croaking to the world, the weakness of

Great Britain and the strength of France. Not long before the event of the late expedition was known, certain personages of some distinction whom I saw, ridiculed all our late measures, and declared we must submit to peace, since we had starved the cause in Germany."[24] Frederick II's remarkable victory a few weeks later blunted that kind of criticism.

Pitt's despondency and his awareness that he had lost control of events in early September 1757, in association with the fact that Frederick II's victory contributed greatly to reducing the secretary's political debits, suggest that to present Pitt otherwise—as a politician whose self-confidence never wavered or as one who always dominated events—is to misconstrue the evidence. Illustrious as Pitt's career became, and as glorious as historians affected by the "disease of admiration" have made it, the minister's terrible self-doubt occurred at a crucial juncture.[25] The failure of the Secret Expedition, along with other setbacks in September 1757, came close to knocking Pitt out of the Newcastle administration on the eve of its most successful enterprises during the Seven Years' War. Unlike Conti, who did not fully recover from his intrigues with the French Protestants, Pitt, who had also tried to help the Huguenots, survived the fiasco of the Secret Expedition and went on to stake his claim on political immortality.

Nor did William Pitt forget the plight of suffering French Protestants. He attempted to make certain that the hidden motivations for the Secret Expedition—the sparking of a Huguenot rebellion—or, that failing, the safe transport of thousands of Huguenot émigrés to England—were not revealed to the public. In this he was quite successful. Moreover, the secretary was aware of plans afoot in late 1757 and early 1758 to try once again to bring thousands of French Protestants to England. Now there was a desperately compelling reason for Huguenots to want to emigrate. Local governmental officials were persecuting them for their alleged involvement with the enemy, the potential English invaders. As the Protestants of the Saintonge and Guyenne lamented, the reprisals carried out by soldiers billeted in their homes were so savage that they felt constrained to flee to the wilderness to escape their tormentors: "The inhumanity was pushed to such an extreme that women on the point of giving birth were imprisoned and all of these vexations reduced the people to extreme misery." In a letter dated February 19, 1758, Antoine Court and his son, Court de Gébelin, wrote to M. Serces in England about the grim situation in the Saintonge and Guyenne and the willingness of thirty thousand Protestants to emigrate to England, where, it was hoped, they would be well received. Then the Courts indicated that "a person whom we made aware of this and who has written about it, as well as Mr. de Vill[ettes], informs us that one of your great men, Mr. Pitt, has already been instructed about this, at least in Part."[26] Pitt's interest in the plight of French Protestants remained undiminished. Sensitive to the religious dimensions of the Seven Years' War, he felt a special responsibility to protect the Protestant religion on the Continent.

Pitt's relations with Pastor Gibert continued for a few more years. Jean-Louis Gibert sent petitions to Pitt, asking that the secretary keep England safe haven for French Protestants who decided to emigrate.[27] In the aftermath of the Rochefort debacle, Gibert had escaped arrest by hiding in a cave.

In the early 1760s, Pastor Gibert, who slipped in and out of France, was still hunted by the French government.[28] A French police notice described Gibert as a pastor who had earlier relied on his contacts at the French court (the prince de Conti) for protection of his intrigues and was still treating with the English about immigration plans.[29] On April 6, 1761, Gibert arrived in London; as a deputy and pastor representing the churches of the Saintonge, he presented a letter to the archbishop of Canterbury (April 21). In the letter, Protestants of the Saintonge appealed to George III and the Protestant powers of the north to arrange with Louis XV that at the time of peace negotiations sixty thousand Huguenots be allowed to expatriate to England before emigrating to the New World as English citizens.[30] The letter was communicated to Hardwicke, Newcastle, and Pitt. The ministry concluded that such a demand by the English government would compromise their peace efforts and allow the French government to seek concessions for Roman Catholics in England.[31] On the other hand, the ministers indicated that they would welcome Protestants who came to England of their own volition. Ultimately, Pastor Gibert led a group of Huguenots to settle in the colony of South Carolina.[32] The police notice alleged that Gibert was in the hire of the English government and received a bounty for each emigrant he enlisted.[33]

As for Thierry, the French Huguenot pilot who had guided the ill-fated Secret Expedition to the coasts of France, he received a pension

of £750 from the English secret service until 1782. In the service's
records, Thierry's name was spelled Querre.[34] He had apparently
served as a valued English agent for some time.

French Protestants

Protestants who experienced the brutality of the government's reprisals in the Saintonge and Guyenne in the fall of 1757 were not in a
position to perceive that this represented the last wide-ranging persecution of their faith during the *ancien régime*. Furthermore, surrounding events precipitated what amounts to a turning point in the history
of the monarchy's attitudes to Protestantism in France. Looking back
from the year 1784 on the travails of the Reformed churches of France,
Pastor Etienne Gibert, the brother and the colleague of Jean-Louis
Gibert, proposed that the beginning of toleration for Protestants began in the Saintonge towards 1755, when Protestants (under the leadership of his brother, Jean-Louis Gibert) became more assertive. They
began purchasing or building stationary churches and demonstrated
a willingness to take up arms to defend these structures. Pastor Etienne
Gibert observed: "In some measure one can date the beginning of toleration in the year 1755 because if my memory serves me well, it is
that year that one began to build churches [*maisons d'oraison*] in Saintonge."[35] Pastor Jean-Louis Gibert also thought that the period when
the government was compelled to tolerate Protestants in the Saintonge began in 1755 and for the same reason.[36] At the Assembly of the
Clergy of 1770, the Catholic bishops, many of whom were still hopeful that Protestantism could be extirpated from France, complained
that the Huguenots were beginning to be tolerated in a de facto way
by the monarchy on account of their assertiveness during the first
years of the Seven Years' War.[37]

These perceptions of the date for the inception of a de facto toleration are not far distant from each other. By September 1757, not only
had Louis XV lost the will and to a large measure the capacity to
prosecute his sacramental policy rigorously against Jansenists, but
he began to retreat from enforcing that same policy against restive
Protestants.

As late as June 12, 1756, Saint-Florentin had informed Moncan at
Montpellier that Louis XV would not tolerate assemblies by Protes-

tants, whom he viewed as animated by a seditious spirit. But in the early fall of 1757, a "melancholic" Louis XV, badly traumatized by the Damiens affair and haunted by the Conti conspiracy, lost much of his earlier resolve. He did not have the heart to prosecute an all-out crusade to eliminate partisans of the "Religion Prétendue Réformée" once and for all. As Jeffrey Merrick observed: "Louis XV, in the end, did not secure the legal identity of Protestants by directing the clergy to register their births, marriages, and deaths or by institutionalizing some alternative to clerical registration. It became clear before the end of his reign, however, that Versailles meant to ignore the bishops' tiresome complaints about nonenforcement of the legislation against nonconformity."[38] With the attenuated enforcement of this legislation, accompanied by a more lenient attitude towards Jansenists, the king's sacramental policy began to fall into desuetude.

This does not mean that Protestants enjoyed full civil rights and toleration after 1757. The thirty-year period (1757–87) when the Edict of Toleration for French Protestants was promulgated by Louis XVI was marked by sporadic outbursts of persecution at the local level. Individual governmental officials, Roman Catholic bishops, and local *curés* still condemned Calvinism and urged harsh measures against the French Protestants.[39] In 1770, the bishops of Languedoc declared: "One can only use force and fear of torture against men [Pastors] of this character."[40] In 1775 at the Assembly of the Clergy, voices were heard urging Louis XVI "to strike this last blow against Calvinism in your States."[41] But no systematic campaign of persecution was ever again instigated. Condorcet remarked, however, that fear of it hung over the heads of Protestants like a sword held by a thread.[42]

According to John Pappas, the last round of systematic persecution took place between 1753 and 1756. We would propose that a powerful wave of persecution struck in the fall of 1757, when Calvinists were hunted down in the Saintonge and Guyenne. Thereafter, the Reformed churches moved into an era of de facto toleration characteristic of the "Second Desert," as opposed to the persecution so prevalent during the "Heroic Desert."

What factors brought about this significant amelioration in the Huguenots' social, political, and religious situation? It is commonly assumed that Voltaire's efforts on behalf of the Protestant community, especially in regard to the Calas Affair, were largely responsible.[43] And undoubtedly in the public mind the Calas Affair was inextricably linked to the wider struggle for Protestant toleration which was mounted to a certain extent by the philosophes.[44] Were the Protestants Jean Calas and the members of his family responsible for the death by hanging of a Calas son, Marc-Antoine, on October 13, 1761, in Toulouse? The Parlement of Toulouse responded in the affirmative, finding Jean Calas guilty of murder and sentencing him to death. The motive for the crime was purportedly this: the Calas family had feared that Marc-Antoine would abjure Calvinism to gain a certificate of Catholicism, required for practitioners of the law. Rather than allow this, the family murdered the erring son. The Calas Affair reached its nadir on March 9, 1762, when Jean Calas' hapless body was broken on the wheel of a cart in Toulouse.

The Calas case caught the attention of Voltaire. After being persuaded that Jean Calas and members of the family were innocent, Voltaire was relentless and eventually successful in his quest to have the name of the Calas family exculpated in the death of Marc-Antoine. In 1765 the Maîtres des Requêtes, a powerful court, reversed the judgments against the family.[45]

Voltaire's taking up the Protestant cause contributed greatly to creating an ambiance in France which made, for many, nationwide persecution of Protestants practically unthinkable. He continued to defend Protestant causes after the Calas Affair: the rehabilitation of the Sirven family; the freeing in 1764 of Claude Chaumont, a Protestant galley-prisoner from Geneva; the liberation of Jacques and Pierre Metayer, arrested in 1768 on their way to the French seminary in Lausanne; the defense of the Protestants of Mauvezin who were troubled for their religious beliefs in 1774; and others.[46]

Indeed, in the early 1760s, an "unnatural alliance" of sorts was formed by Voltaire, a number of other philosophes, and French Reformed pastors, in their united struggle for Protestant toleration.[47] This alliance was "unnatural" because it brought together thinkers who often criticized the Christian faith and pastors and members of the laity who had risked death on account of their faith. However, the "arch-heretic" among the philosophes, Jean-Jacques Rousseau, spent much less effort in this campaign, even though he had once again, in 1754, professed allegiance to the Reformed faith at Geneva. According to Rousseau's own testimony, in response to queries by

Genevan officials about the nature of his faith, he was so nervous that he "behaved at the interview like the stupidest of schoolboys."[48] As for Diderot, he cheered Voltaire's efforts on behalf of the Calas family, but his own public engagement in the affair was relatively meager. He did permit known Protestants, such as the chevalier Louis de Jaucourt to write extensively in the *Encyclopédie*, where they defended freedom of conscience.[49] In fact, the Huguenot Jaucourt was one of Diderot's most dependable editors and indefatigable authors.

In the 1760s, Protestant pastors, including Paul Rabaut, expressed their debt to the philosophes for their help in the struggle for toleration. In 1768, Rabaut wrote: "No one feels more vividly than I do the obligations which we have to Monsieur Voltaire. If the hand which has been troubling us has been released, if we have some tranquillity in our country, it is to this great man that we are indebted."[50] The public's identification of Voltaire with the Protestant cause was demonstrated in an especially poignant fashion when the aged philosophe, upon his triumphant return to Paris in 1778 for the presentation of the play *Irène*, received adulation from crowds as "l'homme aux Calas."[51]

Compared to the prince de Conti, however, Voltaire was a relative latecomer in adopting the specific cause of Protestant toleration as his own. In fact, in the early 1750s, several Reformed pastors were perturbed by the writings of Voltaire and Montesquieu. These philosophes seemed to link Calvinism with the spirit of republicanism and rebellion. Before he became aware of this linkage, Paul Rabaut was an unabashed enthusiast of the philosophes. Writing to Antoine Court on April 16, 1751, he spoke in glowing terms of Voltaire and Montesquieu as proponents of Protestant toleration through the former's *Henriade* and the latter's *Esprit des lois*: "The authority of these great men would be able to make some impression [for tolerance]."[52] But later, having read Voltaire's *Siècle de Louis XIV*, Rabaut was rankled by the charge that a republican spirit is inherent in Calvinism. On October 24, 1755, he wrote to Pastor Paul Moultou of Geneva and expressed his misgivings:

> You are acquainted, Sir, with the *Siècle de Louis XIV* by the famous Voltaire; I do not know if this author wished to court France, but I have viewed with chagrin that in his work, without regard for the sincerity

which history demands, without paying attention to that which he
had said himself in the historical summary which he had placed at the
front of his *Henriade*, without fearing to bring new persecutions to
some people, who have suffered from it so much, the most unjustly in
the world, he has poured out on us the gall of the most malignant
satire. It is that which he has done principally in the article on Calvinism. The more the reputation of the author is great, the more his work
is read, and the more it is important that he be refuted and that it be
[accomplished] in a triumphant fashion.[53]

In the very months of 1755 during which Pastor Paul Rabaut was
negotiating with the prince de Conti regarding the civil rights of
French Protestants, he severely censured Voltaire as an author whose
writings were affecting negatively the quest for toleration.

Montesquieu's *Esprit des lois* perplexed a number of Reformed pastors as well. They had difficulty determining whether this popular
work abetted or did damage to their campaign for religious liberties.
Several Jansenist authors exploited the work selectively as supporting the cause of religious toleration, but a few Catholic prelates had
been quick to capitalize upon the section of the *Esprit des lois* in which
Montesquieu associated Protestantism with rebellion and republicanism.[54] Part 5, book 24, chapter 5, proposes that "the Catholic religion
better suits a monarchy and that the Protestant religion is better
adopted to a republic." Antoine Court took pains to refute this association in his *Lettre d'un patriote sur la tolérance civile des protestants de
France et sur les avantages qui en résulteroient pour le Royaume* (1756).[55] The
author of *L'accord parfait de la Nature, de la Raison, de la Révélation* (1753;
1755) also referred to Montesquieu's *Esprit des lois* and Voltaire's *Siècle
de Louis XIV* as works detrimental to the cause of Protestant toleration: "It is not ecclesiastics alone who are sounding the alarm; diverse
writers of all kinds seem intent on disposing the ministry against us
by representing us under the most odious traits."[56] Nor had the issue
of the philosophes' allegedly anti-Protestant stance run its course,
even by the early 1760s. Court de Gébelin argued in *Les Toulousaines*
(1763) that Montesquieu actually favored Protestant toleration and
that Catholics were "wrong by consequence to oppose us with his
authority."[57]

Undoubtedly, by the mid-1750s, Turgot, Joly de Fleury, the abbé

Prévost, Jean-Pierre-François Ripert de Montclar, Karl Friedrich Baër, Friedrich Grimm, Laurent Angliviel de La Beaumelle, who was himself a Protestant, and other writers of a philosophic bent knew of the suffering that members of the Church of the Desert were experiencing. They felt aggrieved and wrote in favor of toleration for Protestants.[58] In the *Correspondance littéraire* (March 1756), Grimm described how "les sages" and "les vrais hommes d'Etat" were attempting to counter the deadly effects of the revocation of the Edict of Nantes. But they had hardly begun to write, when "obscure priests" rose up "to decry so salutary a project" (April 1756). As for himself, Grimm with remarkable prescience advocated the principle that whatever the beliefs of a citizen, "the moment he fulfills society's duties, he is worthy of enjoying the protection of the government and the privilege of his compatriots" (March 1756).

It is not clear, however, the extent to which Voltaire grasped the harsh nature of the persecution in the Midi.[59] Moreover, he was perceived by the Protestant leadership as a staunch opponent. His correspondence between 1756 and 1758 includes few references to the troubles of French Huguenots; rather, it focuses on his disputes with the Reformed clergy of Geneva and Lausanne.[60] Members of the Genevan clergy suspected him of complicity in the writing of d'Alembert's highly controversial article "Genève," which appeared in the seventh volume of the *Encyclopédie* in 1757. The article in a matter-of-fact manner described the Reformed pastors as proponents of a "perfect Socinianism" and as followers of the "natural religion" of John Locke. Even if the assessment were close to the mark, the Swiss pastors reacted in horror to the characterizations, as did Paul Rabaut. The Swiss pastors angrily turned on Voltaire, with whom they had earlier enjoyed amicable relations. Voltaire did not much care for them either, nor for their religion. In a letter of December 12, 1757, to d'Alembert, he likened "fanatical papists" to "fanatical Calvinists": "tous sont petris de la même m . . . détrempée de sang corrompu."[61]

The philosophes' role in stimulating the extensive de facto toleration that began towards 1757–58, therefore, should not be exaggerated. To contend, for example, that the impact of this early phase of the "philosophic" campaign was determinative in Louis XV's becoming more accommodating towards the Protestants than he had been as late as 1756 is less than a persuasive thesis. John Pappas underscores

the point well: "Certain historians affirm that Louis XV and Choiseul became less severe towards the Protestants because they submitted to the influence of the *Lumières*. According to the documents
[government records] we have just reviewed, it is evident that Louis
XV was not a kind of *'philosophe* without knowing it.'"[62]

A combination of other factors was more instrumental in shaping
Louis XV's new posture. First, the Protestants' own assertiveness in
boldly building churches (*maisons d'oraison*), in a certain measure, compelled the government to tolerate them. Looking back on the 1750s
from the vantage point of the year 1784, Pastor Etienne Gibert made
this pivotal assessment: "I would first observe that it was not toleration that put the churches of France in a position to rise again, but it
was their reestablishment that forced the government to tolerate
them."[63] He was referring to the daring stratagem initiated in 1755 by
his brother, Pastor Jean-Louis Gibert, of purchasing or constructing
buildings for places of worship. In a letter to Etienne, Jean-Louis
explained his own motivations: "I thought we should profit from the
circumstances in which we find ourselves . . . to have public houses.
. . . No one stepped forward to direct the work and pay the masons
but me."[64] On September 20, 1755, a critic complained about Jean-
Louis Gibert's "impudence": "This person has just struck a very bold
blow. . . . Large barns have been bought . . . in which benches and a
pulpit are placed. . . . Well-known in the countryside, M. Gibert
went to Marennes on horseback and walked for a rather long time on
foot in nearly all the roads of the town. If M. Gibert is not in correspondence with someone who is able to reassure him about the risks
he is running, it is an impudence of the first order." Even after the
Rochefort debacle, Gibert was able to convince the Synod of Hautes-
Cévennes in July 1758 that it should resolve "to procure houses in
all locations so that the faithful might render to God their public
cult."[65] Although Sennecterre and other governmental officials had
destroyed several structures, in an attempt to thwart the church-
building program in the fall of 1757, a number survived intact.

As Pastor Etienne Gibert implied, these buildings signified that a
new stage in Protestant assertiveness had been reached: no longer
would some Protestants be content to worship God in carefully concealed open-air assemblies held in the ravines of the Cévennes or on
the windswept coastlines of the Atlantic. They would gather, instead,

in stationary houses of worship. Eventually, their meetings were so "safe" that even wealthy Protestant "notables" became emboldened to form "sociétés particulières" for members of their own social class, refusing to worship with less affluent Protestants.[66] The brazen character of this Protestant building program was not lost on Roman Catholic churchmen and governmental officers.

Second, Louis XV's perception that the prince de Conti, his talented and traitorous cousin, had entered into a conspiracy to incite the Huguenots to a "frondish" revolt when the English troops arrived, ostensibly led him to question if Protestants could be extirpated from France once and for all by force. The specter of the Conti conspiracy was not conducive to thoughts about any new campaign to crush the Protestants, especially during wartime. Even after the failure of the Secret Expedition, Louis XV remained deeply worried about the possibility of a Huguenot revolt. On November 26, 1757, he gave the following secret command to Berryer, recently appointed naval secretary: "Monsieur Berryer, you will continue, even though you are no longer lieutenant of police, to follow the Protestant affair with Monsieur Herrenschwand, as I have earlier ordered."[67] After all, the firebrand Pastor Jean-Louis Gibert had eluded capture.

Third, certain Protestants had provided indisputable proof of their loyalty to the monarch when in September 1757 they defended La Rochelle against the English invaders. As we saw, Louis XV ordered that certain offensive plaques be removed. The king also believed that these loyal Protestants should be recompensed. A blind eye could be turned to their "profanations" of the sacraments. At the same time, Berryer would continue to monitor the activities of rebellious Huguenots.

Louis XV's order that the inscriptions be removed at La Rochelle seemed to symbolize that he recognized the right of these formerly imaginary Protestants to exist in France. Indeed, Paul Rabaut observed to a correspondent that he had it on good authority that the court had been "enchanted" by what the loyal Rochellois had done and that "the King said that he would remember this." Louis XV's sense of debt to loyal Huguenots militated against his taking up the cudgels to rid France of them. Moreover, in the fall of 1757, the spy Herrenschwand was proposing to Berryer a tantalizing idea: wealthy Huguenots might be willing to provide the king a large gift of money.[68]

Fourth, the king often did not have sufficient troops to complete the potentially explosive task of ridding France of Huguenots by force of arms. Saint-Florentin encouraged governmental officers in the south to follow the policy of containing rather than subduing religionnaires. He feared that rash attacks with undermanned contingents might incite Protestants to rebellion. Governmental officers in the south understood the problem only too well. In February 1759, Thomond explained to Saint-Florentin why it would not be wise to attempt to arrest Pastor Paul Rabaut: "I do not know if, in the general circumstances where we are and in the particular position where we find ourselves in this region in relation to the few troops we have here, Paul Rabaut could be arrested without causing ferment."[69] The diminished number of troops cut down the options the king had for punishing Protestant "disobedience" or for keeping them from worshiping as they pleased.

A Breach in the Monarchy's Sacramental Policy

The prince de Conti's quixotic dealings with the French Protestants between 1755 and 1757, in which he eventually attempted to exploit them for his own ends, went badly astray; many of them in the Saintonge and Guyenne became suspects and the targets of terrible reprisals. But fears of the prince's intrigues and reports about Pastor Gibert's partisans and the possibility of a Fronde-like rebellion, along with other factors (previously noted), helped snuff out Louis XV's ardor for upholding the sacramental stipulations that were critical to the maintenance of his own political orthodoxy. A breach in the king's sacramental policy towards Protestants yawned more openly.

De facto toleration quickly appeared in the south, and that before the Calas Affair. In a "Very humble and very respectful request of the Protestants of Languedoc," dated February 1761, Reformed pastors already looked back on the days of rude persecution as a bygone epoch. They gratefully acknowledged the arrival of this new era, which reflected a remarkable shift in the government's attitude: "This unfortunate generation, known in the Ordinances under the name of Nouveaux Convertis, is passed; another has succeeded it, which, having horror of the dissimulation of the one which preceded it, makes a public profession of its faith, under the shelter of a

Government for whom equity and moderation form its character."[70]

Despite his change of perspective, Louis XV continued to employ traditional rhetoric about enforcing the anti-Protestant jurisprudence. The Assembly of the Clergy in 1760 bitterly complained about the emerging "toleration" for Calvinism: "Nearly all the barriers opposed to Calvinism have been successively breached. Ministers, preachers, trained in heretical schools and in foreign nations, have inundated several of our provinces. It was asked at first that Calvinists be able to celebrate their marriages in a form which was purely civil and profane; and although one feigned to ask only for this permission, it was evident that such would lead to complete toleration of Calvinism. Today, toleration is being preached aloud."[71]

The king's response echoed earlier messages of reassurance: "I will always maintain exactly the execution of ordinances, edicts and declarations concerning the religionnaires; I do not cease to give orders to prevent and break up their assemblies, and to destroy all the prejudices with which they may have been inspired to hold about a toleration opposed to my true sentiments."[72] But this kind of rhetoric began to lose the force generated by conviction.

In 1765, the Assembly of the Clergy submitted remonstrances to Louis XV that reaffirmed a traditional premise: "There is, Sire, in your Kingdom, only one master, one single monarch whom we obey: there is only one single cult and one single faith. . . . The King has always repressed the audacity of innovators in constantly opposing error by the just severity of the laws."[73] The assembly's analysis captured well the thinking of Louis XIV; it did not accurately reflect the changing religious political situation in France.

Despite reassurances to the clergy, Louis XV was backing away from the enforcement of his sacramental ideology. In 1766, the king secretly commissioned Gilbert de Voisins, his *conseiller d'état*, to create a "plan relative to the religionnaires of the Kingdom."[74] In response to this request Voisins crafted *Mémoires sur les moyens de donner aux protestants un état civil en France*. But Voisins died in 1769, and political exigencies pushed the project aside.[75] As we saw, Protestants believed that Louis XV had also asked the prince de Conti and Loménie de Brienne to work on an undisclosed project in favor of the Protestants. A number of magistrates in the parlements of France, seeking to make natural law mesh with civil law, also devised various strategies to circumvent anti-Protestant legislation. David Bien commented: "By 1770 the parlements had decided to seek every available subterfuge which would permit them not to enforce the laws which proscribed Protestant marriage."[76] Understandably, complaints from individual churchmen and the Assemblies of the Clergy about the Protestant menace, often denounced as concealing a "republican plot," continued apace with these developments.

When Louis XV died in 1774, Gal-Pomaret, a Reformed pastor in Ganges, paid homage to the king for the vastly improved conditions Huguenots enjoyed in the 1770s. In a letter to Pastor Olivier Desmont of Bordeaux, Gal-Pomaret declared: "We have lost, Monsieur, a good King, in losing Louis XV. The prisons, the galleys, all were filled with our confessors when he mounted the throne; and when he left it, none of our brothers is to be found in captivity. The good prince had his weaknesses, even his vices. Ah! but what man does not have his own."[77] Louis XV, who had initially denied that Protestants even existed in his kingdom, and who had attempted to enforce anti-Protestant legislation until 1757, had by the end of his reign earned the plaudits of a well-respected pastor of the "Church of the Desert," one who corresponded with Voltaire.[78]

A Shift in Sacramental Policy

The repercussions of Louis XV's actual change in attitude regarding sacramental policy were monumental. In *The Damiens Affair,* Van Kley studies among other themes the Jansenist quest to escape the effects of the bull *Unigenitus* in the refusal of sacraments conflict. He argues that by September 1757, the Jansenists began to benefit from a victory they and the Parlement of Paris had won on the sacramental front.[79] In that month the Parlement of Paris returned triumphantly from exile and "under cover of the king's Law of Silence, thereafter ordered priests to administer the sacraments to appellants of *Unigenitus* and harried them out of the land if they refused."[80] The Parlement of Paris had gained authority over the Church's sacraments. Interestingly enough, the improvement of the Jansenists' situation emerged nearly in tandem with the inception of de facto toleration for Protestants. And obviously the prince de Conti was the critically important common figure to whom many Jansenists and the Huguenots looked for leadership and counsel. Even though many of the Protestant pastors were largely unaware of the intricacy of the Jansenists' campaign for "ecclesiastical toleration" (coupled, on occasion, with an appeal for "civil toleration" for Protestants), they undoubtedly benefited from it.[81]

Van Kley perceptively notes how the monarchy began to back away from enforcing its own sacramental policy against both the Jansenists and the Protestants towards 1756–57:

> Less conjectural and more immediate is the momentous shift in royal ecclesiastical policy with regard to appellants of the bull *Unigenitus*, which we have located in September 1757. If moreover, the clergy's remonstrances of 1770 are correct in pointing to the onset of the Seven Years' War (1756–1757) as the beginning of the Protestants' new assertiveness and the non-enforcement of the declaration of 1724 against them, then the year of Damiens marks a sacramental moment of the greatest significance in France. Not only would the monarchy have ceased supporting the clergy in its attempt to withhold the sacraments from those who persisted in regarding themselves as orthodox Catholics but it would have also begun to distance itself from the campaign to foist the sacraments of baptism and marriage upon those who in spite of a century of persecution persisted in their refusal to regard the second of these as a sacrament at all. A de facto policy of sacramental live-and-let-live seems to have taken root at this date.[82]

In Van Kley's view, the overthrowing of Louis XV's sacramental policy in 1756–57 had much to do with the unraveling of the *ancien régime*.

Many factors, political, economic, and intellectual, undoubtedly worked to undo the threads that held French society together before the Revolution. Historians have proffered finely tuned syntheses regarding how these multiple forces interacted with each other.[83] But as Van Kley and Merrick have convincingly demonstrated, politicoreligious controversies should be factored into any overarching synthesis regarding "origins." They played no small role in subverting the ideology of the monarchy.[84] The fabric of the *ancien régime* unraveled to a certain degree because the sacramental threads, believed so essential to political unity, began to give way. With the parting of these threads, numbers of contemporaries became convinced that other bases for establishing unity and other criteria for defining citizenship would have to be sought.

Louis XV felt constrained to make concessions to Protestants, thereby contributing to the undoing of his own sacramental policy. With these concessions, the king inadvertently cleared the way for another remarkable round of concessions by his successor, his grandson, Louis XVI.

Initially, Louis XVI's reign did not augur well for a change in the civil status of Protestants. During his *sacre* (coronation) at Rheims in June 1775, Louis XVI disappointed Turgot and other partisans of toleration for Protestants by taking the traditional oath to "extirpate heresy." Hermann Weber has suggested that members of the clergy and the king hoped that a strengthening or a renewal of the monarchy's political authority in the kingdom could be achieved by revivifying Roman Catholicism as the national religion. In that light, Louis XVI's dismissal of Turgot's proposal to "modernize" the *sacre* becomes more understandable. In an obverse fashion, the king attempted to emulate the most holy and traditional patterns for the *sacre*, thereby emphasizing the divine character of his religious and political union with the nation; he went so far as to exercise his healing function as *Roi thaumaturge,* touching some twenty-four hundred persons with scrofula, much to the disgust of several nobles who witnessed the king's "healing" ceremony.[85] Once again seeking reassurance, the Assembly of the Clergy also asked the king to indicate "that he is not in the disposition to accord any favor or protection to the 'self-styled Reformed Religion' and the rumors which circulate regarding this subject are without foundation, his Majesty having made no proposition in this regard."[86]

The next year, Jakob Heinrich Meister commented in the *Correspondance littéraire* (April 1776) about a resurgence of Roman Catholic devotion that had swept through Paris: "It is notable that the Jubilee had been celebrated in Paris with a devotion and with a regularity capable of astonishing times less corrupted than our own. Could this religious effervescence prove that *philosophie* had not made all the progress so much touted about it? Perhaps."[87] Little wonder that Paul Rabaut's son, Rabaut Saint-Etienne, did not think France in 1779 was "ripe for a project of universal tolerance" because neither "the laws, nor the priests, nor the nation and perhaps the government" were properly predisposed towards it.[88]

Nonetheless, in the early 1780s the king was confronted by forces seeking Protestant toleration. On May 12, 1782, the Parlement of Toulouse allowed curés to inscribe the births of children in their registers without the parents producing a marriage certificate.[89] Two Assemblies of the Clergy (Assemblée extraordinaire du Clergé, 1782; Assemblée du Clergé, 1785) drew up remonstrances against this ruling; their members believed that it undermined the Church's control of births, marriages, and deaths through the sacraments.

Then again, Louis XVI faced a coterie of "Magistrats–Philosophes," including the baron de Breteuil, secretary of state for the king's household, Claude-Carloman de Rulhière, Malesherbes, and the marquis de Lafayette, along with Rabaut Saint-Etienne, the son of Pastor Paul Rabaut, who skillfully manipulated a literary and political campaign in favor of toleration for French Protestants. Abetting the campaign were several Jansenist parlementarians and lawyers, with the indomitable warhorse, Adrien Le Paige, in their midst, and writers for the Jansenist underground journal, *Nouvelles Ecclésiastiques*.[90] It was as if cobelligerent factions from earlier rounds in the struggle for Protestant rights, with several of the same individuals, had regrouped to make a final push for toleration.[91]

In 1785, Lafayette visited Paul Rabaut in Nîmes and became acquainted with Rabaut Saint-Etienne.[92] That same year, Lafayette informed George Washington that he was going to engage in new efforts to improve the civil status of Protestants.[93] Malesherbes, a veteran of earlier bouts in the struggle, drew up the *Mémoire sur le mariage des protestans* (1785 and 1786), in which he analyzed the benefits that would accrue to the kingdom if Protestants received a number of rights other citizens enjoyed. Moreover, he shrewdly argued that Louis XIV had never intended to deprive French Protestants of their civil rights; in consequence, these rights should once again be accorded them. As Malesherbes remarked, "One can easily recognize that it is to be faithful to the principles which were in the heart of Louis XIV to give to Protestants a civil status and the rights common to all other citizens."[94] Whether or not apologists for Protestant toleration forged new "fictions" in describing Louis XIV's motivations is a moot point.

The baron de Breteuil provided Louis XVI with a report in October 1786 on possible remedies for improving the situation of Protestants in France.

On February 9, 1787, in the Parlement of Paris, Robert de Saint-Vincent, having struggled for toleration of Jansenists, delivered a critically important address for Protestant toleration. He reviewed the history of intolerance in France, joining the persecution of oppressed Protestants to that of oppressed Jansenists at Port-Royal, lavishly praised as the "fertile nursery of all talents, of all sciences, and of all virtues."[95] Saint-Vincent argued that Jansenists and Protestants had suffered at the hands of the same individuals—by implication, the Jesuits. At the time of the Revocation of the Edict of Nantes, Louis XIV had wanted Protestants to remain in the kingdom until "it might please God to enlighten them . . . and dissipate their darkness." But an unnamed group (the Jesuits) persuaded the king to change his mind: "Those who destroyed Port-Royal are the same ones who have been the ardent persecutors of the Protestants."[96] They convinced an aged Louis XIV to endorse the "fiction" that there were no longer any Protestants in France and induced Louis XV in his youth to renew this "fiction" in the Declaration of 1724. These blunders by the monarchy forced Protestants to flee, much to the benefit of France's neighbors. But if toleration were permitted to flourish, young Protestants would learn in public schools to appreciate the true sanctity of Catholicism, "rid of all political and ultramontane [Jesuit] prejudices," and thereby "create a new nursery of citizens who will prove useful both to the church and the state." After hearing Saint-Vincent's speech, his colleagues approved the motion that the king be urged to consider, in his wisdom, "the surest way to give a civil status to Protestants."[97]

Lafayette also convinced his colleagues on the second committee in the Assembly of Notables to petition the king on the matter.[98] Surmounting some vacillation, on November 17, 1787, Louis XVI, encouraged by the queen, appended his signature to the Edict of Toleration, drawn up principally by Malesherbes with counsel from some members of the Parlement of Paris, "talented experts," and Rabaut Saint-Etienne.[99]

The edict gave the appearance of showcasing the conviction of the clergy and the Parlement of Paris that Roman Catholicism should remain the state religion in public worship and that it served as the basis for the kingdom's unity. In the preamble to the edict, the king reiterated the traditional premise: "We shall always favor with all our power the means of instruction and persuasion which tend to tie together our subjects by the common profession of the ancient faith of our Kingdom." Later in the document, however, he conceded that use of force had not brought his non-Catholic subjects to that faith, and they should now be given certain civil rights while awaiting the time when they would come to the faith.[100] Essaying to fade this concession into the background of his exaltation of the Roman Catholic Church, Louis XVI declared: "I see with satisfaction that the clergy render homage to the ways of humanity which have dictated my edict concerning non-Catholics; in according them a civil status, I took care to maintain the unity of public worship in my Kingdom, the faith that I received from my fathers will be the national and dominant faith in my States."[101] In reality, the king had widened the breach in his own sacramental ideology.

After heated debate, the edict was registered by the Parlement of Paris on January 29, 1788.[102] One source gave the vote as 97 to 16. On this occasion, d'Eprémesnil, a member of the Parlement, turned to a crucifix and dramatically declared that Christ had been crucified again.[103] The Parlement of Toulouse, which had put Jean Calas to death in the 1760s, dutifully registered the edict on March 17, 1788. Three other parlements — Bordeaux, Besançon, and Douai — refused to do so.

The quest of some 500,000 to 600,000 "imaginary" Protestants for rights that would allow them to be incorporated into French society and yet worship God according to the dictates of conscience, had contributed to the subversion of the sacramental ideology that Louis XV attempted to buttress until the fall of 1757. This theory stipulated that society was founded on contracts between God and the king and between the king and his Catholic subjects and that the sacraments of the Catholic Church knit society into a civic and religious whole. The monarchy's definition assumed that all French citizens or subjects were loyal Roman Catholics, excluding Jansenist appellants to the bull *Unigenitus*. Particularly after September 1757 and largely on account of stark political realities, Louis XV began to waver, not so much in word as in practice, in his support for this vision of French society and citizenship. In this context, de facto toleration began to spread for Jansenists and Huguenots who "profaned" the Church's sacraments. Despite early hearty efforts, Louis XVI could not reverse the continued subversion of the sacramental view of citizenship and national unity. Even if the monarchy's sacramental ideology may not have had universal acceptance in French society before the crisis of 1756–57, the significance of these developments for the French kings was profound.

EIGHT

Epilogue:
Of Revolt, the Conti Conspiracy,
and French Citizenship

✢ ✢ ✢

T he Conti conspiracy invites comparisons between the prince's imaginative stratagems for revolt and the plots of frondeur nobles from the seventeenth century. Indeed, the formal similarities are sometimes striking. In 1653, for example, one of Conti's forebears, another prince de Conti, secretly pondered plans for a rebellion involving nobles like himself and "republican" French Huguenots from southern France, supported by Cromwell's military forces. Cloak-and-dagger agents scurried as messengers between the conspirators.[1]

By contrast, the Conti conspiracy may seem strangely misplaced in the political, intellectual and social landscape of the Siècle des lumières, or the French Enlightenment, if it is assumed that France at the middle of the eighteenth century was politically placid and stable and that the French people, imbued with a "philosophic" spirit, had largely turned their backs on things religious. France as painted by the Conti conspiracy does not easily accord with this familiar portrait.

The conspiracy belies, for example, the commonplace that the reign of Louis XV "was untroubled by civil unrest."[2] In reality, Louis XV became deeply despondent about the seemingly unending political and religious crises of 1756–1757. The spirit of revolt or resistance to his authority appeared all too sinister and pervasive in Paris and among the prince de Conti's Huguenot partisans. Damiens' attack on his royal person and the prince de Conti's machinations traumatized the king almost beyond what he could bear.

The Conti conspiracy discloses that, at least until the 1750s, religion played a far more significant role in French politics than is often supposed. Divergent interpretations of Catholic teaching provided both the prince de Conti and Louis XV with several of the arguments they used to defend their respective political theories. From Jansenist ideology as mediated by Adrien Le Paige, the prince de Conti culled a justification for his "frondish" opposition to his "tyrannical" cousin, Louis XV. But Louis XV also looked to Catholic teaching to brace royal authority with divine sanction. And it was the king's incapacity or lack of resolution to uphold his sacramental ideology by enforcing anti-Protestant legislation or the bull *Unigenitus* as a law of the state that ultimately proved so subversive to the monarchy's claim that only orthodox Roman Catholics were French citizen-subjects.

The conspiracy also makes clear that eighteenth-century French Huguenots were not as uniformly quiescent and loyal to the king as their spokesmen claimed. Undoubtedly, during the Seven Years' War the majority of Huguenots did remain Louis XV's loyal subjects. Like the Camisards before them, thousands of others were restive and willing to take up arms and fight for freedom of conscience. They believed themselves to be a people of God, but a people without a country. They were prepared to participate with Gibert and other militant pastors in a Conti-inspired revolt.

And, finally, the Conti conspiracy signals the fact that the memory of rambunctious frondeur nobles from the seventeenth century had not been completely eradicated in the eighteenth. Through his Jansenist advisor Adrien Le Paige, the prince de Conti ferreted out arguments and stratagems from writers for the Parlements of France and the frondeur nobles in his own revolt against "tyranny." And what was he himself, if not an eighteenth-century frondeur noble?

Ideological continuities, therefore, flowed between the prince de Conti and his frondeur predecessors. But continuities also emerged between Conti's partisans of the 1750s who defended the rights of the parlements of France against the alleged encroachments of a "despotic" king, Louis XV, and a number of clerics, politicians, and writers in the 1780s who mounted a renewed campaign for Huguenot civil rights or challenged the royal authority of another "despotic" king, Louis XVI. These continuities should be explored more fully.

In May 1789, with his own reform program in shreds, Louis XVI turned to the Estates General for relief. The coffers of the government were, for all practical purposes, bare. The king sought some means to extricate the nation from the economic, political, and social crisis into which it had obviously plunged. Whereas the government stared at a yearly national debt service that had soared to an estimated 285 million livres, many French workers had the agonizing personal experience of watching the price of bread and other staples surge upward in relation to earning power. These prices spiraled beyond levels with which people's wages, if they had work, could keep pace. Food supplies seemed unevenly distributed, if they were available at all. For many, the specter of famine haunted even menial chores. Portions of the population were hungry, poverty-stricken, and desperate. Hatred of privileged orders seemed intense, fueling the popularity of the Third Estate. The Réveillon Riots in late April 1789, when perhaps three hundred were killed, provided singularly bloody testimony to the unrest in the capital.[3] Disorders had erupted earlier in other parts of the kingdom. The cahiers de doléances, drawn up by the constituencies of deputies to the Estates General, were stuffed with grievances large and small, sometimes running at cross-purposes — far too many to be cured by a cumbersome body such as the Estates General.

And yet even the "patriotic" deputies to the Estates General still regarded Louis XVI as the king of France. None of the deputies' cahiers proposed the outright abolition of the monarchy. Many cahiers however, did want to place severe limitations upon the powers of the king and demanded a "constitution." But if the word choices and the style of the cahiers de doléances represent an accurate test of the political sensitivities of Louis XVI's subjects, the majority of the French people remained committed monarchists.[4] If anything in May 1789, they had inflated expectations of what the king and the Estates General could accomplish in this much-publicized national emergency.

After Louis XVI's reception of the deputies on May 2, 1789, and other inaugural events, the working sessions of the Estates General opened on May 5, in the Hôtel des Menus Plaisirs at Versailles. The physical setting of the Chateau de Versailles was, of course, spectacular; not so, the makeshift hall where the delegates met. Even if the king and members of the privileged orders flaunted disdain for the Third Estate, how could delegates, especially those from the provinces, not be at least somewhat awed by all the stunning pomp and ceremony displayed before their curious eyes? And would not the king give them counsel regarding how the nation might be pulled out of its misery?

But Louis XVI's oration in which he warned the assembly against "the exaggerated desire for innovation" seemed both disappointing and lackluster. Nonetheless, the deputies repeatedly interrupted the speech with applause. After all, the deputies viewed themselves as subjects of the royal orator, even though they frequently used the word *citizen* to describe themselves. The speech by Barentin, Garde des Sceaux (Minister of Justice), could hardly be heard. This was probably just as well, given his criticism of "dangerous innovations which the enemies of the public welfare seek to confuse with those desirable and necessary changes that are to bring about our regeneration." For thirty minutes, Jacques Necker, the king's director-general of finance, addressed issues of economic reform before his voice gave out; the rest of his three-hour recital was read for him. As Necker's tiresome speech lumbered on, the king yawned and dozed, and many of the delegates became restless.[5]

All in all, however, May 5 was not a bad day for the king. At its conclusion, Louis XVI could have scarcely foreseen that by the end of the next month, he would have surrendered most of his effective authority to members of this same Estates General. He could hardly have imagined that many members of the Third Estate, boldly supported by his frondeur cousin, Louis-Philippe Joseph, the duc d'Orléans, would come to believe that they in particular and not the king represented the nation. In this momentous transfer of power, the events of another day, June 23, 1789, were especially significant.

At 11:00 A.M. on June 23, 1789, after an early-morning rainstorm, Louis XVI arrived at the Salle des Etats, to which he had invited members of the Estates General. An hour and a quarter earlier, the duc d'Orléans had preceded the king. Just as the prince de Conti opposed his cousin, Louis XV, in the politicoreligious crisis of 1756–57, so the duc d'Orléans was playing a prominent role in opposing his cousin, Louis XVI, in 1789.

For many Parisians, d'Orléans, a Grand Master of a Masonic lodge, was a wildly popular personage. In a royal session of November 19, 1787, had he not withstood the king's desire to register in the Court of Peers an edict designed to raise 120,000,000 livres the first year and 420,000,000 over five? Had he not boldly attempted to restrain the king's absolutist reach by stammering (he spoke with difficulty), "Sire, it's illegal." The startled king could only mumble the nakedly absolutist words: "It's up to you . . . it's legal because I wish it." Thereafter an angry Louis XVI converted the session into a *lit de justice* and got his way with the edict. As to d'Orléans, the next day the king ordered him and two others into temporary exile. But reaction against these arbitrary acts provoked a tremendous backlash against the king, especially from the parlements of France. Protesting the exile, the Parlement of Paris proclaimed: "Sire, if M. le duc d'Orléans is guilty, so are we all."[6]

By the fall of 1787, the duc d'Orléans' reputation as a frondeur opponent of the king's "despotic" designs had a brilliant sheen. For many contemporaries, he was an authentic hero. Others, however, cursed him as an irresponsible renegade who somehow single-handedly unleashed the turmoil of 1789.

D'Orléans' popularity was enhanced by his exorbitant wealth and the generosity with which he sometimes shared a portion of it. In April 1789, the workers associated with the Réveillon Riots cheered him heartily: "Long live d'Orléans, our father, the only true friend of the people." In response, he emptied his purse and threw money to them, much to the disgust of several nobles accompanying him. Earlier, in 1780, he had opened up the refurbished Palais-Royal, one of his properties, to the people. And there an "oppositional" spirit to Versailles sprang up. Camille Desmoulins described its essence well: "At the Palais-Royal those who have stentorian voices take it in turn, every night, to climb up on to a table, around which people crowd to hear them read. They read out the most forceful statements on current affairs. The silence is only broken by applause at the most daring places. Then the patriots shout Encore!"[7]

In the crowded cafés, dress shops, jewelry stores, political clubs, theaters, bookshops, and bordellos along the promenades and galleries of the Palais-Royal, an army of Parisians could meander, hustle, buy, barter and sell, bet and borrow, proposition, and indulge a passion for free speech. They risked little recrimination because the property belonged to d'Orléans and was off-limits to the police. The Palais-Royal quickly took on the trappings of the capital's largest rumor-mill: writers, publishers, political hacks, and others pushed their way through the daily sea of humanity in a frantic quest to chase down the hottest rumor and latest scandal. The atmosphere of the Palais-Royal seemed to capture the spirit of its patron, the worldly minded duc d'Orléans.

By some accounts, when arriving at the critical meeting of the Estates General on June 23, 1789, the duc d'Orléans was the only noble among his rain-soaked colleagues of the Second Estate to be greeted by sustained applause and cheers—"bravo" and "vive Monseigneur d'Orléans."[8] Just like the prince de Conti, the frondeur and powerful noble was much loved by many citizens of Paris.

Nearly two weeks earlier, on June 10, 1789, the Third Estate had provocatively summoned the First and Second Estates to join it. Three days later, a trickle of clergy from the First Estate accepted the offer; on June 19, the trickle became a flood—149 members of the First Estate voted to follow the same course. Also on June 17, by a vote of 491 to 89, the Third Estate changed its name to the Assemblée nationale and renewed its claim to represent the nation. A British ambassador sagely commented to his foreign secretary: "If His Majesty once gives His decided approbation of the proceedings, such as they have hitherto been, of the Tiers-Etat, it will be little short of Laying His Crown at their feet."[9]

Louis XVI was not prepared to do that—at least, not yet. On June 19, in response to these ominous developments, the king called for a royal session with the Estates General to be held on June 23. The king intended to enforce his royal will that the three Orders remain separate.

On the morning of June 20, finding their meeting hall closed for repairs and guarded by troops, members of the Third Estate suspected a duplicitous gambit of Louis XVI—a prelude to the dissolution of their Order. Undaunted, nearly 600 of them trudged to an indoor tennis court on the rue du vieux Versailles. There Jean-Joseph Mounier called them to swear an oath "to God and the Patrie never to be separated until we have formed a solid and equitable Constitution as our constituents have asked us to." Those who took this oath numbered 577. The Englishman Arthur Young sensed the revolutionary import of their gesture: it represented nothing less than "an assumption of all authority in the Kingdom."[10]

Louis XVI and the Royal Session, June 23, 1789

These coups and countercoups fed the high tension enveloping the king's plenary royal session. Louis XVI, self-proclaimed "common father of all my subjects," delivered a thirty-five-point declaration, including several elements of genuine compromise regarding the confirmation of the deputies' credentials. But underneath any apparent velvet, two hard-fisted objectives seemed plain enough: to quash the burgeoning power of the Third Estate and to smother the creation of a united Estates General. He bluntly commanded the Estates General "to separate immediately, and to return tomorrow, each to the chambers of your Order, so that you can recommence your seances." He declared void "all the deliberations taken by the Deputies of the Order of the Third Estate, from May 17 until this month."[11]

After the king had finished his speech and exited, many clergy and nobles from the First and Second Estates did obey His Majesty's command and filed out. Other deputies of the Third Estate and some clerics, stunned by the king's audacious speech, remained seated. Finally, the royal master of ceremonies, the twenty-seven-year-old marquis de Dreux-Brézé, approached Jean Sylvain Bailly, the president of the Assemblée, and asked if he had heard the king's order to retire. The president replied that he could not adjourn the session without some discussion.

At first a deafening silence engulfed the hall. Then the silence was dramatically punctured. Honoré-Gabriel Riqueti, the comte de Mirabeau, hurled a defiant retort at the royal master of ceremonies: "Yes, we have heard the King's proposed intentions; . . . you have no right to be his mouthpiece in the National Assembly, you have no place here, no right to speak, you are not qualified to remind us of his words. However, in order to avoid all equivocation and delay, I declare that if you have been ordered to make us leave, you must seek orders to employ force, for we shall not leave except by force of bayonets."[12] Shouts of approval erupted from Mirabeau's colleagues. Then Armand-Gaston Camus (1761–1804), a Jansenist veteran of parlementary confrontations with royal authority, boldly declared that "a free nation cannot be imposed upon without its consent"; he then made a motion that validated the Third Estate's transformation into the National Assembly. The motion passed unanimously. Thereafter Antoine-Pierre Barnave (1761–93), a Protestant, also delivered a fiery speech in which he challenged the deputies to stay what they were—the National Assembly: "It only remains to the executive power to separate you, but it is your dignity to persist, and to persist upholding the title of National Assembly." Finally Mirabeau spoke again, and at his urging, the National Assembly approved the motion that the "person of each of the Deputies is inviolable" and could not be sought out or arrested for any opinions held or propositions made in the Estates General.[13]

In these moments of supreme defiance of the king's dictates, the same combination of confessional and social forces, so disruptive in the politicoreligious revolt of the mid-1750s had reappeared. Mirabeau was a sort of "philosophic" frondeur noble; Camus, a Jansenist; and Barnave, a Protestant. This time, it was directly instrumental in absolutism's last agony.[14]

Upon hearing the news that the Third Estate would not yield, Louis XVI shrugged off this disobedience. Then he himself reportedly said: "Oh well, let them stay." With this concession, the king's authority, already grievously compromised, suffered yet another crippling blow. It was not enhanced when word reached the streets of Paris that Necker had resigned (a misleading rumor, as it turned out—he had withdrawn his resignation). Popular unrest continued to seethe in Paris.

Nor did the king strengthen his political hand when four days later he invited "his loyal clergy and his loyal nobility" to join the Third Estate to make a new constitution. J. F. Bosher aptly observes: "The king was to reign for three more years, but his rule had come to an end."[15]

The troops Louis XVI surreptitiously ordered to Paris in late June were unable or unwilling to restore his authority. Already on June 24, 1789, two companies of the gardes-françaises had announced that they would not perform their duties. Then on July 14, 1789, members of the gardes-françaises, urged on by the agitator Hulin, aided citizens of Paris in taking the Bastille. At least ninety-one Parisians were killed in the assault, and many others wounded. After his surrender, Governor de Launay, the commander of the Bastille, was savagely attacked and murdered by members of a mob. As more blood blotted the streets of Paris, emotions became even more highly charged. The capital was quickly turning into a hotbed of revolt, which only the late-evening downpours seemed capable of temporarily dousing.

Louis XVI's diary entry for July 14 was indeed ironic. Probably referring to the lack of game he had killed that day, he summarized the day with the simple word "Nothing."[16] Still overconfident, the king was apparently planning to hold another royal session of the Estates General on July 16, during which he would ask the members to accept his proposals of June 23, 1789, or risk having their assembly dissolved. Only by the morning of July 15, after talking with Broglie, did Louis XVI begin to realize just how politically impotent he had become, just how many elements of the military, including the gardes-françaises, had abandoned him. On July 17, Louis XVI made a chastened political trip to pay homage to the new order in Paris. Bailly, the mayor of Paris, presented the king with the keys to the city at Porte de Chaillot. Moreover, in front of the Hôtel de Ville, Louis XVI valiantly pinned a cockade of red and blue, the colors of the duc d'Orléans and the city of Paris, on his hat. Nonetheless, it was clear that monarchy in the old style had died. Simon Schama put it this way: "With his court virtually abolished and his royal ceremonial stripped from him, Louis XVI had become, at last, just another *père de famille.*"[17] He remained the kingly father of the French, but his children boasted that they were free.

Was it mere coincidence that at the critical royal session of June 23, 1789, a "philosophic" frondeur noble, a Jansenist, and a Protestant spoke defiantly against the dictates of Louis XVI? Perhaps. Then again, continuities between the politicoreligious revolt of the 1750s and the tumultuous unrest of the late 1780s give the apparent happenstance less of the allure of an accident. The same kinds of people, a frondeur noble, Jansenists, and Protestants, promoting broadly similar agendas, were involved in each of these political crises.

As we saw, another popular cousin of the king, the duc d'Orléans, was present at the June 23 session. Like the prince de Conti before him, this prince of the blood possessed a frondeur spirit. He had cultivated alliances with parlementary and Jansenist malcontents and sponsored publications on the importance of religious opinions. He had played a pivotal role in the prerevolutionary defiance of the king's wishes. This temerity earned for the duc d'Orléans a lettre de cachet, which ordered what became a temporary exile. A number of contemporaries believed that the duc d'Orléans' opposition to Louis XVI was stimulated more by a spirit of vengeance against the royal couple than by adherence to political principle. Or his goal may have been to keep "any king, any church, and code of manners [from telling] him, or kindred spirits, how or where they must pass their time."[18] Whatever his ultimate motives in the contest of wills played out on June 23, 1789, the duc d'Orléans led the party of nobles of the Second Estate who joined themselves to the Third Estate.

The same kind of arguments, once stemming from the prince de Conti's advisor, Adrien Le Paige, and other Jansenists, resurfaced on the eve of the Revolution: Jansenist-oriented Robert de Saint-Vincent and d'Eprémesnil directed sharp criticisms towards "ministerial despotism" in association with the pamphlet warfare between the proparlementary "patriotic party" and the "ministerial" pamphleteers.[19] These arguments had also been exploited by Le Paige and other partisans of the parlements against Maupeou's "reform" in 1771. In fact, Le Paige's *Lettre sur les lits de justice*, written during the days of intense opposition of a segment of the Parlement de Paris and the prince de Conti to the "arbitrary" power of Louis XV (1756), was deemed so appropriate for the political situation of 1787 that it was published again under the title *Réflexions d'un citoyen sur les lits du justice*. Certainly some modification of these arguments occurred in the debates in 1787–88, as Van Kley said: "Le Paige's version of parliamentary constitutionalism ceded dominance to Mey's and Maultrot's, which recast the parlements as mere mandatories of the temporarily defunct Estates General. A constitutionalism which featured the parlements as lineal descendants of Frankish legislative assemblies — and therefore as the nation's chief 'representatives'— fell victim to Maupeou's *coup*."[20] Nonetheless the destruction of the ancient constitution in 1789 was definitely adjoined to the political and religious battles at mid-century — the ones in which the prince de Conti had starred so melodramatically.[21]

Louis XV and the *Lit de Justice* of December 13, 1756

Louis XVI's effort to crush the power of the Estates General on June 23, 1789, evokes memories of Louis XV's histrionic attempt to quash the power of the Parlement de Paris on December 13, 1756, with a *lit de justice*. On both occasions, the kings of France faced a restless public, a cousin who was a defiant but popular noble, and a recalcitrant assembly, some of whose members were influenced by Jansenist ideology and rhetoric. As in June 1789, so in December 1756, *mauvais discours* were ripe with news of conspiracies. Placards rudely lampooned and lambasted both Bourbon kings.

But of course many cultural, economic, and political variables did distinguish the two quandaries from which Louis XV and Louis XVI tried to extricate themselves, respectively, in 1756 and 1789. For one, much of the sacramental ideology buttressing the authority of Louis XV, until the confessional and political crisis of 1756–57, had been compromised in that very same crisis. Although Louis XVI tried to infuse new life into the myth of a sacred and inviolable bond between himself and the nation, during his coronation or *sacre* at Rheims in 1775, he was only partially successful. Too much of the monarchy's sacred aura had been obliterated during the politicoreligious revolt against Louis XV; too many "enlightened" and "frondish" views of the state now contested this sacred ideology in both clandestine and licit literature.

For another, Louis XVI had to face a much more virulent form of public opinion than did his predecessor, Louis XV. Once again, it was during the politicoreligious revolt of 1756–57 that public opinion seemed to gain its particular license and strength. In 1789, it blew with gale-like force, whipped up by the duc d'Orléans and other malcontents and focused far more on political, social, and economic concerns than on the more specifically politicoreligious issues of the mid-1750s.

In the months before December 1756, the spirit of revolt had been stirred by the Jansenist refusal of sacraments controversy, the more radical Huguenots' quest for freedom of conscience, the battle of the princes and peers with Louis XV, and the Parlement de Paris contentious claim that Louis XV should be bound by the kingdom's laws whose guardians and interpreters were members of the parlements. Starring as chief agitator was the charismatic prince de Conti, patron and strategist for the Parlement de Paris, beloved hero of the people of Paris, and renegade feared by the king and Madame de Pompadour.

As a frondeur noble who had tried to incite Huguenots to revolt earlier in 1756, as a victim of slights—whether real or imaginary—

inflicted by Madame de Pompadour and Louis XV, and as a partisan of Le Paige's oppositional views of the French constitution, the prince de Conti broke histrionically with the king in late November 1756. Despondent about the loss of this former confidant, Louis XV almost pathetically begged his cousin, the prince de Conti, not to forsake him. But if Conti remained resolutely hostile, the king said he would try to carry on without the prince, realizing that for him, His Majesty, things were going from bad to worse. And indeed they went to worse. On December 13, 1756, Louis XV attempted to force his royal will on the Parlement de Paris with a *lit de justice*. He ordered the Parlement of Paris to register his edict that was designed to bring about a compromise solution to the intractable politicoreligious crisis. Instead, Louis XV's *lit de justice* inflamed members of the Parlement, further convinced the prince de Conti that Louis XV was a despot, and failed to placate conservative Roman Catholic bishops. Some members of the Parlement promptly abandoned their posts.

D'Argenson was greatly alarmed by what happened at the royal session on December 13, 1756: "Here we are, then, completely at loggerheads with the King, and a chief [the prince de Conti] completely ready to participate in the movement of resistance and revolt which could follow." He continued: "In fact, all this announces to us some kind of revolt. . . . All the people have become partisans of the Parlements: they see in them the only remedy for their vexations; they have a hatred for priests. Thus it is feared that at Paris Jesuits and priests will be massacred one of these days."[22]

Was there a possibility that an armed revolt of sizable proportions would take place in early 1757, as it did soon after the climactic session of June 23, 1789? Would the "people of Paris" rally to the Parlement and the prince de Conti against the king, as d'Argenson speculated they might? We know that the prince de Conti could envision a revolutionary situation in which the throne of France would become vacant. We know that a rumor flew to Frederick II about an alleged revolt of the people of Paris led by the prince de Conti. We know that on January 5, 1757, a domestic named Damiens, an enigmatic character, familiar to Conti's associates, stabbed Louis XV. But we also know from the perspective of hindsight that d'Argenson's "movement of resistance and revolt" did not follow, at least not in Paris.

But contemporary Parisians had no prophetic gift with which to discern what loomed on their political horizons in December 1756 and January 1757. Little wonder that many Frenchmen were so anxious to learn who Damiens' coconspirators might have been and to determine whether Damiens' attempt on the life of the king signaled the beginning of a much larger revolt. Little wonder, too, that afterwards the king became even more deeply distressed and "melancholic."

If anything, Louis XV's woes only intensified in the summer months of 1757. Herrenschwand, Madame de Pompadour's spy, now linked the prince de Conti to a potentially massive Huguenot revolt in the south of France—one supported by thousands of invading English soldiers. Traumatized by Damiens' attack and by the larger Conti conspiracy, "melancholic" Louis XV seriously considered resigning the throne of France—or so a spy reported to Holdernesse.

Unlike Louis XVI, who eventually perished in the French Revolution, Louis XV survived the various crises associated with the politicoreligious revolt of 1756–57. The Secret Expedition failed miserably, Pastor Gibert's Huguenot "revolt" was countermanded, and the prince de Conti was essentially exiled, losing his power base at court. Even the people of Paris seemed less volatile in the remaining years of Louis XV's kingship.

But Louis XV did not survive the politicoreligious revolt of 1756–57 unscathed. As noted, he had possibly considered the drastic step of abdicating. The sacred aura of his own kingship was badly tarnished. The "desacralization" of the king and his person became more evident among the people of France in the wake of that revolt.[23]

Moreover, Louis XV's ability and resolve to defend his own sacramental ideology of citizenship diminished. After 1757, Jansenists and Huguenots, previously hounded and harassed by the government, began to enjoy de facto toleration. This significant development undercut the king's rhetoric that orthodox Roman Catholicism alone constituted the one faith of his realm.

Stimulated at least in part by Louis XV's incapacity to enforce acceptance of his view of citizenship and the state, and by what Roger Chartier prefers to call "an affective rupture" between the people of France and the monarchy, a shift in the locus of authority, away from the monarchy and towards the emerging powerful force of public opinion, gathered momentum.[24] Although participants in the Republic of Letters often considered "popular opinion," or the opinion of the "people," to be unstable and subject to manipulation, they sometimes characterized "public opinion" as establishing its base in self-evident universal and rational truths. Rulhière believed this force had emerged in the late 1740s; Malesherbes placed its origins at the founding of the Académie française.[25] Agreement among scholars on its ultimate provenance remains elusive.

Appeals to "public judgment" crop up in the Republic of Letters during the late seventeenth century and appeals to "public opinion" are apparent in discourse about finance and the theater before 1750, but it is the latter that became especially prominent in the Jansenist religious political controversies of the 1750s. Men of letters, pamphleteers, and the lawyers and politicians who drew up the *rémonstrances* of the parlements often shaped its ever-changing contours.[26] The convivial salons of Paris, where the art of conversation was pursued with such assiduity by members of various social classes, constituted another venue for a display of public opinion's expansive force.[27]

In 1775, Malesherbes described public opinion: "A tribunal has been raised independent of all powers and respected by all powers, which evaluates all talents, and pronounces on all people of merit. And in an enlightened century, in a century in which each citizen can speak to the entire nation by means of print, those who have the talent for instruction of men and gift of moving them—men of letters, in a word—are, among the dispersed public, what the orators of Rome and Athens were in the midst of the public assembly."[28] Before this tribunal, writers such as Louis-Sébastien Mercier, Le Fuel de Mericourt, and Pidansat de Mairobert attempted to disseminate frondeur journalism in the 1770s, only to have their clandestine efforts chastised not unexpectedly by Fréron but also by the philosophe Grimm. In the early 1780s the government effectively quashed this frondeur journalism and suppressed many "bad" or "pernicious" books.[29] Even though their standards for what constituted an illicit work were frittering away, book censors and the police kept doggedly at their posts during that decade. As late as 1788, the domestic press was still censored by a paternalistic government seeking to protect its own interests. Much philosophic-pornographic literature circulated "under the cloak," because of the real dangers book peddlers and printers encountered in trafficking in this literature. Robert Darnton reminds us: "The

Old Regime in its last years was not the jolly, tolerant, laissez-faire sort of world imagined by some historians, and the Bastille was no three-star hotel."[30]

Nonetheless, appeals to public opinion could not ultimately be stifled by the Crown. In the 1770s and the 1780s, individuals like the younger Mirabeau, Necker, Calonne, and Linguet, as well as bodies such as the parlements of France (1771–74; 1788), appealed to public opinion as they sought to have one form of abuse or another redressed. Even Louis XVI took it seriously: "I must always consult public opinion, it is never wrong."[31]

During the years 1787 to 1789, writers attempted to curry favor with public opinion through the periodical press, cahiers de doléances, memoirs, letters, and pamphlets. Apologists offered wide-ranging and often contradictory theories of the nature of the French "constitution." Traditionalist monarchists, obliged to interact with the potent power of public opinion, tried to bolster the sovereign authority of the monarchy by finding its historical roots in a misty Merovingian past and its ultimate warrant in divine sanction; on the contrary, several writers claimed that the constitution was yet to be created.[32] Whether of Jansenist (Le Paige's writings, for example), "philosophic," Physiocratic, or Rousseauist inspiration, innovative and often hybrid theories regarding social contracts, fundamental laws, representative governments, and the rights of citizens were debated in clubs, cafés, shops, salons, Masonic lodges, *cabinets de lecture*, town squares, and public gardens in Paris and in the provinces.

Impassioned writers often seized upon cheap, uncensored pamphlets as the vehicle of choice for getting their polemical agendas before a public that was hungry for the latest rumor, tantalizing tidbit of gossip, and political opinion. Recourse to pamphlet warfare was by no means a novel tactic for propagandists in the history of print.[33] In the recent past, pamphleteers had attempted to engage public opinion during the politicoreligious debates of the 1750s as well as during the Maupeou coup in the early 1770s.[34] The pamphleteers of 1787 to 1789 turned out pamphlets at a furious pace, trying to direct the rapidly changing course of prerevolutionary politics. As many as ten million copies of pamphlets rained down upon France in that two-and-one-half-year period.[35]

Arthur Young visited the Palais-Royal on June 9, 1789, at the time the Third Estate was bidding to become the voice of the Estates General. His comments provide a sense of the high excitement provoked by this swelling sea of pamphlets: "I went to the Palais-Royal to see what new things were published, and to procure a catalogue of all. Every hour produces something new. Thirteen came out today, sixteen yesterday, and ninety-two last week. . . . One can scarcely squeeze from the door to the counter. . . . Nineteen-twentieths of these productions are in favour of liberty, and commonly violent against the clergy and nobility."[36]

Among the major themes cascading through this flood of printed matter was debate over the controversial Edict of Toleration for Protestants. Linguet observed that pamphlets hostile to Protestant toleration could inspire "terror in timorous minds."[37]

Thoroughly alarmed by the edict, *dévot* defenders of the monarchy and the Church rushed into print. A number were convinced that the edict was the deadly fruit of a conspiracy among philosophes, Jansenists, and Protestants. These writers were certain that toleration for Protestants would have grave consequences: it would put the monarchy's own survival in doubt. A sampling of their pamphlets reveals great dismay. In his *Lettre à un magistrat du parlement de Paris, au sujet de l'édit sur l'état civil des protestans* (Avignon, 1787), a pamphleteer argued that the edict constituted a segment of a great conspiracy of "philosophisme" to introduce "tolerantisme" into France. The philosophes were using toleration and the Protestant cause as a front for their real goals—the subversion of Roman Catholicism and the monarchy. Protestantism was a sect "republican by essence, tending naturally to anarchy, the enemy of all authority."[38] He stated that "nothing disunites a country more than diversity of opinions in religion."[39] Then he pulled back the veil on the philosophes' true goals: "They know very well that all coups delivered against the Catholic religion, the true religion of the Monarchy, strike the Monarchy itself, that the weakening of one brings about the weakening of the other, and that they will fall when they cease mutually to sustain each other."[40] For this pamphleteer, toleration for Protestants could lead directly to the destruction of the monarchy.

The author of *Le secret révélé: ou Lettre à un magistrat de province sur les Protestans* (1787) shared similar alarmist sentiments. He contended that the edict would bring about the "subversion of civil and religious principles" and would prompt a "deadly revolution which was going to hasten the corruption of morals and change the form of the Government and the Constitution." Whereas Louis XIV and Louis XV had viewed the unity of religion, government, and legislation as the basis of the national pact, "the new law inverted this admirable relationship by separating the religious order from the natural and civil law."[41] The author proposed that the philosophes were partisans of the postulate that no one could be deprived of civil status for failing to adhere to the national religion. They complained that any "national pact which has religion as its basis would be barbarous, unjust, tyrannical, injurious to dignity, and contrary to natural law, the first and most august of all laws." The philosophes were attempting to foist this atrocious system on France in the name of toleration for Protestants; in reality, they were seeking to gain the right for skeptics and atheists to become citizens and "to enjoy the advantages of the social pact, without having any relationship with the national religion."[42] The pamphleteer urged that there be no change in the constitution that until the present had placed the plentitude of power and authority in the monarchy and allowed no admixture of truth and error in the national religion.[43]

Other Roman Catholics, however, applauded the edict. The Roman Catholic author of *Lettre impartiale, sur l'édit des protestans; à M. le Comte de Xxx* (Paris, 1788) discounted the claim that an alliance existed among Protestants, philosophes, and Jansenists.[44] For this pamphleteer, the real question was whether the king would continue to deprive Protestants of the rights of citizenship while he forced them by law to remain in France.[45] A Jansenist pamphleteer offered *Deux mots au discours d'un prétendu ministre patriote* (N.p., 1788) as a defense of the Edict of Toleration against the sharp criticisms of the abbé Jacques-Julien Bonnaud's *Discours à lire au Conseil*. In sum, staunch defenders of the monarchy's older definition of citizenship entered the fray to influence public opinion and ran up against governmental ministers, Protestants, Jansenists, "moderate Catholics," and writers of various "philosophic" stripes who were partisans of Protestant toleration. A number of authors relied on arguments drawn from several ideological arsenals to bolster their case.

The charge by the *dévot* or ultramontane pamphleteers that Protestants in the 1780s had collaborated with Jansenists and philosophes in the struggle for civil rights contained more than a modicum of truth. Rulhière, who wrote *Eclaircissemens historiques sur les causes de la Révocation de l'Edit de Nantes et sur l'Etat des protestans en France* (1788), envisioned the establishment of a national religion. Its creed seemed to refract various ideologies associated with the coalition of Jansenists and Gallicans, Protestants, and philosophes. He hailed his broadly ecumenical religion as "l'Eglise réformée gallicane." This "philosophic" faith was designed to replace ultramontane Roman Catholicism, and the king was designated as its "Chef Suprême," thereby avoiding domination from the pope.[46] In a letter of June 16, 1788, Rulhière thanked another member of the coalition, Pastor Rabaut Saint-Etienne: "It is to you that I owe the fact that I have conserved my belief as a philosophe regarding toleration, independence of opinion."[47]

Rabaut Saint-Etienne, who lionized Court de Gébelin, his friend and mentor, as well as Voltaire and other philosophes, viewed himself as one of the main organizers of the coalition.[48] On February 12, 1788, he explained to fellow Protestants in Bordeaux how he had enlisted writers in the struggle for toleration: "I sought and I succeeded in forming relations with diverse writers who are concerned about these matters; in enlightening their fellow citizens, they indirectly helped our affairs, their means should work side by side with ours." The pastor believed that it was necessary to organize this campaign for Protestants' "incorporation into the nation" because "writings in favor of toleration had absolutely ceased since the death of Voltaire [1778]." "No one," he asserted, had come along to fill the place of the philosophes. All it would take to proscribe Protestants' rights would be the arrival of a *dévot* ministry or king. Moreover, the clergy of the Roman Catholic Church and antiphilosophes were attempting to bring back the "old opinion." The pastor intemperately scored Roman Catholics by claiming that "every Catholic is a persecutor by nature due to his maxim: no salvation outside of the Church."[49] Burdened by this gloomy assessment of the Protestant situation in the early 1780s, Rabaut Saint-Etienne felt constrained to enlist "philosophic" governmental leaders and writers to reverse the deteriorating conditions. And as we saw earlier, a number of Jansenists, such as Robert de Saint-Vincent, also helped sponsor the campaign for toleration of Protestants.

The *dévot* charge, however, that Protestants had conspired with

Jansenists and philosophes to undermine the monarchy by subverting the exclusive claims of the national religion is a more complex indictment to adjudicate.[50] On one hand, participants in the loosely knit coalition often proclaimed themselves to be monarchists. The Magistrats-Philosophes Malesherbes and Rulhière supported royal authority. The Jansenist party, though reduced in numbers in the Parlement of Paris, was by no means politically impotent. Its members generally remained monarchists, even if their ideological beliefs could take on republican and seditious hues.[51] In the early years of the Revolution, the principal Protestant leader Rabaut Saint-Etienne, who admired the constitutional monarchy in England, professed to be a monarchist as well. On September 1, 1789, at the Constituent Assembly, he scoffed at the idea of a "republican" France: "It is impossible to think that anyone in the Assembly had conceived of the ridiculous project of converting the Kingdom into a republic."[52] Moreover, the Protestant author of *Discours sur l'édit de bienfaisance, à l'usage des Protestans de la Campagne* (1788) appealed to his coreligionists to extol Louis XVI's virtues as the king who had promulgated the Edict of Toleration: "That he deserves to be loved, he who, sensible to our miseries, placed us under the protection of the laws! We bless you, clement Monarch, inheritor of the royal virtues which brought about a flourishing peace under a glorious reign."[53] When the Bastille fell, on July 14, 1789, few Protestants were public proponents of republicanism or had criticized divine right political theory, whatever their private sentiments and whatever their "republican" and "rebellious" past.

On the other hand, a willingness to defy the king's wishes characterized certain members of the coalition who had struggled for freedom of conscience. It was, we recall, Mirabeau, a "philosophic" frondeur noble; Armand-Gaston Camus, a Jansenist; and Antoine-Pierre Barnave, a Protestant, who on June 23, 1789, had so blatantly defied Louis XVI's order for the Third Estate to quit the Salle des Etats. It was the rebellious duc d'Orléans, the cousin of the king, who led a number of the nobles to join the Third Estate and who had also worked for religious toleration. He had also been Mirabeau's patron and supporter. Within this coalition, then, differing perceptions of what constituted an appropriate attitude to the monarchy existed and were transmuted regularly. One set of perceptions resembled closely the sentiments of those who had directly challenged the authority of Louis XV during the politicoreligious revolt in 1756–57.

The Revolution and Protestant Freedom of Conscience

Once a "revolution" seemed in the offing in 1789, Protestants commonly viewed it favorably. They anticipated that it might create a political context in which the remaining legal restrictions the monarchy imposed upon their lives might be removed. On January 25, 1789, Jean Gachon, pastor of the influential Reformed Church of Nîmes, declared: "It [his church] dares again hope that the Nation taking at this same epoch a great step towards liberty, the cause of Protestants will become more and more favorable, and that profiting with prudence and circumspection from the general revolution, Protestants will be able to bring about the elimination of the restrictions which the law of November 1787 maintained."[54]

In the August 1789 debates surrounding *The Declaration of the Rights of Man and Citizen*, Rabaut Saint-Etienne delivered a searing criticism of the Edict of Toleration. He designated it "more celebrated than just." He argued that 120,000 out of the 360,000 people from the *sénéchausée* he represented wanted a complement to the edict. When he made this pronouncement, according to a contemporary account, "a crowd of Députés cried out that their cahiers bore the same wish."[55] Rabaut Saint-Etienne complained that the edict allowed Protestants a civil state but deprived them of the liberty "to profess their cult." Penal laws against public worship had not been abolished. Saint-Etienne made his demand explicit. He directly linked freedom of conscience for Protestants to liberty and equality of rights for all Frenchmen: "I am asking, thus, Messieurs, for French Protestants and for all non-Catholics in the Kingdom, what you are asking for yourselves: *la liberté, l'égalité des droits.*" He was sorely disappointed that Article 10 of *The Declaration of the Rights of Man and Citizen* (August 26, 1789), assuring non-Catholics freedom of conscience, did not permit them freedom of public worship.[56]

Frustrated by this omission and the inadequacies of the Edict of Toleration, Rabaut Saint-Etienne led a campaign that gained admission for his coreligionists to all employment and civil and military positions (December 24, 1789) and the restitution of properties belonging to the heirs of Protestant refugees (July 10 and December 15, 1790). And finally, in 1791, Protestants were granted the right to worship God publicly.[57] At long last, the arduous quest was over: before the law, Protestants had become the equals of Romans Catholics. In a special service at Paris, on October 13, 1791, celebrating the Protestants' new legal status, Pastor Paul-Henri Marron paid homage to the Revolution, which "has not made us change our master: it has rendered us free." In the same address he proclaimed: "Henceforth France is one; all the inhabitants of this vast empire are friends and brothers."[58]

The struggle of Jews, another religious minority, seemed to end in the same year. On September 27, 1791, Jews were enfranchised. The abbé Gregoire and Jacques-Pierre Brissot were instrumental in this breakthrough. Brissot proposed that to deny Jews such rights would violate *The Declaration of the Rights of Man and Citizen*.[59] At least on paper, freedom of opinion, even of religious beliefs, had gained legal warrant in France.[60]

The Huguenots' social, religious, and political world had been transformed from what it had been in the summer of 1755 when Paul Rabaut, an outlawed pastor of the "Church of the Desert," ventured to Paris to attend clandestine meetings with the prince de Conti, Louis XV's mighty but rambunctious cousin. In the mid-1750s the jurisprudence of the kingdom did not even acknowledge the existence of Protestants. Conti's interest in the Protestant cause appeared so promising and yet so isolated. Relatively few men of letters and governmental officials wanted to or dared to espouse that cause, including Voltaire himself.

But by the year 1791, Paul Rabaut's son, Rabaut Saint-Etienne, though recognized as a Protestant pastor, had emerged as a political leader in a national government. On March 14, 1790, he became president of the Constituent Assembly. His electoral successes undoubtedly symbolized for many Protestants their own emergence into the public arena in France. With the Revolution they began to figure much more prominently in local governments, especially in the Languedoc. A number of Huguenots participated in national governments as well.

Neither Paul Rabaut nor the prince de Conti could have predicted the outcome of the prince's efforts to win toleration for them or the "storm" (a contemporary expression of Antoine Court and Court de

Gébelin) that would batter Huguenots, especially in the south of France, in the wake of the prince de Conti's conspiracy against Louis XV.

As we have seen, this "storm" was intimately connected with wider politicoreligious fronts that menaced French political life in the mid-1750s. Paradoxically, the particular storm associated with the Conti conspiracy helped clear the way for a patch of relatively calm weather during which Protestants enjoyed de facto toleration. So grateful was a much-relieved Louis XV that at least some of his Protestant subjects at La Rochelle had remained loyal in September 1757, and so desirous was he not to incite another Huguenot rebellion by forcing others to comply with the anti-Protestant legislation, he began to look the other way when it came to implementing that legislation. In the context of the ensuing de facto toleration, Protestants could live more comfortably in France. They could not shake the fear, however, that at any time (the Calas Affair, for example) they might fall victim to another round of repression.

This concern renewed in their leaders the resolve to struggle for civil rights with other members of their loosely knit coalition, the Jansenists, the philosophes, and the Magistrats-Philosophes. Upon the promulgation of the Edict of Toleration and the nation's adoption of a new definition of citizenship, the world changed even more dramatically for Protestants. In Rabaut Saint-Etienne's poignant words, Protestants finally "became Frenchmen."[61] More generally, the Revolution witnessed the birth of a new political culture.[62]

A New Definition of Citizenship

During the Revolution, the French people redefined who they were.[63] The monarchy's ideology positing the rights of citizenship dependent upon a proper observance of Roman Catholic sacraments had already frayed badly; now it unraveled completely. According to the new definition of citizenship, Frenchmen were equal before the law.[64] Ideally, neither parentage, wealth, nor religion should henceforth exclude them from access to citizenship or determine how they could function in society. *The Declaration of the Rights of Man and Citizen* (August 26, 1789) reads: "Les Français naissent et demeurent libres et égaux en droits." In reality, access to voting and other rights were severely curtailed by qualifications of gender and wealth, even after the promulgation of *The Declaration of the Rights of Man and Citizen* (it became the preamble for the Constitution of September 1791). The struggle for women's rights, for example, was far from over in 1789, let alone in 1791.[65]

In their struggle for freedom of conscience, Protestants, albeit a religious minority, had played a pivotal role in a larger battle waged by philosophes, Jansenists, and magistrates in the parlements of France over the nature of the "constitution" and the "fundamental laws" of France and over what criteria should be used to determine who could be a French citizen. Jeffrey Merrick notes: "Jansenists, Protestants, and parlementaires all undermined the linkage of civil status and religious conformity during the controversies of the eighteenth century."[66] Even if the "cause of Protestants" did not become "the cause of all good citizens," as one rhetorically indulgent pamphleteer had proclaimed, it became at least the cause of a coterie of adroit politicians and writers. For these reformers, this religious minority, some 500,000 to 600,000 strong (Rabaut Saint-Etienne boasted that there were two million Protestants), could not be ignored if genuine equality before the law were to exist in France. Any criteria for establishing citizenship had to be construed, as Mirabeau advised, to protect the "right of man" that no one should be "troubled in the exercise of one's religion."[67] The religious faiths of minorities, including the followers of the "Religion Prétendue Réformée," Jansenists, and Jews, were to be respected.

Although having little impact on the lives of most French persons earlier in the century, the Huguenot struggle for freedom of conscience eventually took on political significance for the entire nation. This struggle prompted segments of the Huguenot population to be swept up in the politicoreligious revolt of the 1750s in which a desperate prince de Conti conspired against Louis XV. The revolt, with its many fronts, nearly overwhelmed the king of France, Louis XV. Moreover, it provided a precedent of sorts and arguments for revolt for some of those who defied another king in the turbulent days preceding a much larger "revolution" three decades later. The struggle also helped elicit from the French people a revolutionary transformation of what it meant to be a citizen.

Chapter One. The Huguenot Struggle for Freedom of Conscience

A portion of this chapter is based on my doctoral thesis, "L'influence des philosophes français sur les pasteurs réformés du Languedoc pendant la deuxième moitié du dix-huitième siècle" (University of Toulouse, 1969).

1. French Protestants compared their difficult lives with those of the wandering Children of Israel described in the Bible. Thus, the Huguenots spoke of the "Church of the Desert," or the "Church of the Wilderness." The French Protestant historian Emile Léonard made the distinction between the *premier Désert,* or *Désert héroïque,* 1685–1760, when French Protestants were persecuted, and the *second Désert,* 1760–87, when they began to enjoy a tacit tolerance. A number of historians still employ this distinction. See Philippe Joutard, "Les déserts (1685–1800)," in *Histoire des protestants en France,* ed. Robert Mandrou (Toulouse, 1977), p. 189. Consult the following studies concerning the "Church of the Desert": Charles Coquerel, *Histoire des églises du désert chez les protestants de France depuis la fin du règne de Louis XIV jusqu'à la révolution française,* 2 vols. (Geneva, 1841); Edmond Hugues, *Antoine Court: Histoire de la restauration du Protestantisme en France au XVIIIe siècle d'après des documents inédits,* 2 vols. (Paris, 1872); Emile Léonard, *Histoire ecclésiastique des réformés français au XVIIIe siècle* (Paris, 1940); Samuel Mours, *Les Eglises Réformées en France: Tableaux et cartes* (Paris, 1958); Herbert Lüthy, *La Banque Protestante en France de la Révocation de l'Edit de Nantes à la Révolution,* 2 vols. (Paris, 1961).

2. See J. Vienot, *Histoire de la réforme française: Des origines à l'Edit de Nantes* (Paris, 1926); Mark Greengrass, *The French Reformation* (Oxford, 1987), pp. 14–20; Henry Heller, *The Conquest of Poverty: The Calvinist Revolt in Sixteenth Century France* (Leiden, 1986), pp. 27–69, 111.

3. Greengrass, *The French Reformation,* pp. 9–14. See James K. Farge, *Orthodoxy and Reform in Early Reformation France: The Faculty of Theology of Paris, 1500–1543* (Leiden, 1985).

4. See Robert Kingdon, *Geneva and the Coming of the Wars of Religion in France, 1555–1563* (Geneva, 1956).

5. Cited in Greengrass, *The French Revolution,* p. 63. On Jean Morély's controversy with Theodore Beza over ecclesiastical discipline, see Henry Heller,

Iron and Blood: Civil Wars in Sixteenth-Century France (Montreal, 1991), pp. 72–74.

6. Barbara Diefendorf, *Beneath the Cross: Catholics and Huguenots in Sixteenth-Century Paris* (New York, 1991), p. 54.

7. See Denis Crouzet, *Les guerriers de Dieu: La violence au temps des troubles de religion*, 2 vols. (Paris, 1990); Heller, *Iron and Blood,* p. 13; Janine Estèbe, "Vers une autre religion et une autre église (1536–1598)," in *Histoire des protestants en France,* ed. Robert Mandrou, pp. 87–90.

8. See Robert Kingdon, *Myths about the St. Bartholomew's Day Massacres, 1572–1576* (Cambridge, Mass., 1988).

9. Greengrass, *The French Reformation,* p. 80. See Kingdon, *Geneva and the Wars of Religion in France;* Robert Kingdon, *Geneva and the Consolidation of the French Protestant Movement, 1564–1572* (Geneva, 1967).

10. Cited in Roland Mousnier, *The Assassination of Henry IV: The Tyrannicide Problem and the Consolidation of the French Absolute Monarchy in the Early Seventeenth Century,* trans. Joan Spencer, (London, 1973), Appendices, p. 320.

11. R. M. Golden, ed., *The Huguenot Connection: The Edict of Nantes, Its Revocation, and Early French Migration to South Carolina* (Dordrecht, 1988), p. 15. For background on the Huguenots at the end of the sixteenth century and the beginning of the seventeenth, see Léonce Anquez, *Histoire des assemblées politiques des réformés de France (1573–1622)* (Geneva, 1970 [1859]).

12. Philip Benedict, *The Huguenot Population of France, 1600–1685: The Demographic Fate and Customs of a Religious Minority* (Philadelphia, 1991), p. 102.

13. Menna Prestwich, "The Huguenots under Richelieu and Mazarin, 1629–61: A Golden Age?" in *Huguenots in Britain and Their French Background, 1550–1800: Contributions to the Historical Conference of the Huguenot Society of London, 24–25 September 1985,* ed. Irene Scouloudi (Totowa, N. J. 1987), pp. 175–97. On Louis XIV's attitude towards the Roman Catholic Church and the Reformed faith, see H. G. Judge, "Louis XIV and the Church," in *Louis XIV and the Craft of Kingship,* ed. John C. Rule (Columbus, Ohio, 1969), pp. 240–64.

14. Solange Deyon, "La destruction des temples," in *La Révocation de l'Edit de Nantes et le protestantisme français en 1685,* ed. Roger Zuber and Laurent Theis (Paris, 1986), p. 242.

15. For a careful analysis of the meaning of *republicanism* in the context of seventeenth-century French Protestantism, see Arthur Herman, "The Huguenot Republic and Antirepublicanism in Seventeenth-Century France," *Journal of the History of Ideas* 53 (1992): 249–69. Elisabeth Labrousse argues that French Protestants of the seventeenth century became especially suspected of propagating republicanism after Charles I was put to death in England by Protestants (Labrousse, "Understanding the Revocation of the Edict of

Nantes from the Perspective of the French Court," in *The Huguenot Connection*, p. 51).

16. Cited in Mousnier, *The Assassination of Henry IV*, pp. 88–89 (a paraphrase of John Calvin, *Institutes of the Christian Religion*, IV, XX, 32). For a discussion of John Calvin's views of "the duty to resist" as well as those of his followers, see Quentin Skinner, *The Foundations of Modern Political Thought*, vol. 2, *The Age of Reformation* (London, 1978), pp. 191–94, 210–17, 220.

17. For an even-handed review of this literature, see Kingdon, *Myths*, pp. 136–72.

18. See Elisabeth Labrousse, "The Wars of Religion in Seventeenth-Century Huguenot Thought," in *The Massacre of St. Bartholomew: Reappraisals and Documents*, ed. Alfred Soman (The Hague, 1974), pp. 243–55.

19. Herman, "The Huguenot Republic," p. 265. See also William Beik, *Absolutism and Society in Seventeenth-Century France: State Power and Provincial Aristocracy in Languedoc* (New York, 1985; Cambridge, Eng., 1992), pp. 168–72.

20. A statement by Elisabeth Labrousse, cited by Philippe Joutard, "1685: Une fin et une nouvelle chance pour le protestantisme français," in *Le Réfuge huguenot*, ed. M. Magdelaine and R. von Thadden (Paris, 1985), p. 17.

21. Odile Martin, "Prosélytisme et tolérance à Lyon du milieu du XVIIe siècle à la Révocation de l'Edit de Nantes," *Revue d'histoire moderne et contemporaine* 25 (April–June 1978): 310. See also Odile Martin, *La conversion protestante à Lyon (1659–1687)* (Geneva, 1986).

22. Henri Basnage, Sieur de Beauval, *Tolérance des Religions*, ed. Elisabeth Labrousse (New York, 1970), pp. xvi–xvii. On the dragonnades see Georges Frèche, "Contre-Réforme et dragonnades (1610–1689): Pour une orientation statistique de l'histoire du Protestantisme," *B.S.H.P.F.* 119 (April–June 1973): 362–83.

23. Philip Benedict, "La population réformée française de 1600 à 1685," *Annales: Economies, Sociétés, Civilisations* 42 (November–December 1987): 1433. For maps indicating the countries and towns where Huguenots settled outside of France, see Janine Garrisson, *L'Edit de Nantes et sa révocation: Histoire d'une intolérance* (Paris, 1985), pp. 182–87. Other Huguenots had left France in the previous century. See Baron F. de Schickler, *Les Eglises du Réfuge en Angleterre*, 3 vols. (Paris, 1892).

24. See the superb study by Erich Haase, *Einführung in die Literatur des Refuge: Der Beitrag der französischen Protestanten zur Entwicklung analytischer Denkformen am Ende des 17. Jahrhunderts* (Berlin, 1959).

25. Philippe Joutard, "The Revocation of the Edict of Nantes: End or Renewal of French Protestantism?" in *International Calvinism*, ed. Menna Prestwich (Oxford, 1985), pp. 343–44.

26. Jean Orcibal, *Louis XIV et les protestants* (Paris, 1951), p. 1.

27. Regarding the revocation, see Elisabeth Labrousse, *La Révocation de*

l'Edit de Nantes: Une foi, une loi, un roi? (Payot, 1985); Garrisson, *L'Edit de Nantes; Jean Queniart, La Révocation de l'Edit de Nantes: Protestants et catholiques français de 1598 á 1685* (Paris, 1985); Jean-Robert Armogathe, *Croire en liberté: L'Eglise catholique et la révocation de l'Edit de Nantes* (Paris, 1985).

28. Queniart, *La Révocation de l'Edit de Nantes*, pp. 118–19. For example, 17,600 were "converted" within six days at Montauban. See Elisabeth Labrousse's description of the difficulties "Nouveaux convertis" experienced when they did not fully practice their new faith (*La Révocation de l'Edit de Nantes*, pp. 202–11).

29. Cited in Joutard, "Les déserts," p. 198.

30. See Philippe Joutard, *La légende des Camisards: Une sensibilité au passé* (Paris, 1977).

31. Samuel Mours and Daniel Robert, *Le protestantisme en France du XVIIIe siècle à nos jours* (Paris, 1972), p. 82. For discussions of the French prophets, see Hillel Schwartz, *The French Prophets: The History of a Millenarian Group in Eighteenth-Century England* (Berkeley, 1980), pp. 22–36; Michael Heyd, "La réaction à l'enthousiasme et la sécularisation des sensibilités religieuses au début du dix-huitième siècle," in *Sécularisation*, ed. Michèle Mat (Brussels, 1984), pp. 5–38.

32. See the "Déclaration du Roy du 8 mars 1715," in Léon Pilatte, ed., *Edits Déclarations et Arrests concernant la religion réformée, 1662–1751* (Paris, 1885), p. 483.

33. Cited in Geoffrey Adams, *The Huguenots and French Opinion, 1685–1787: The Enlightenment Debate on Toleration* (Waterloo, Ontario, 1991), p. 39. The fear that Huguenots would form a state within a state was also well entrenched in the thinking of antirepublican writers of the seventeenth century (Herman, "The Huguenot Republic," 252–53).

34. Concerning the death penalty for pastors, see "Déclaration du Roy, du 14 mai 1724," Article 2 (in Pilatte, ed., *Edits Déclarations et Arrests*, pp. 536–37). Consult also Archives consistoriales de l'Eglise Réformée de Nîmes, L 47, "Complaintes contre les morts des Pasteurs."

35. *B.S.H.P.F.*, 36 (1887): 506.

36. Mours and Robert, *Le protestantisme en France*, p. 157.

37. Hugues, *Antoine Court*, 1:20.

38. See G. Edouard Guiraud, "Le séminaire de Lausanne et le pastorat en France pendant la période du Désert 1715–1787 (d'après les manuscrits Court)" (Thesis, University of Geneva, 1913), p. 25; Jules Chavannes, "Une école libre de théologie des temps passés: Notes historiques sur le séminaire protestant à Lausanne," *Le Chrétien Evangélique: Revue religieuse de la Suisse Romande* 15 (1872): 35.

39. Hélène Kern, "Le séminaire de Lausanne et le Comité Genévois," *B.S.H.P.F.* 108 (October–December 1962): 202.

40. Besides the study by Edmond Hugues regarding the career of Antoine Court, see Joutard, *La légende des Camisards,* pp. 137–62.

41. John G. Clark, *La Rochelle and the Atlantic Economy during the Eighteenth Century* (Baltimore, 1981), p. 53.

42. A spy for the government in the Languedoc named Puechmille (surname-Lagarde) provided an analysis of the attitude prevalent among "notables" towards the holding of worship assemblies. Although this description was written in 1761, it undoubtedly captures accurately the spirit of these same people in the 1750s, the period of our special interest: "J'y ay la façon de penser des protestans surtout des notables. Ils m'ont paru ne demander pas mieux que se soumettre aux vues du gouvernment, ils avouent que les assemblées sont à juste raison suspectes dans un état bien policé, non seulement ils n'y vont pas euxmêmes mais ils sont indignes contre les gens du public qui y vont" (AN, TT 442, doc. 200, Lettre de Lagarde à Monseigneur, February 15, 1761).

43. Mours and Robert, *Le protestantisme en France,* pp. 134–35.

44. C. Devic and J. Vaissette, *Histoire générale du Languedoc* (Toulouse, 1878), 13: 1078.

45. Cited in Michel Péronnet, "Les assemblées du clergé et les protestants," *Dix-huitième siècle* 17 (1985): 146.

46. Abbé Dedieu, *Histoire politique des protestants français, 1715–1794* (Paris, 1925), 1: 193; John Pappas, "La répression contre les protestants dans la seconde moitié du siècle, d'après les registres de l'ancien régime," *Dix-huitième siècle* 17 (1985): 112–13.

47. Dedieu, *Histoire politique des protestants français,* 1: 227.

48. AN, TT 440, doc. 143, Lettre de l'Evêque d'Uzès à Saint-Florentin, August 18, 1752.

49. BN, Salle des manuscrits, FF 7047; AN, TT 440, doc. 257.

50. AN, TT 440, doc. 8, "Mémoire de Puechmille à Saint-Florentin"; "Note d'un traitre fournissant à l'Intendant de Languedoc des indications sur les ministres du désert et leurs familles, 1751(?)," *B.S.H.P.F.* 7 (1858): 461–65. Soulier de Puechmille, from Anduze, had spent some time in Lausanne preparing for the Reformed ministry. He returned to France and was received as a proposant of the Reformed churches. Then he converted to Catholicism without Protestant pastors being aware of this. He became a remarkable informer. The archbishop of Avignon who arranged for him to be hired described his assets in this fashion: "Cet homme-là est parfaitement au fait de tout ce qui se passe non seulement à Genève, mais encore chez les Religionnaires du Languedoc et autres contrées voisines, et que sur cette connoissance il se trouve en état de rendre de très grands services à la Religion et à l'Etat" (AN, TT 440, doc. 2, Lettre de l'Archevêque d'Avignon à Saint-Florentin [April 1, 1750]).

51. AN, TT 440 doc. 8.

52. The sermons of these pastors were seized and are presently housed in the Archives du Département de l'Hérault: those of Pastor Bénézet—C. 232; and those of Pastor Molines—C. 233. Pastor Molines's abjuration of the Reformed faith was published under the title *Lettre curieuse et intéressante aux Catholiques romains et aux Protestants* (Saint-Quentin, 1757).

53. AN, TT 440 doc. 129, "Mémoire abregé, concernant l'état où se trouvent les Protestans, en France dans le mois de juin mil sept-cens cinquante deux"; see also AN, TT 440, doc. 41.

54. Dedieu, *Histoire politique des protestants français*, 1, p. 258.

55. BN, Salle des manuscrits, FF 7047, fol. 375. It is indeed likely that Louis XV commanded the publication of the ban. Saint-Florentin indicated this to Richelieu: "Le roi juge qu'il faut absolument leur faire perdre le goût et l'habitude de s'assembler" (cited in G. de Félice, *Histoire des Protestants de France depuis l'origine de la Réformation jusqu'au temps présent* [Paris, 1850], p. 507).

56. BN, Salle des manuscrits, FF 7047, Article 4; see also Articles 6, 9, 10, 11, 13, 15, 16, which treat the subject of Reformed pastors.

57. Cited in Edmond Hugues, ed., *Les Synodes du Désert: Actes et réglements des synodes nationaux et provinciaux tenus au Désert de France de l'an 1715* (Paris, 1891), 2: 41–42 n2.

58. Concerning the details of the arrest and judgment of Pastor Teissier, consult the Archives du Département de l'Hérault, C. 236.

59. Regarding the careers of Jean-Louis Gibert and his brother, Etienne, see Daniel Benoît, *Les frères Gibert: Deux pasteurs du Désert et du Réfuge (1722–1817)* (Toulouse, 1889).

60. Ibid., pp. 64–65; Bibliothèque de l'Université de Genève (B.U.G.), CF7, Collection Antoine Court, fols. 55v–56r.

61. AN, TT 447, docs. 170, 173.

62. Benoît, *Les frères Gibert*, p. 78.

63. Ibid., p. 79; B.U.G., Collection 7XIII, fols. 263–64 (letter of Antoine Court to Dugas, March 2, 1755).

64. Benoît, *Les frères Gibert*, p. 80.

65. Ibid., pp. 86–95.

66. Cited in Camille Rabaud, *Paul Rabaut, Apôtre du Désert* (Paris, 1920), p. vii.

67. Ibid., p. 31. Paul Rabaut retained his title as the minister of the Reformed Church of Nîmes until his death on September 25, 1794. Due to Rabaut's health problems, the church relieved him of his formal pastoral responsibilities in 1785 (Archives consistoriales de l'Eglise Réformée de Nîmes, B 91/20, p. 78). On Rabaut's preaching, see Albert Monod, *Les sermons de Paul Rabaut: Pasteur du Désert (1738–1785)* (Mazamet, 1911).

68. See especially Philippe Joutard's discussion of Court's *L'histoire des troubles des Cévennes,* in *La légende des Camisards,* pp. 144–59.

69. On the debate between Jurieu and Bayle, see Walter Rex, *Essays on Pierre Bayle and Religious Controversy* (The Hague, 1965), pp. 197–255; Elisabeth Labrousse, "The Political Ideas of the Huguenot Diaspora (Bayle and Jurieu)," in *Church, State, and Society under the Bourbon Kings of France,* ed. Richard M. Golden (Lawrence, Kan., 1982), pp. 222–83; Guy Howard Dodge, *The Political Theory of the Huguenots of the Dispersion with Special Reference to the Thought and Influence of Pierre Jurieu* (New York, 1972 [1947]). See also Geoffrey Adams, "Monarchistes ou républicains?" *Dix-huitième siècle* 17 (1985): 83–95.

70. John T. O'Connor, "Republican Conspiracies in the Old Regime" (paper presented at the International Congress on the History of the French Revolution, Georgetown University, Washington, D.C., May 6, 1989). In 1719, Jacques Basnage, an eminent French Protestant pastor residing in the United Provinces, recommended to his brethren back in France that they be satisfied with their *culte domestique* and that they should abandon their religious assemblies (Adams, "Monarchistes ou républicains?" p. 88).

71. Joutard, *La légende des Camisards,* pp. 124–29.

72. Eighteenth-century apologists seeking toleration for French Protestants sometimes claimed that the number of Huguenots who had emigrated ranged into the millions (versus the more reasonable figure of 200,000). For a reassessment of the thesis that the emigration of French Protestants caused grave damage to the French economy, see W. C. Scoville, *The Persecution of Huguenots and French Economic Development, 1680–1720* (Berkeley, 1960). But for a renewal of the claim (contra Scoville) that the emigration did severe damage to the economic well-being of France, see Robin D. Gwynn, *Huguenot Heritage: The History and Contribution of the Huguenots in Britain* (London, 1985), pp. 157–59.

73. See Antoine Court, *Lettre d'un patriote sur la tolérance civile des protestants de France et sur les avantages qui en résulteroient pour le Royaume* (N.p., 1756).

74. Cited in Marc Chalamet, *Un collaborateur d'Antoine Court–Pierre Peirot Pasteur du Désert (1712–1772)* (Paris, 1923), p. 38.

Chapter Two. Religious Political Disputes at Mid-Century

1. See the somewhat partisan but valuable account of Conti's career, G. Capon and R. Yves Plessis, *Paris galant au dix-huitième siècle: Vie privée du prince de Conty Louis-François de Bourbon (1717–1776)* (Paris, 1907); see also "Conti, Louis-François de Bourbon, prince de," in *Dictionnaire de biographie française,* ed. Roman d'Amat (Paris, 1961), 9: 543.

2. Prince de Ligne, *Lettres et Pensées*, pp. 9–10, cited in Capon and Plessis, *Paris galant au dix-huitième siècle*, p. 2.

3. On Conti's forebear, Armand de Bourbon, the prince de Conti, and his involvement in the Fronde, see Philip A. Knachel, *England and the "Fronde": The Impact of the English Civil War and Revolution on France* (Ithaca, N.Y., 1967), pp. 197–201, 207–10; A. Lloyd Moote, *The Revolt of the Judges: The Parlement of Paris and the Fronde, 1643–1652* (Princeton, N.J., 1971), pp. 178–79, 190–92, 198, 206, 209, 215, 217–18, 320.

4. J. L. Soulavie, *Suite des mémoires du maréchal duc de Richelieu* (Paris, 1791), pp. 31–32; Louis Dutens, *Memoirs of a Traveller, Now in Retirement* (London, 1806), 4: 157–58.

5. Dutens, *Memoirs of a Traveller*, 4: 32–33.

6. *Galérie de l'ancienne cour, ou Mémoires anecdotes pour servir à l'histoire des règnes de Louis XIV et de Louis XV* (N.p., 1788), 4: 382.

7. Rohan Butler, *Choiseul*, vol. 1, *Father and Son 1719–1754* (Oxford, 1980), p. 1068.

8. Cited in Capon and Plessis, *Paris galant au dix-huitième siècle*, p. 3.

9. Butler, *Choiseul*, 1: 518, 547.

10. Ibid., p. 564.

11. Dutens, *Memoirs of a Traveller*, 3: 80–81. Several accounts claim that the prince de Conti killed the maréchal de Saxe in a duel in 1750. For a refutation of this accusation, see Capon and Plessis, *Paris galant au dix-huitième siècle*, pp. 75–81.

12. Earlier, on November 26, 1742, Louis XV had written to the maréchal de Noailles: "Monsieur the prince de Conti asked me for counsel concerning what he was going to become; . . . he certainly has a strong will and an extreme desire to succeed" (cited in Didier Ozanam and Michel Antoine, eds., *Correspondance secrète du comte de Broglie avec Louis XV [1756–1774]* [Paris, 1956], 1: xvi–xvii n2).

13. M. E. Boutaric, *Correspondance secrète inédite de Louis XV sur la politique étrangère avec le comte de Broglie, Tercier . . .* (Paris, 1866), 2: 404; Ozanam and Antoine, eds., *Correspondance secrète*, 1: xvi–xxvi. One of the prince de Conti's forebears, François-Louis de Conti, had been elected king of Poland in 1697 but was displaced by a rival.

14. Boutaric, *Correspondence secrète*, 2: 405.

15. Antonia White, *The Memoirs of Chevalier d'Eon* (London, 1970), p. 127.

16. René-Louis de Voyer, marquis d'Argenson, *Journal et mémoires du marquis d'Argenson*, ed. E.-J.-B. Rathery (Paris, 1859–67), 5: 167; Charles-Philippe d'Albert, duc de Luynes, *Mémoires du duc de Luynes, sur la cour de Louis XV, 1735–1758*, ed. L. Dussieux and E. Soulié (Paris, 1860–65), 13: 424.

17. Comte de Broglie, *Politique de tous les cabinets de l'Europe pendant les règnes de Louis XV et de Louis XVI* (Hamburg, 1794), pp. 31–32. On Conti's

own designs, see Michel Antoine, *Louis XV* (Paris, 1989), pp. 645–58.

18. Duc de Luynes, *Mémoires,* 13: 435. On the career of Madame de Pompadour, see Nancy Mitford, *Madame de Pompadour* (New York, 1984); Tibor Simanyi, *Madame de Pompadour: Eine Biographie* (Düsseldorf, 1979); Pierre de Nolhac, *Madame de Pompadour et la politique* (Paris, 1928).

19. M. Duclos, *Mémoires secrets sur le règne de Louis XIV, la régence et le règne de Louis XV* (Paris, 1805), 2: 296–97; Emile Campardon, *Madame de Pompadour et la cour de Louis XV au milieu du dix-huitième siècle* (Paris, 1867), p. 160.

20. Duclos, *Mémoires secrets,* 2: 296–97. In his *Madame Pompadour et la politique,* Pierre de Nolhac argued against the supposition that Madame de Pompadour had a major role in the "important decisions of Louis XV and his ministers." To my mind this assessment is less than convincing.

21. Jeffrey Merrick, "Conscience and Citizenship in Eighteenth-Century France," *Eighteenth Century Studies* 21 (fall 1987): 49.

22. Malesherbes cited in Jeffrey Merrick, *The Desacralization of the French Monarchy in the Eighteenth Century* (Baton Rouge, La., 1990), p. 138; Merrick, "Conscience and Citizenship," pp. 52–53.

23. Nor could civil rights to Jews be accorded. On the status of Jews in eighteenth-century France, see Arthur Hertzberg, *The French Enlightenment and the Jews* (New York, 1968).

24. Jean-Pierre-François Ripert de Monclar, *Mémoire théologique et politique au sujet des mariages clandestins des protestants en France* (N.p., 1755, 1756), pp. 4, 8, 121–22. Contemporary scholarship has raised questions regarding the attribution of this piece to Monclar. See my bibliography.

25. *Vie privée et politique de Louis-François-Joseph, Prince de Conti, Prince du Sang Par J. P**** (Paris, 1790), p. 27. Louis Dutens, who knew Conti well, described him as "indévot sans être athée" (Capon and Plessis, *Paris galant au dix-huitième siècle,* p. 5).

26. BN, NAF 1799, fol. 12v.

27. For background on the princes and peers see Jean-Pierre Labatut, *Les ducs et pairs de France au XVIIe siècle* (Paris, 1972); Franklin L. Ford, *Robe and Sword: The Regrouping of French Aristocracy after Louis XIV* (Cambridge, Mass., 1953), pp. 173–87.

28. Charles O'Brien, "Jansenists on Civil Toleration in Mid-Eighteenth Century France," *Theologische Zeitschrift* 37 (1981): 73. For analyses of differences between the Jansenist movement in the seventeenth century and Jansenism as "a kind of vague political front" (Dale Van Kley's description) in the eighteenth, see Bernard Plongéron, "Une image de l'église d'après les 'Nouvelles Ecclésiastiques': 1728–1790," *Revue d'histoire de l'Eglise de France* 16 (1967): 241–68; Yann Fauchois, "Jansénisme et politique au XVIIIe siècle: Légitimation de l'état et délégitimation de la monarchie chez G. N. Maultrot," *Revue d'histoire moderne et contemporaine* 34 (1987): 473–91; Dale Van Kley,

The Jansenists and the Expulsion of the Jesuits from France, 1757–1765 (New Haven, Conn., 1975); Dale Van Kley, *The Damiens Affair and the Unraveling of the Ancien Régime, 1750–1770* (Princeton, N.J., 1984).

29. Louis Cognet, *Le jansénisme* (Paris, 1968), p. 34.

30. Ibid., p. 13.

31. Dale Van Kley, "The Jansenist Constitutional Legacy in the French Prerevolution," in *The French Revolution and the Creation of Modern Political Culture,* vol. 1, *The Political Culture of the Old Regime,* ed. Keith Baker (Oxford, 1987), p. 171.

32. Van Kley, *The Jansenists and the Expulsion of the Jesuits,* p. 21; Monique Cottret, "Aux origines du républicanisme janséniste: Le mythe de l'église primitive et le primitivisme des lumières," *Revue d'histoire moderne et contemporaine* 31 (1984): 99–115. Jansenists' emphasis upon the rights and obligations of the laity, coupled with the accent some placed on priests' rights to participate with bishops in deciding church matters (Richerism), seemed radically subversive to many defenders of papal monarchy. Edmond Richer, elected syndic of the Sorbonne in 1608, had argued that the whole of the Church represented in a council had authority greater than the papacy's and that priests had a spiritual authority equal to that of bishops.

33. Arnauld cited in Alexander Sedgwick, "Seventeenth-Century French Jansenism and the Enlightenment," in *Church, State, and Society under the Bourbon Kings of France,* ed. Richard M. Golden (Lawrence, Kan., 1982), pp. 136–37.

34. Jacques Le Brun, "La conscience et la théologie moderne," in *La Révocation de l'Edit de Nantes et le protestantisme français en 1685,* ed. Roger Zuber and Laurent Theis (Paris, 1986), p. 126.

35. Feelings of animosity lingered from the battle between the Jansenists Arnauld and Pierre Nicole and the Protestant pastor of Charenton, Jean Claude, over the perpetuity of the Eucharist. On this debate, see Richard Simon, *Additions aux Recherches curieuses sur la diversité des langues et religions d'Edward Brerewood,* ed. Jacques Le Brun and John Woodbridge (Paris, 1983), pp. 15–29.

36. On the Jansenists' use of the distinction between *de droit* and *de fait,* see Van Kley, *The Jansenists and the Expulsion of the Jesuits,* pp. 14, 19, 22, 126.

37. Merrick, *The Desacralization of the French Monarchy,* p. 63.

38. Ibid.; Van Kley, *The Damiens Affair,* p. 106.

39. Van Kley, *The Jansenists and the Expulsion of the Jesuits,* pp. 25–26. For various definitions of Gallicanism, see Merrick, *The Desacralization of the French Monarchy,* p. 31; Aimé Georges Martimort, *Le gallicanisme de Bossuet* (Paris, 1953).

40. B. Robert Kreiser, *Miracles, Convulsions, and Ecclesiastical Politics in Early Eighteenth-Century Paris* (Princeton, N.J., 1978), pp. ix–xi.

41. O'Brien, "Jansenists on Civil Toleration," pp. 71–83.

42. Dale Van Kley, "The Estates General as Ecumenical Council: The Constitutionalism of Corporate Consensus and the *Parlement*'s Ruling of September 25, 1788," *Journal of Modern History* 61 (March 1989): 21–30; David Bell, *Lawyers and Citizens: The Making of a Political Elite in Old Regime France* (New York, 1994), pp. 68–88, 115–17.

43. The chronological divisions and themes of these phases were graciously provided to me by Dale Van Kley in a letter of June 26, 1990.

44. Philippe Godard, *La querelle des réfus de sacrements, 1730–1765* (Paris, 1937), pp. 73–81.

45. Butler, *Choiseul*, 1: 1013.

46. Moreau cited in Merrick, *The Desacralization of the French Monarchy*, p. 135. On Moreau's career, see Dieter Gembicki, *Histoire et politique à la fin de l'Ancien Régime: Jacob-Nicholas Moreau, 1717–1803* (Paris, 1979).

47. Consult Choiseul's fascinating account of the creation of the encyclical: Maurice Boutry, *Choiseul à Rome: Lettres et mémoires inédits, 1754–1757* (Paris, n.d.). Louis XV believed that the new law reflected "the same spirit of conciliation" as Benedict XIV's encyclical. Choiseul was surprised that the pope seemed to think that refusing to accept the bull *Unigenitus* was only a venial sin.

48. Jules Flammermont and Maurice Tourneux, eds., *Rémonstrances du Parlement de Paris au XVIIIe siècle* (Paris, 1895), 2: xxiii–xxvi; Antoine, *Louis XV*, pp. 706–9.

49. Daniel Carroll Joynes, "Parlementaires, Peers, and the *Parti Janséniste*: The Refusal of Sacraments and the Revival of the Ancient Constitution in Eighteenth Century France," in *Proceedings of the Eighth Annual Meeting of the Western Society for French History, October 23–25, 1980, Eugene, Oregon*, ed. Edgar Leon Newman (Las Cruces, N. M., 1981), p. 229.

50. Ibid. Precedents gave peers the right to sit as councillors to the Parlement, but few were exercising this prerogative (Ford, *Robe and Sword*, p. 175).

51. Van Kley, *The Jansenists and the Expulsion of the Jesuits*, pp. 26–27.

52. Julian Swann, "Parlement, Politics and the Parti Janséniste: The Grand Conseil Affair, 1755–1756," *French History* 6 (December 1992): 435. Swann's study affords a careful analysis of this "affair."

53. BN, Lb. 38 659, "Réclamation présentée au Roi le 20 Fév. 1756 par M. le Duc d'Orléans, au nom des Princes et des Pairs," pp. 1–2.

54. BN, NAF 36, fol. 1.

55. BN, Lb. 38 693, *Lettre sur les lits de justice*. For background on this letter, see Joynes, "Parlementaires, Peers, and the *Parti Janséniste*," pp. 233–35. On Conti's presence at court in August 1756, see AM, Correspondance Politique, Prusse 185: letters of Knyphausen to Frederick II, August 1, 3, 5, 8, 1756. The Prussian ambassador believed that Conti's brief stay at court was precip-

itated by his desire to deal with the disputes between the Parlement of Paris and the king.

56. Le Paige, *Lettre sur les lits de justice*, p. 2.

57. On the "fundamental laws" of France, see André Lemaire, *Les lois fondementales de la monarchie française d'après les théorticiens de l'Ancien Régime* (Paris, 1907). Conti's hostility towards Louis XV was apparently directed at both the person of the king as well as at His Majesty's view of kingship. For background on the concept of kingship, see Ernst H. Kantorowicz, *The King's Two Bodies: A Study in Medieval Political Theory* (Princeton, N.J., 1957).

58. Knachel, *England and the "Fronde,"* pp. 207–10. See the multiple references to the prince de Conti in Ernst Kossmann, *La Fronde* (Leiden, 1954).

59. Richelieu cited in Herman, "The Huguenot Republic," p. 254.

60. Mark Motley, *Becoming a French Aristocrat: The Education of the Court Nobility, 1580–1715* (Princeton, N.J., 1990), pp. 54–55, 58.

61. Duclos, *Mémoires secrets*, 2: 297–98; Mitford, *Madame de Pompadour*, p. 219.

62. *Politique de tous les cabinets de l'Europe*, p. 32; Mitford, *Madame de Pompadour*, pp. 220–21.

63. Comte de Broglie, cited in *Politique de tous les cabinets de l'Europe*, p. 33. On the diplomatic revolution, consult Richard Waddington, *Louis XV et le Renversement des Alliances* (Paris, 1896).

Chapter Three.   The "Secret" Negotiations between the Prince de Conti and Pastor Paul Rabaut

Portions of this chapter are based on my article, "La conspiration du prince de Conti," *Dix-huitième siècle* 17 (1985): 97–109.

1. On Protestant pastors as recruiters, see AN, TT 441, doc. 312; on Frederick II's "emissaries," see AN, O'453, fol. 200v (letter of Saint-Florentin to Saint-Priest, August 20, 1757); on the prayers of Protestants for Frederick II, see AN, TT 442, doc. 70 (letter of Thomond to Saint-Florentin, November 21, 1758).

2. AN, TT 442, doc. 72 (letter of Thomond to Saint-Florentin, dated December 25, 1758). The song is found in doc. 72. Protestant apologists argued that the song was forged by their enemies.

3. D'Amat, ed., *Dictionnaire de biographie française*, 9: 543.

4. On Le Cointe, see A. Pichéral-Dardier, ed., *Paul Rabaut, ses lettres à Antoine Court (1739–1755)* (Paris, 1884), 2: 375 n2. Le Cointe served as the Protestants' representative in Paris before Court de Gébelin replaced him.

5. See the minutes for this letter, B.S.H.P.F., MS Coquerel 309, fol. 2r.

6. Ibid., fol. 8r; "Journal de Paul Rabaut," *B.S.H.P.F.* 28 (1878): 176.

7. B.S.H.P.F., MS Coquerel 309, fols. 8r, 8v.

8. Pichéral-Dardier, ed., *Paul Rabaut*, 2: 376–77.

9. B.S.H.P.F., MS Coquerel 310 B, fols. 10r–10v.

10. Charles Dardier, ed., *Paul Rabaut, ses lettres à divers* (Paris, 1892), 1: 106, 108.

11. Pichéral-Dardier, ed., *Paul Rabaut*, 2: 380.

12. Dardier, ed., *Paul Rabaut*, 1: 115.

13. B.S.H.P.F., MS Coquerel 309, fol. 10r.

14. B.S.H.P.F., MS Coquerel 310 B, fols. 11r–12v. In a letter dated October 8, 1755, Pradel described the emerging division of opinion to Antoine Court: "Il y a eu une triste partage d'opinions parmi nos avocats; les uns soutenant qu'il faut se borner à demander la confirmation des mariages & des Batêmes, et les autres affirmant qu'il falloit solliciter le redressement des principaux griefs des Eglises Réformées de France" (B.U.G., Collection Antoine Court 1/28, fol. 775v).

15. Pichéral-Dardier, ed., *Paul Rabaut*, 2: 381 n2.

16. B.U.G., CF 29/3, fol. 127 (extract of letters from Pradel to Rabaut).

17. B.U.G., Collection Antoine Court 1/28, fol. 825.

18. Pichéral-Dardier, ed., *Paul Rabaut*, 2: 384 n3.

19. "Journal de Paul Rabaut," 180; B.S.H.P.F., MS Coquerel 310 C, fol. 13v.

20. B.S.H.P.F., MS Coquerel 311, fols. 122v–23v, 123r.

21. On Jean Georges Lefranc de Pompignan, see René Pomeau, *La religion de Voltaire* (Paris, 1969), pp. 319, 344.

22. B.S.H.P.F., MS Coquerel 311, fol. 122v.

23. Marquis d'Argenson, *Journal et mémoires,*, 9: 172–73.

24. BN, NAF 36, fol. 1.

25. B.U.G., Collection Antoine Court 1/28, fol. 811v.

26. BN, NAF 1799, fols. 10r–10v. See also Edmond Hugues, "Un épisode de l'histoire du protestantisme au XVIIIe siècle," *B.S.H.P.F.* 26 (1877): 297.

27. I have not located a copy of Rabaut's letter of March 17, 1756. It is referred to in Antoine Court and Court de Gébelin's response, dated March 30, 1756 (B.S.H.P.F., MS Coquerel 311, fol. 127r).

28. B.S.H.P.F., MS Coquerel 311, fol. 127r.

29. BN, NAF 1799, fol. 11r.

30. Ibid., fols. 11v–12r.

31. B.S.H.P.F., MS Coquerel 311, fols. 125r–25v, 126r.

32. Ibid., fol. 130r.

33. Dedieu, *Histoire politique des protestants français,* 1: 290–92.

34. In a letter to Saint-Florentin, dated March 11, 1757, Saint-Priest described Mirepoix's "moderate" approach: "Il m'a fait l'honneur de me répondre qu'il fallait traiter les religionnaires avec beaucoup de douceur de peur de les aigrir" (AN, TT 441, doc. 216).

35. AN O'452, fol. 21r.

36. BN, NAF 1799, fols. 11v–12r.
37. AN, O'452, fol. 144r.
38. AN, TT 441, doc. 141.
39. "Journal de Paul Rabaut," 180.
40. AN, TT 441, doc. 159.
41. AN, O'452, fols. 193v, 194r.
42. AN, TT 441, doc. 191.
43. Archives du Département de la Gironde, C. 4683, "Copie d'une lettre du Sr. Thibaut, Prieur d'Auriac de Boursan en Perigord."
44. Duc de Luynes, *Mémoires*, 15: 212, 214.
45. Archives du Département de la Gironde, C. 4683.
46. Ibid.
47. AN, TT 441, doc. 191.
48. Horace Walpole, *Letters from Hon. Horace Walpole to George Montagu, Esq., from the Year 1736 to the Year 1770* (London, 1819), pp. 130–31.
49. AN, TT 441, doc. 191.
50. Benoît, *Les frères Gibert*, pp. 106–7.
51. Van Kley, *The Damiens Affair*, p. 146.
52. AM, Correspondance politique, Prusse 185.
53. Duc de Luynes, *Mémoires*, 15: 339–40.
54. Ibid., p. 339.
55. B.U.G., CF 29/3, fol. 129 (letter of December 1756 from Pradel to Paul Rabaut).
56. This same correspondent was critical of Saint-Priest.
57. BN, NAF 1799, fol. 5r.
58. Madame de Pompadour, *Mémoires de Madame la Marquise de Pompadour . . . Ecrites par elle-même* (Liege, 1756), p. 23.
59. BN, NAF 1799, fols. 28r–28v.
60. Boutaric, *Correspondance secrète*, 1: 73.
61. Ibid., pp. 73–74.
62. Marquis d'Argenson, *Journal et mémoires*, 9: 354 (entry for December 2, 1756).
63. BPR, 547, fol. 3r.
64. Marquis d'Argenson, *Journal et mémoires*, 9: 369–70 (entry for December 23, 1756).

Chapter Four. The Prince de Conti "Embroiled" in Damiens' Attempt on the Life of Louis XV

1. Marquis d'Argenson, *Journal et mémoires*, 9: 370. Chancellor Lamoignon de Blancmesnil, the father of Malesherbes, declared: "Il y a longtemps que je vois notre état menacé d'une révolution. Je ne croyais pas cependant que ma vieillesse dut la voir; mais à présent elle me paraît se préparer tellement

que, quelque vieux que je sois, je commence à croire que j'aurai la douleur d'en être le témoin" (Flammermont and Tourneux, eds., *Rémonstrances du Parlement de Paris*, 2: xxvi). For Barbier's comment about the pervasive spirit of revolt in Paris during December 1756, see Gilles Perrault, *Le secret du roi* (Paris, 1992), pp. 380–81.

2. R. Koser, ed., *Politische Correspondenz Friedrich Des Grössen* (Berlin, 1886), 14: 227.

3. AN, Y 15813 (Interrogatory, March 1757).

4. Edmond-J. F. Barbier, *Journal historique et anecdotique du règne de Louis XV, 1718–1763,* ed. A. de la Villegille (Paris, 1857–66), 4: 172; see also Pierre Rétat, ed., *L'attentat de Damiens: Discours sur l'événement au XVIIIe siècle* (Paris, n.d.), pp. 255–57.

5. Rétat, *L'attentat de Damiens,* p. 193.

6. Van Kley, *The Damiens Affair,* pp. 65–68.

7. *Pièces originales et procédures du procès fait à Robert-François Damiens, tant en la prévôté de l'Hôtel qu'en la cour du parlement* (Paris, 1757), p. 103: "[Damiens] said that it was he alone who had committed the crime, that no one had participated in it, that there had been no conspiracy, that no one took part, that it would be very malapropos to trouble people."

8. J. L. Soulavie, *Mémoires historiques et anecdotes de la cour de France pendant la faveur de la marquise de Pompadour* (Paris, 1802), p. 172.

9. Charles Collé, *Journal historique ou Mémoires critiques et littéraires* (Paris, 1807), 2: 171 (entry under March 1757).

10. Van Kley, *The Jansenists and the Expulsion of the Jesuits,* pp. 68–69.

11. Van Kley, *The Damiens Affair,* p. 65.

12. *Gazette d'Amsterdam* cited in Rétat, *L'attentat de Damiens,* p. 91.

13. Boutaric, *Correspondance secréte,* 1: 75.

14. Van Kley, *The Damiens Affair,* p. 91.

15. "Précis historique concernant Robert-François Damiens," in *Pièces originales,* p. xxxii.

16. Soulavie, *Mémoires historiques,* pp. 183–84.

17. Van Kley, *The Damiens Affair,* p. 92.

18. Capon and Plessis, *Paris galant au dix-huitième siècle,* pp. 92–93.

19. AN, Y 15813 (Interrogatory, March 1757). This documentation was graciously provided to me by Professor Dale Van Kley.

20. BN, FF 10,628, fol. 75r.

21. Van Kley, *The Damiens Affair,* p. 71.

22. Soulavie, *Mémoires historiques,* p. 138.

23. Duc de Luynes, *Mémoires,* 16: 291.

24. On Damiens' execution, see Rétat, *L'attentat de Damiens,* pp. 241–66.

25. Frédéric Masson, ed., *Mémoires et lettres de François Joachim de Pierre Cardinal de Bernis (1715–1758)* (Paris, 1878), 2: 225.

26. French Protestant historian Edmond Hugues published large segments of Berryer's notebook and Herrenschwand's correspondence. See "Un épisode," pp. 289–303, 338–50. He omitted small sections of the original manuscripts and did not indicate where the manuscripts were housed. Hugues was quite critical of the idea that Conti's conspiracy was of interest to Protestants.

27. *Pièces originales*, p. 82.

28. In *The Prince*, Machiavelli argued that once a "Turkish despot" was vanquished, the conqueror should wipe out the despot's family. This was a familiar theme in discussions of Turkish despotism. See Melvin Richter, "Despotism," in *Dictionary of the History of Ideas*, ed. Philip P. Wiener (New York, 1973), 2: 7–9, 13.

29. BN, FF 10,628, fol. 74r.

30. This is the first page of Herrenschwand's memoir.

31. Ozanam and Antoine, eds., *Correspondance secrète*, 1: xli.

32. Pierre Grosclaude, "Une négociation prématurée: Louis Dutens et les protestants français, 1775–1776," *B.S.H.P.F.* 104 (April–June, 1958): 81.

33. Dutens, *Memoirs of a Traveller*, 3: 74–75.

34. Ibid., pp. 76–77.

35. B.S.H.P.F., MS 358 III, fol. 16IV: "Msr. Le Prince de Conti l'honore non seulement de son estime mais même de cette noble familiarité qui rapproche les mérites en faisant disparaître le rang."

36. On Taaffe, see J. Hovyn de Tranchère, ed., *Le dessous de l'histoire curiosités judiciares administratives, politiques et littéraires* (Paris, 1886), p. 304. A police record of April 10, 1761, reads: "M. Taaffe, gentilhomme irlandais agé d'environ 45 ans, est membre du Parlement d'Angleterre vit en France depuis longtemps. Il a fait autrefois grande figure dans cette ville et étoit très bien . . . surtout chez le Prince de Conti" (Arsenal, 12022, nos. 109–10). The materials on Taaffe from the Arsenal were graciously provided by Professor Dale Van Kley.

37. Hovyn de Tranchère, ed., *Les dessous de l'histoire*, p. 308; Arsenal, 12022, nos. 14–20. There are also traces of payments made to spies in France in the records of Lord Holdernesse (Add. MSS 32,997, fol. 72). François de Bussey, known in the English secret service as No. 101, was a highly ranked French diplomat, occasionally in the pay of the English (Evan Charteris, *William Augustus Duke of Cumberland and the Seven Years' War* [London, 1920], p. 153). On Bussey (1699–1780), who was "prémier commis des Affaires étrangères" (April 1, 1749–May 21, 1766), see Jean-Pierre Samoyault, *Les bureaux du sécretariat d'état des affaires étrangères sous Louis XV* (Paris, 1971), pp. 50–57, 278. Bussey was privy to the "secret du roi" and apparently worked with the prince de Conti.

38. François Ravaisson-Mollien, *Archives de la Bastille d'après des documents*

inédits (Geneva, 1975), 17: 114–15 (letter of Buchot to Sartine, April 10, 1761).

39. Arsenal, 12022, nos. 64–69.

40. B.S.H.P.F., MS Coquerel 311, fol. 127r.

41. *General Court-Martial* (Published by Authority, London, 1758), p. 9.

42. Soulavie, *Mémoires historiques,* pp. 139–41.

Chapter Five.   William Pitt and the Secret Expedition

1. On the career of William Cavendish (1720–1764), fourth duke of Devonshire and marquis of Hartington, see William Gould, ed., *Lives of the Georgian Age, 1714–1837* (New York, 1978), p. 82. When Pitt left the Devonshire ministry in April 1757, it was a "mutilated, enfeebled, system," quite incapable of handling the war effort.

2. George II cited in Reed Browning, *The Duke of Newcastle* (New Haven, Conn., 1975), p. 259. Regarding the negotiations pursued by Newcastle to establish a new ministry, see pp. 257–60 of Browning's work. See also the detailed analysis of the negotiations in J.C.D. Clark, *The Dynamics of Change: The Crisis of the 1750s and English Party Systems* (Cambridge, Eng., 1982), pp. 423–47.

3. Consult W.C.B. Tunstall, *Admiral Byng and the Loss of Minorca* (London, 1928). Pitt left the Devonshire ministry in the wake of the Byng affair. See also Marie Peters, *Pitt and Popularity: The Patriot Minister and London Opinion during the Seven Years' War* (Oxford, 1980), pp. 46–47, 69–70.

4. Gerhard Ritter, *Frederick the Great: A Historical Profile* (Berkeley, 1970), p. 110.

5. How to deal with George II's commitments to the elector of Hanover was one of Pitt's most vexing problems, given his own reputation as an "anti-Hanoverian" (Richard Middleton, *The Bells of Victory: The Pitt-Newcastle Ministry and the Conduct of the Seven Years' War, 1757–1762* [Cambridge, Eng., 1985], p. 11). On England's relationship with Hanover, see the many references in Ragnhild Hatton, *George I, Elector and King* (Cambridge, Mass., 1978); and J. H. Plumb, *The First Four Georges* (London, 1977), pp. 83, 93.

6. On the career of Pitt, see Stanley Ayling, *The Elder Pitt, Earl of Chatham* (London, 1976); Peter Douglas Brown, *William Pitt, Earl of Chatham: The Great Commoner* (London, 1978).

7. O'Connor, "Republican Conspiracies in the Old Regime," p. 14.

8. Pitt studied papers related to this expedition in planning the "Secret Expedition" of 1757 (Brian Tunstall, *William Pitt, Earl of Chatham* [London, 1938], p. 194). For further discussion of the "Secret Expedition," see Middleton, *The Bells of Victory,* pp. 26–31, 40–44.

9. Charteris, *William Augustus Duke of Cumberland,* p. 239.

10. William Pitt, *Correspondence of William Pitt, Earl of Chatham,* ed. John, Earl of Chatham (London, 1888), 1: 206.

11. BM, Add. MSS 6839, fol. 55r.

12. On the career of Ligonier, see Rex Whitworth, *Field Marshal Lord Ligonier: A Story of the British Army, 1702–1770* (Oxford, 1958).

13. Ibid., pp. 211–12.

14. Ibid., p. 220. See Clerk's report: PRO 30/8/85 I, fols. 19r–21r.

15. Horace Walpole, *Memoirs of the Reign of King George the Second,* ed. Lord Holland (London, 1846), 3: 43.

16. The memoir came from one of the ministry's "most confidential correspondents" in France. Pitt and others relied upon it heavily (*General Court-Martial,* pp. 9–10).

17. Jean Baptiste Honoré Raymond Capefigué, *Oeuvres de Capefigué: Louis XV et la société du XVIIIe siècle* (Brussels, 1845), p. 285.

18. For background on the political significance of George II as a defender of Protestantism, see J.C.D. Clark, *English Society 1688–1832: Ideology, Social Structure and Political Practice during the Ancien Régime* (Cambridge, Eng., 1985), pp. 173–85.

19. BM, Add. MSS 32,872, fol. 103r.

20. The description of Pitt's requisitions comes from Basil Williams, *The Life of William Pitt, Earl of Chatham* (New York, 1913), 1: 340.

21. PRO 30/8/48 I, fol. 120r.

22. Pitt, *Correspondence,* 1: 241–42 (dated August 13, 1757). This letter (a copy) is found in the BM, Add. MSS 32,873, fol. 50r.

23. Charles Chenevix Trench, *George II* (London, 1973), pp. 283, 284. For a more detailed treatment of George II's concerns about Hanover, see Uriel Dann, *Hanover and Great Britain, 1740–1760: Diplomacy and Survival* (London, 1991), pp. 113–15.

24. Charteris, *William Augustus Duke of Cumberland,* p. 284.

25. Basil Williams, *The Life of William Pitt,* 1: 340.

26. BM, Add. MSS 32,872, fol. 365r.

27. Ibid., fol. 434r.

28. Admiral Hawke also received a communication on September 5, in which Pitt prodded him to embark. Hawke replied that "I needed no spur in the Execution of his Orders" (Ruddock Mackay, *Admiral Hawke* [Oxford, 1965], p. 168).

29. BM, Add. MSS 32,872, fol. 367r (Copie d'une lettre du Roy de Prusse à Monsieur Michel du 30 d'Août 1757).

30. *A Genuine Account of the Late Grand Expedition to the Coast of France, under the Conduct of the Admirals Hawke, Knowles, & Broderick, and of General Mordaunt . . . By a Volunteer . . .* (1757), a segment of which was reprinted in translation in the *Mercure historique et politique* (November 1757): 530–31.

31. Emily J. Climenson, ed., *Elizabeth Montagu, The Queen of the Blue Stock-*

ings: Her Correspondence from 1720 to 1761 (London, 1906), 2: 116 (letter from Mrs. Donnellan to Montagu, September 15, 1757).

32. BM, Add. MSS 32,997, fol. 257r.

33. Whitworth, *Field Marshal Lord Ligonier,* p. 219.

34. Tunstall, *William Pitt,* p. 197.

35. Trench, *George II,* p. 284.

36. Basil Williams, *The Life of William Pitt,* 1: 345.

37. BM, Add. MSS 32,874, fol. 11v.

38. BM, Add. MSS 32,873, fol. 83r.

39. PRO 30/8/85 I, fols. 33r, 33v.

40. PRO 30/9/85 I, "Lettre particulière de Paris," fol. 37v.

41. Archives Historiques de la Guerre, MR 1086 doc. 19, fol. 28.

42. B.U.G., Collection Antoine Court 46, doc. 47.

43. Tourny referred to this ordinance in a letter he wrote to Saint-Florentin, the summary of which is found in the Archives du Département de la Gironde, C. 192.

44. B.U.G., Collection Antoine Court 46, doc. 47.

45. Archives du Département de la Gironde, C. 192, letter of Saint-Florentin to Tourny, dated October 5, 1757. See Françoise Arduin, "Un subdélégué de Libourne au XVIIIe siècle: Léonard Bulle (1748–1773)," *Revue historique de Bordeaux et du Département de la Gironde* 16 (1923): 213.

46. B.S.H.P.F., MS 358 III, fol. 101r (letter from "Nogaret" to Chiron, dated January 4, 1759).

47. *Mercure historique et politique* (November 1757): 507–8.

48. *The Secret Expedition Impartially Disclosed . . .* (London, 1757), pp. 1–2.

49. William Pitt, *Authentic Memoirs of the Right Honourable the late Earl of Chatham* (London, 1778), p. 12. In contrast, Almon described the cause of the Great Expedition's failure in these terms: "The cause of the miscarriage was not precisely ascertained. Mr. *Pitt* ascribed it to the inactivity of Sir *John Mordaunt,* who had the command of the troops. The friends of that officer ascribed it to the plan, which in derision, they called 'one of Mr. Pitt's visions'" (John Almon, *Anecdotes of the Life of the Right Hon. William Pitt* [London, 1810], 1: 232).

50. Rex Whitworth, Ligonier's modern biographer, points out: "As a Huguenot refugee he knew that there were a great number of disaffected French subjects in the area of Rochefort which probably swayed his judgement in favour of recommending an attack on the much more important, but ill defended, harbour and arsenal 10 miles up the Charente" (*Field Marshal Lord Ligonier,* p. 220).

Chapter Six.   The Failure of the Secret Expedition

1. John G. Clark, *La Rochelle and the Atlantic Economy,* p. 51. For the tenuous status of wealthy Huguenot merchants in Roman Catholic La Rochelle, consult J. F. Bosher, "The Political and Religious Origins of la Rochelle's Primacy in Trade with New France, 1627–1685," *French History* 7 (September 1993): 305.

2. The plaques had been attached to the gate "des Minimes."

3. Dardier, ed., *Paul Rabaut,* 1: 178 n6.

4. Ibid., p. 178.

5. Archives du Département de la Gironde, C. 198 (résumé of letter of Tourny to Saint-Florentin, October 5, 1757).

6. Frédéric Gardy, ed., *Correspondance de Jaques Serces* (London, 1956), 2: 225–26.

7. Ibid., p. 226. The Courts quoted extracts from the supplication the Protestants of the Saintonge and Guyenne sent to Louis XV.

8. B.U.G., Collection Antoine Court 46, fol. 51.

9. Archives du Département de la Gironde, C. 315 (Interrogatory of Michel Leboeuf).

10. Ibid., Interrogatory of Michel Frappier. See Arduin, "Un subdélégué de Libourne," p. 217.

11. Archives du Département de la Gironde, C. 315 (Interrogatory of Isabeau Frégère).

12. Ibid., letters of March 24, April 28, 1758.

13. Ibid., letters of April 10, March 24, 1758.

14. Pierre Dez, *Histoire des Protestants et de l'Eglise Réformée de l'Ile de Ré* (La Rochelle, 1926), p. 110.

15. BM, Add. MSS 32,874, fol. 115v.

16. BM, Add. MSS 6839, fols. 74v, 75v.

17. Ibid., fol. 79r.

18. Romney Sedgwick, "Letters from William Pitt to Lord Bute: 1755–1758," in *Essays Presented to Sir Lewis Namier,* ed. A.J.P. Taylor (London, 1956), p. 132.

19. Ibid., pp. 132–33.

20. Walpole, *Memoirs of the Reign of George the Second,* 3: 75. Potter later advertised that it was against his wish that Pitt's letter had been printed in the *Bath Journal.*

21. Romney Sedgwick, "Letters from William Pitt to Lord Bute," p. 137.

22. Whitworth, *Field Marshal Lord Lignoier,* p. 224. Ligonier seconded Pitt's idea that the fleet should return to the coast off Rochefort.

23. Pitt, *Correspondence,* 1: 277, 281 n1.

24. BM, Add. MSS 32,875, fol. 124r.

25. John Bradshaw, ed., *The Letters of Philip Dormer Stanhope, Earl of Chesterfield* (London, 1893), 3: 1185. Earlier, on October 10, 1757, Lord Chesterfield had commented to his son: "As the expectations of the whole nation had been raised to the highest pitch, the universal disappointment and indignation have arisen in proportion; and I question whether the ferment of men's minds was ever greater. Suspicions, you may be sure, are various and endless; but the most prevailing one is, that the tail of the Hanover neutrality, like that of a comet, extended itself to Rochefort" (ibid., 3: 1180).

26. Philip C. Yorke, ed. *The Life and Correspondence of Philip Yorke Earl of Hardwicke, Lord High Chancellor of Great Britain* (Cambridge, Eng., 1913), 3: 186.

27. Mackay, *Admiral Hawke*, p. 178.

28. Lord John Russel, *Correspondence of John, Fourth Duke of Bedford* (London, 1843), 2: 280. On October 4, 1757, General Mordaunt had written to Pitt: "I cannot help repeating my concern that the Affair of Rochefort did not succeed, and I shall be doubly unhappy, if upon reading the Council of War, you do not think we acted right" (PRO 30/8/78 II, fol. 274v).

29. Yorke, ed., *The Life and Correspondence,* 3: 187.

30. Pitt, *Correspondence,* 1: 279 n1.

31. Ibid., pp. 277–78.

32. Peters, *Pitt and Popularity,* p. 97.

33. Ibid. Newcastle implied that the date Pitt's letter was published in the *Gazette* was October 15, 1757.

34. BM, Add. MSS 32,875, fol. 124v.

35. Peters, *Pitt and Popularity,* p. 96.

36. Ibid., p. 97.

37. BM, Add. MSS 32,875, fol. 124r (letter from Newcastle to Hardwicke, dated October 14, 1757): "Mr. Pitt is very violent, upon the behaviour of the Land Officers, which he attributed to a formed design in great Part of the Army against Him. He told me yesterday, that He, or (or and) Sr. John Mordaunt, must be tried."

38. Ibid., fol. 124v. See Mackay, *Admiral Hawke,* pp. 179–80.

39. Newcastle noted this in a letter to Hardwicke, dated October 23, 1757 (BM, Add. MSS 32,875, fol. 227v).

40. Walpole, *Memoirs of the Reign of King George the Second,* 3: 76.

41. *The Report of the General Officers, Appointed By his* MAJESTY's *Warrant of the First of November 1757, to enquire into the Causes of the Failure of the late Expedition to the Coasts of France* (London, 1758), p. 20.

42. Ibid., p. 22.

43. Ibid., p. 43.

44. Ibid., p. 58.

45. Walpole, *Memoirs of the Reign of King George the Second,* 3: 77, 62.

46. BM, Add. MSS 32,997, fols. 297v–98r.

47. Walpole, *Memoirs of the Reign of King George the Second*, 3: 78–79.

48. Yorke, ed., *The Life and Correspondence*, 3: 188, 186 (letters of the duke of Newcastle to the earl of Hardwicke, October 12, 8, 1757).

49. Andrew Bisset, ed., *Memoirs and Papers of Sir Andrew Mitchell* (London, 1850), 1: 275.

50. PRO 30/8/78 II, fol. 202r.

51. G. Tulau, ed., "La flotte anglaise sur les côtes d'Aunis et de Saintonge en 1757," *Revue maritime et coloniale* 114 (July–September 1892): 111–18.

52. *General Court-Martial*, p. 52.

53. Claiming that all Protestants of Saintonge and Aunis and in neighboring provinces had contributed to the common defense, a commentator then noted the rumor in question: "On doit donc envisager comme des calomnies outrées ce qu'insinuent quelques rélations où l'on voudroit faire croire que les *Anglais* ont pratiqué des intelligences dans le pais, & qu'ils destinent la quantité d'Uniformes verds, qu'ils ont embarquez sur leur Flotte, à en revetir ceux des habitans qui se joindroient à eux. La fausseté de ces suppositions paroîtra encore mieux dans son jour en se rappellant ce qui est rapporté ci-dessus du premier projet des *Anglois*, & en faisant reflexion que, depuis le moment qu'ils ont tourné leur vues contre les Côtes de *France*, ils n'ont guere eu le tems de pratiquer les intelligences que la malignité leur suppose gratuitement" (*Mercure historique et politique* [October, 1757]: 387).

54. BM, Add. MSS 6839, fol. 80r (letter of October 14, 1757).

55. Mackay, *Admiral Hawke*, pp. 173, 174–76.

56. *Candid Reflections on the Report (As Published by Authority) of the General Officers Appointed by his Majesty's Warrant of the First of November last, to enquire into the CAUSES of the FAILURE of the late Expedition to the Coasts of FRANCE* (London, 1758), p. 35.

Chapter Seven.   The Conspiracy of the Prince de Conti against Louis XV: The Aftermath

A small portion of this chapter is based on my article, "An 'Unnatural Alliance' for Religious Toleration: The Philosophes and the Outlawed Pastors of the 'Church of the Desert,'" reprinted with permission from *Church History* 42 (December 1973): 505–23.

1. BM, Add. MSS 32,872, fol. 451r.

2. Horace Walpole, *Memoirs of King George II*, vol. 2, *March 1754–1757*, ed. John Brooke (New Haven, Conn., 1985), p. 272.

3. Etienne François Choiseul, *Mémoires du duc de Choiseul* (Paris, 1983), p. 134.

4. Conti was obviously aware of the Fronde, in which his forebears had participated so significantly. Moreover, Conti's Jansenist advisor, Adrien Le

Paige, utilized arguments drawn from pamphlets distributed during the Fronde.

5. Hugues, "Un épisode," p. 340.

6. Madame de Pompadour, *Mémoires,* pp. 27–28. The authenticity of these memoirs is somewhat in doubt.

7. Antoine, *Louis XV,* pp. 640, 641; on Louis XV's mistresses, pp. 500–506.

8. Ibid., p. 640.

9. Boutaric, *Correspondance secrète,* p. 74. See also pp. 290, 293.

10. Ibid. p. 224 (letter of September 15, 1757).

11. AM, Correspondance politique, Pologne 236, fol. 416r.

12. Cited in White, *The Memoirs of Chevalier d'Eon,* p. 48.

13. Capon and Plessis, *Paris galant au dix-huitième siècle,* pp. 111–63.

14. *Galérie de l'ancienne cour,* 3: 318–19; Jean Guéhenno, *Jean-Jacques Rousseau,* trans. John Weightman and Doreen Weightman (New York, 1967), 2: 61, 205–6, 212.

15. Capon and Plessis, *Paris galant au dix-huitième siècle,* pp. 167–87; Durand Escheverria, *The Maupeou Revolution: A Study in the History of Libertarianism in France, 1770–1774* (Baton Rouge, La., 1985), pp. 18, 23, 24.

16. Hugues, "Un épisode," p. 343.

17. B.S.H.P.F., MS 358 III, fol. 16ir.

18. Cited in Antoine, *Louis XV,* p. 971.

19. Peters, *Pitt and Popularity,* p. 95.

20. Bisset, ed., *Memoirs and Papers of Sir Andrew Mitchell,* 1: 164.

21. Horace Walpole, *The Letters of Horace Walpole, Fourth Earl of Oxford,* ed. Paget Toynbee (Oxford, 1903), 4: 108–9.

22. Robert Spector, *English Literary Periodicals and the Climate of Opinion during the Seven Years' War* (The Hague, 1966), p. 51. On October 22, 1757, William Beckford stated: "To attack and destroy one of the principal naval arsenals and docks of France was a noble project: success in the undertaking would have made amends for all our losses and disappointments. I do from my soul believe, that if courage or conduct had not been wanting, we must have succeeded. Heaven and earth seemed to favour us" (Pitt, *Correspondence,* 1: 280).

23. Ritter, *Frederick the Great,* p. 115.

24. Pitt, *Correspondence,* 1: 279.

25. Middleton, *The Bells of Victory,* pp. 219–32 (Appendix, "Pitt and the Historians").

26. AN, TT 441, doc. 288; Gardy, ed., *Correspondance de Jaques Serces,* 2: 225–26.

27. Benoît, *Les frères Gibert,* pp. 162–66.

28. AN, TT 447, docs. 167, 169, 170.

29. Ibid., doc. 173 ("Il apuya beaucoup sur les correspondances et les protections qu'il avoit à la Cour").

30. Fr. Waddington, "Projet d'émigration du pasteur Gibert pour les protestants de la Saintonge et des provinces voisines d'après des documents inédits, 1761–1764," *B.S.H.P.F.* 6 (1858): 371–72.

31. Ibid., p. 373.

32. Daniel Robert, "La fin du 'Désert héroïque'—Pourquoi Jean-Louis Gibert a-t-il émigré (1761–1763)?" *B.S.H.P.F.* 98 (October–December, 1951): 238–47.

33. Ibid., p. 240. See the dossier on Gibert for a description of the sums of money he was allegedly receiving from the English government (AN, TT 447, doc. 170).

34. Lewis Namier, *The Structure of Politics at the Accession of George III* (London, 1961), pp. 229–30.

35. B.S.H.P.F., Fonds Farelle, Languedoc XIX, Cévennes 449, fol. 114v. Gibert's date for the inception of this building program is confirmed by the marquis d'Argenson (*Journal et mémoires,* 9: 156 [entry for December 25, 1755]).

36. Waddington, "Projet d'émigration du pasteur Gibert," p. 271.

37. Van Kley, *The Damiens Affair,* p. 269.

38. Merrick, *The Desacralization of the French Monarchy,* p. 151.

39. Timothy Tackett, *Priest and Parish in Eighteenth-Century France: A Social and Political Study of the Curés in a Diocese of Dauphiné, 1750–1791* (Princeton, N.J., 1977), pp. 215–19.

40. Archives du Département de l'Hérault, C. 467, "Messieurs du Clergé."

41. B.S.H.P.F. 36 (1887): 532. Oddly enough, this statement is attributed to Loménie de Brienne who on occasion worked for Protestant toleration.

42. Marie Jean Antoine Nicolas de Condorcet, *Recueil de pièces sur l'état des protestants en France* (London, 1783), p. 4.

43. See David Bien, *The Calas Affair: Persecution, Toleration, and Heresy in Eighteenth-Century Toulouse* (Princeton, N.J., 1960).

44. See especially Adams, *The Huguenots and French Opinion.*

45. Edna Nixon, *Voltaire and the Calas Case* (New York, 1961), p. 193. Voltaire had intervened on behalf of other Protestants before the Calas Affair. See Charles Dardier, "Voltaire agissant en faveur des protestants en 1754," *B.S.H.P.F.* 32 (1883): 528–29; Daniel Benoît, "Ribaute Charon, Voltaire et Rousseau," *Recueil de l'Académie des sciences, belles-lettres et arts de Tarn-et-Garonne* 21 (1905; published 1906): 41–56.

46. Graham Gargett, *Voltaire and Protestantism* (Oxford, 1980), p. 353.

47. "Unnatural alliance" is David Bien's well-chosen expression, noted in *The Calas Affair,* p. 25.

48. Jean-Jacques Rousseau, *The Confessions of Jean-Jacques Rousseau,* trans. J. M. Cohen (New York, 1978), pp. 365–66. On Rousseau's reluctance to become a principal figure in the struggle for Huguenots' freedom of conscience, see Adams, *The Huguenots and French Opinion,* pp. 147–62.

49. Arthur M. Wilson, *Diderot* (New York, 1962), pp. 441–42. The cheval-

ier de Jaucourt did write a twelve-page article entitled "Tolérance," which was taken out of the *Encyclopédie* (Madelaine F. Morris, *Le Chevalier de Jaucourt: Un ami de la terre* [Geneva, 1979], p. 86). On the Encyclopedists and Calvinists, see Adams, *The Huguenots and French Opinion,* pp. 103 –15.

50. Dardier, ed., *Paul Rabaut,* 2: 79 (letter of February 29, 1768).

51. Haydn Mason, *Voltaire: A Biography* (Baltimore, 1981), p. 141.

52. Pichéral-Dardier, ed., *Paul Rabaut,* 2: 133.

53. Rabaut's letter cited in Coquerel, *Histoire des églises du désert,* 2: 197.

54. See, for example, *Lettre de M. l'Evêque d'Agen à M. Le Controleur Général contre la tolérance des Huguenots* (N.p., 1751).

55. It should be noted that Antoine Court had already launched an attack against Montesquieu and Voltaire for the same reason, in *Le patriote français et impartial ou réponse à la Lettre de M. l'Evêque d'Agen . . .* , 2 vols. (Villefranche, 1753). But Court's criticisms of the philosophes were not as severe in this work as in his *Lettre d'un patriote.*

56. [Chevalier de Beaumont], *L'accord parfait de la Nature, de la Raison, de la Révélation . . .* (Göttingen, 1755), p. 11.

57. Court de Gébelin, *Les Toulousaines ou lettres historiques et apologétiques en faveur de la Religion Réformée . . .* (Edimbourg [Lausanne], 1763), p. 283.

58. See Armand Lods, "Biographie: Les partisans et les adversaires de l'Edit de Tolérance: Etude bibliographique et juridique, 1750–1789," *B.S.H.P.F.,* 36 (1887): 551–65; Adams, *The Huguenots and French Opinion;* Claude Lauriol, *La Beaumelle: Un protestant cévenol entre Montesquieu et Voltaire* (Geneva, 1978), pp. 129–31.

59. Gargett, *Voltaire and Protestantism,* p. 274.

60. Ibid., p. 276. See also Paul Chaponnière, *Voltaire chez les Calvinistes* (Paris, 1936).

61. Voltaire, *Correspondance* (Paris, 1978), 4: 1187.

62. Pappas, "La répression contre les protestants," p. 122.

63. B.S.H.P.F., Fonds Farelle, Languedoc XIX, Cévennes 449, fol. 112v.

64. Robert, "Pourquoi Jean-Louis Gibert a-t-il émigré?" p. 241 n7.

65. Ibid., pp. 241 n8, 242. On the other hand, Paul Rabaut warned the National Synod of 1758 that building churches in this fashion was too provocative. The synod apparently accepted his advice. Once again, Gibert and Rabaut found themselves at odds on an important issue.

66. Archives consistoriales de l'Eglise Réformée de Nîmes, C 8, "Articles au Consistoire en 1782," Article 4; "Montauban en 1773–1774: Trois lettres de Jeannette-Philippine Le Clerc," *B.S.H.P.F.* 52 (1903): 69.

67. BN, NAF 1799, fol. 4r.

68. Herrenschwand's notion was that Protestants would give money in exchange for better treatment. The plan fell through. Nonetheless, according to the maréchal de Belle-Isle, a Protestant emissary from Languedoc

offered 35 million livres, payable on January 1, 1759, and two thousand armed men for the duration of the war, in exchange for two towns in each province where Protestantism could be practiced. Much of the money was to come from foreign Protestant sources. Belle-Isle advised Louis XV not to accept the offer because it would allow republican "enemies into the Kingdom." After further discussion of the offer in the Conseil, the king rejected it ([François Antoine Chevrier], *Testament politique du maréchal duc de Belle-Isle* [Paris, 1762], pp. 35–42).

69. AN, TT 442, letter of Thomond to Saint-Florentin, dated February 28, 1759.

70. Ibid., doc. 197, fol. 3.

71. Cited in de Félice, *Histoire des Protestants de France*, p. 521.

72. Cited in Péronnet, "Les assemblées du clergé et les protestants," 146.

73. Cited in Michel Péronnet, "Loménie de Brienne, archevêque de Toulouse, principal ministre du roi et l'Edit des Non Catholiques de novembre 1787," *B.S.H.P.F.* 134 (April–June, 1988): 262.

74. Antoine, *Louis XV*, p. 866; Paul Del Perugia, *Louis XV* (Paris, 1975), pp. 506–7. Lutherans in Alsace did receive certain civil rights at this time.

75. Antoine, *Louis XV*, p. 866.

76. David Bien, "Catholic Magistrates and Protestant Marriages in the French Enlightenment," *French Historical Studies* 2 (fall 1962): 427.

77. "Lettres écrites par divers pasteurs au sujet des églises réformées de France," *B.S.H.P.F.* 19–20 (1870–71): 33 (letter of Pomaret to Desmont, dated May 31, 1774). In fact a few Protestants were still in jail.

78. See Daniel Benoît and Emile du Cailar, *Gal-Pomaret, Pasteur de Ganges: Son temps, son ministère, ses écrits* (Paris, 1899).

79. Van Kley, *The Damiens Affair*, p. 259.

80. Dale Van Kley, "Church, State, and the Ideological Origins of the French Revolution: The Debate over the General Assembly of the Gallican Clergy in 1765," *Journal of Modern History* 51 (December 1979): 632.

81. See O'Brien, "Jansenists on Civil Toleration," pp. 71–93. For a later period, see Charles O'Brien, "The Jansenist Campaign for Toleration of Protestants in Late Eighteenth-Century France: Sacred or Secular?" *Journal of the History of Ideas* 46 (1985): 523–38.

82. Van Kley, *The Damiens Affair*, p. 269. In 1751–52 several governmental officers had attempted to moderate somewhat the impact of the anti-Protestant legislation.

83. For a valuable review of literature since 1939 on the origins of the French Revolution, see William Doyle, *Origins of the French Revolution* (Oxford, 1982), pp. 7–40. See also Sarah Maza, "Politics, Culture, and the Origins of the French Revolution," *Journal of Modern History* 61 (December 1989): 704–23. On the relationships between the parlements of France and the

French Revolution, see the carefully nuanced analysis of Bailey Stone, *The French Parlements and the Crisis of the Old Regime* (Chapel Hill, N.C., 1986), pp. 252–69. Both Stone and Doyle have emphasized the "conservative" tendencies of the members of the parlements during the second half of the eighteenth century.

84. Jeffrey Merrick, "'Disputes over Words' and Constitutional Conflict in France, 1730–1732," *French Historical Studies* 14 (fall 1986): 518.

85. Hermann Weber, "Le sacre de Louis XVI," *Actes du colloque international de Sorèze: Le règne de Louis XVI et la Guerre d'Indépendence américaine* (Dourgne, 1977), pp. 16–20.

86. Péronnet, "Loménie de Brienne," p. 263.

87. Meister cited in François Bluche, *La vie quotidienne au temps de Louis XVI* (Paris, 1980), p. 166. For Le Paige's involvement in the campaign for Protestant toleration even in the mid-1770s, see Adams, *The Huguenots and French Opinion*, pp. 232–33.

88. Claude Lauriol, "L'Edit de 1787 et la tolérance à la fin de l'Ancien Régime," *B.S.H.P.F.* 134 (April–June 1988): 428.

89. Péronnet, "Loménie de Brienne," 263.

90. O'Brien, "The Jansenist Campaign for Toleration of Protestants," pp. 526–38.

91. A definitive study of how the belligerents orchestrated their campaign awaits its author. See Claude Lauriol's helpful review on this subject, "L'Edit de 1787," pp. 425–33; see also Jean Egret, *The French Prerevolution, 1787–1788*, trans. Wesley D. Camp (Chicago, 1977), pp. 77–87; Adams, *The Huguenots and French Opinion*, pp. 231–94.

92. Adams, *The Huguenots and French Opinion*, pp. 267–70.

93. *Mémoires, correspondance et manuscrits du général Lafayette*, published by his family (Paris, 1837), 2: 182.

94. Malesherbes, *Mémoire sur le mariage des protestans* (N.p., 1785), p. 21.

95. Newberry Library, Case FRC 1161, "Aux Chambres Assemblées, Un de Messieurs Conseiller de Grand Chambre, a dit," p. 32. For Robert de Saint-Vincent's earlier efforts to win toleration for Protestants, see Charles H. O'Brien, "Jansenists and Civil Toleration of Protestants in France, 1775–1778: Lepaige, Guidi, and Robert de Saint-Vincent," in Roland Crahay, ed., *La tolérance civile* (Brussels, 1982), pp. 183–99.

96. Newberry Library, Case FRC 1151, "Aux Chambres Assemblées," pp. 7, 34.

97. Ibid., pp. 27, 36.

98. The record of the meeting on May 25, 1787, reads: "M. de Lafayette a proposé de supplier Sa Majesté d'accorder l'état civil aux protestans, et d'ordonner la réforme des lois criminelles" (*Mémoires, correspondance et manuscrits du général Lafayette*, p. 179).

99. See Pierre Grosclaude, "Comment MALESHERBES élabore sa doctrine sur le problème des Protestants," *B.S.H.P.F.* 103 (July–September 1957): 149–72; Joseph Hudault, *Guy-Jean-Baptiste Target et sa contribution à la préparation de l'Edit de novembre 1787 sur l'état civil des protestants* (Paris, 1966). Jean Egret observes that Malesherbes and Rabaut Saint-Etienne disputed sharply (Egret, *The French Prerevolution,* p. 81). Nigel Aston links the Edict of Toleration to the "practical necessity too of absorbing thousands of Dutch Calvinists who were the victims of the victorious Stadtholder in 1787, when all French influence in the United Provinces ended in the most humiliating circumstances" (*The End of an Elite: The French Bishops and the Coming of the Revolution, 1786–1790* [Oxford, 1992], p. 93.).

100. Burdette Poland, *French Protestantism and the French Revolution: A Study in Church and State, Thought and Religion, 1685–1815* (Princeton, N.J., 1957), p. 79.

101. "Le Clergé Catholique et les protestants français, 1775, 1780, 1788," *B.S.H.P.F.* 36 (1887): 539.

102. For the Parlement of Paris's concerns with the edict, see Newberry Library, Case FRC 6495, "Rémonstrances du Parlement de Paris concernant les non-Catholiques. Arretées le 18 Janvier 1788." Consult especially Henri Dubief, "La réception de l'Edit du 17 novembre 1787 par les Parlements," *B.S.H.P.F.* 134 (April–May, 1988): 281–93.

103. Dubief, "La réception de l'Edit," p. 285.

Chapter Eight.   Epilogue

1. Knachel, *England and the "Fronde,"* pp. 197–210.

2. Yves-Marie Bercé, *History of Peasant Revolts: The Social Origins of Rebellion in Early Modern France,* trans. Amanda Whitmore (Ithaca, N.Y., 1990), p. 315.

3. Jacques Godechot, *The Taking of the Bastille, July 14th, 1789,* trans. Jean Stewart (London, 1970), p. 147.

4. Emmet Kennedy, *A Cultural History of the French Revolution* (New Haven, Conn., 1989), pp. 294–96.

5. Simon Schama, *Citizens: A Chronicle of the French Revolution* (New York, 1989), pp. 346–47.

6. George A. Kelly, "The Machine of the Duc d'Orléans and the New Politics," *Journal of Modern History* 51 (December 1979): 669.

7. *Mémoires pour servir à l'histoire de l'année 1789* (Paris, 1789), 2: 231.

8. Ibid.

9. Ibid. William Doyle, *The Oxford History of the French Revolution* (Oxford, 1990), p. 105.

10. Schama, *Citizens,* pp. 359–61.

11. *Mémoires pour servir à l'histoire de l'année 1789,* 2: 240.

12. Cited in Barbara Luttrell, *Mirabeau* (Carbondale, Ill., 1990), p. 12.

13. An account of this session is found in Bertrand Barère's *Le point du jour, ou Résultat de ce qui s'est passé la veille à l'assemblée nationale* (Paris, 1789), 1: 41–43 (Newberry FRC 5.1201). Dale Van Kley graciously informed me of the existence of these accounts.

14. This theme is developed more fully in Dale Van Kley's forthcoming book on the religious origins of the French Revolution.

15. J. F. Bosher, *The French Revolution: A New Interpretation* (London, 1989), p. 132.

16. Schama, *Citizens,* p. 419.

17. Ibid., p. 424.

18. Kelly, "The Machine of the Duc d'Orléans," p. 668.

19. See especially Dale Van Kley, "New Wine in Old Wineskins: Continuity and Rupture in the Pamphlet Debate of the French Prerevolution, 1787–1789," *French Historical Studies* 17, (fall 1991): 447–65.

20. Dale Van Kley, "The Religious Origins of the Patriot and Ministerial Parties in Pre-Revolutionary France: Controversy over the Chancellor's Constitutional *Coup,* 1771–1775," *Historical Reflections / Réflexions historiques* 18 (summer 1992): 61.

21. Keith M. Baker, *Inventing the French Revolution: Essays on French Political Culture in the Eighteenth Century* (Cambridge, Eng., 1990), p. 152.

22. D'Argenson, *Journal et mémoires,* 9: 370.

23. See Roger Chartier's careful analysis of the meaning of "desacralization" as it relates to the kings of France, in *The Cultural Origins of the French Revolution,* trans. Lydia G. Cochrane (Durham, N.C., 1991), pp. 111–35. This turning point in French political, religious, and social life is also associated with the struggle over the publication of Helvétius' controversial book, *De l'esprit,* in July 1758. See D. W. Smith, *Helvétius: A Study in Persecution* (Westport, Conn., 1982).

24. Chartier describes this "affective rupture" as a disenchantment "that accustomed people to dissociate ordinary existence from the destiny of the sovereign" (*The Cultural Origins of the French Revolution,* p. 122). He does not, however, believe this disenchantment was "completely new" in the 1750s. See also the discussion of Louis XV's waning popularity in Arlette Farge and Jacques Revel, *Logiques de la foule: L'affaire des enlévements d'enfants, Paris 1750* (Paris, 1988).

25. Mona Ozouf, "'Public Opinion'" at the End of the Old Regime," *Journal of Modern History* 60, supp. (September 1988): S6 n17. See Keith M. Baker, "Politique et opinion publique sous l'Ancien Régime," *Annales: Economies, Sociétés, Civilisations* 42 (January–February 1987): 41–45, 59–64; Jürgen Habermas, *L'espace public* (Paris, 1986); Chartier, *The Cultural Origins of the French Revolution,* pp. 20–37.

26. Ozouf, "'Public Opinion,'" S6. See also Thomas E. Kaiser, "Rhetoric in the Service of the King: The Abbé Dubos and the Concept of Public Judgment," *Eighteenth-Century Studies* 23, (winter 1989–90): 182–99; Thomas E. Crow, *Painters and Public Life in Eighteenth Century Paris* (New Haven, Conn., 1985); Sarah Maza, "Le Tribunal de la Nation: Les mémoires judiciares et l'opinion publique à la fin de l'ancien régime," *Annales: Economies, Sociétés, Civilisations* 42, (January–February, 1987): 73–90.

27. Dena Goodman, "Enlightenment Salons: The Convergence of Female and Philosophic Ambitions," *Eighteenth-Century Studies* 22 (spring 1989): 329–50.

28. Cited by Ozouf, "'Public Opinion,'" p. S9 n17 (from Malesherbes, *Discours prononcé dans l'Académie française le jeudi 16 février* [Paris, 1775], p. 5). See also Raymond Birn, "Malesherbes and the Call for a Free Press," in *Revolution in Print: The Press in France, 1775–1800*, ed. Robert Darnton and Daniel Roche (Berkeley, 1989), pp. 50–66.

29. Nina Gelbart, "'Frondeur'" Journalism in the 1770s: Theatre Criticism and Radical Politics in the Prerevolutionary French Press," *Eighteenth-Century Studies* 17 (summer 1984): 493–514; Daniel Roche, "Censorship and the Publishing Industry," in *Revolution in Print*, pp. 3–26.

30. Robert Darnton, "Philosophy under the Cloak," in *Revolution in Print*, p. 29.

31. Baker, *Inventing the French Revolution*, p. 189. Louis XVI's statement is cited by John Hardman, *Louis XVI* (New Haven, Conn., 1993), p. 35; see also p. 166.

32. Jeremy Popkin, "Pamphlet Journalism at the End of the Old Regime," *Eighteenth-Century Studies* 22 (spring 1989): 351–67; Jack Censer, *Prelude to Power: The Parisian Radical Press, 1789–91* (Baltimore, 1976); Marina Valensise, "The French Constitution in Prerevolutionary Debate," *Journal of Modern History* 60, supp. (September 1988): S22–S57.

33. See, for example, Joseph Klaits, *Printed Propaganda under Louis XIV: Absolute Monarchy and Public Opinion* (Princeton, N.J., 1976), pp. 86–112.

34. Baker, *Inventing the French Revolution*, p. 152.

35. Jeremy Popkin, *The Revolutionary News: The Press in France, 1789–1799* (Durham, N.C., 1990), p. 26. See also Dale Van Kley and Jeremy Popkin, "The Pre-Revolutionary Debate," sec. 5, in *The French Revolution Research Collection* (Oxford, 1990), pp. 1–40.

36. Cited in Doyle, *The Oxford History of the French Revolution*, p. 104. The duc d'Orléans had a stable of propagandists or "idea men" with whom he worked; they "moved in steady succession through the Palais Royal" (Kelly, "The Machine of the Duc d'Orléans," p. 671).

37. Cited in Adams, *The Huguenots and French Opinion*, p. 296. See his

discussion of the pamphlet debate regarding the Edict of Toleration, pp. 295–300.

38. Newberry Library, Case FRC 4623, *Lettre à un magistrat du parlement de Paris, au sujet de l'édit sur l'état civil des protestans* (Avignon, 1787), p. 6.

39. Newberry Library, Case FRC 4623, pt. 2, *Seconde lettre à un magistrat du parlement de Paris sur l'édit concernant l'état civil des protestans* (Avignon, 1787), p. 12.

40. Ibid., pp. 27–28.

41. Newberry Library, Case FRC 8208, *Le sécret révélé: ou Lettre à un magistrat de province sur les Protestans* (s. l., sn., ca. 1787), pp. 1, 3.

42. Ibid., pp. 11, 14.

43. Ibid., p. 69.

44. Newberry Library, Case FRC 4964, *Lettre impartiale, sur l'édit des protestans; à M. le Comte de xxx* (Paris, January 8, 1788), pp. 6, 35–36.

45. Ibid., pp. 27–28.

46. B.S.H.P.F., Collection 1085: "Lettre philosophique sur la religion Protestante."

47. B.S.H.P.F., MS Coquerel 337, doc. 237.

48. On Rabaut Saint-Etienne's favorable attitude towards the "philosophic" movement, see Woodbridge, "L'influence des philosophes français sur les pasteurs réformés du Languedoc," pp. 299–305.

49. Dardier, ed., *Paul Rabaut*, 2: 409–10.

50. Michelet, Jaurès, and others were attracted to the thesis that Jansenists, for example, had participated in a conspiracy that led to the Revolution. René Taveneaux denies that Jansenists were involved in such a plot, but he proposes that their political theory could easily take on a "revolutionary" character (*Jansénisme et politique* [Paris, 1965], pp. 45–48).

51. See Dale Van Kley, "The Jansenist Constitutional Legacy," pp. 169–201.

52. Armand Lods, "Quelques notes sur les opinions politiques de Rabaut de Saint-Etienne," *La Révolution française* 40 (January–June, 1901): 356.

53. *Discours sur l'édit de bienfaisance, à l'usage des Protestans de la Campagne* (N.p., 1788), p. 16.

54. Archives consistoriales de l'Eglise Réformée de Nîmes, B33: "Note du Consistoire de Nîmes pour servir de réponse à l'arrêté du Consistoire de Bordeaux du 6 9bre 1788."

55. "Opinion de M. Rabaut de Saint-Etienne sur la motion suivante de M. le comte de Casteltane, 'Nul homme ne peut être inquieté pour ses opinions, ni troublé dans l'exercice de sa religion,'" in *Procès-verbal de l'Assemblée nationale* (Paris, 1789), 3: 7, 5 and note.

56. Ibid., pp. 8, 9.

57. This does not mean that Huguenots in France were necessarily treated as equals by their fellow citizens. In its session of August 17, 1790, the

National Assembly indicated that Protestants of the Helvetic Confession and Augsburg Confession in Alsace were guaranteed that their rights would remain as they had been since the time of their reunion with France (*Collection générale des décrets rendus par l'Assemblée nationale* [Paris, 1790], 2: 202).

58. Newberry Library, Case FRC 3474: "Discours prononcé au service extraordinaire célébré par les Protestans de Paris . . . A l'occasion de l'achèvement de la Constitution et de son acceptation par the Roi. Le jeudi 13, Octobre 1791," pp. 12, 14. Ironically, the "movement of dechristianization" (1793–94) would take away from Protestants the freedom of worship. See, for example, John Woodbridge, "The Reformed Pastors of Languedoc Face the Movement of Dechristianization (1793–1794)," in *Sécularisation,* ed. Michèle Mat, (Brussels, 1984), pp. 77–89; Michel Vovelle, *Religion et Révolution: La déchristianisation de l'an II* (Paris, 1976).

59. Ruth F. Necheles, "The Abbé Grégoire's Work in Behalf of Jews, 1788–1791," *French Historical Studies* 6 (fall 1969): 172; Jacques Godechot, "La Révolution française et les juifs (1789–1799)," in *Les Juifs et la Révolution Française: Problèmes et aspirations,* Bernard Blumenkranz and Albert Soboul, eds. (Toulouse, 1976), pp. 47–86; Myriam Yardeni, "Les Juifs dans la polémique sur la tolérance des protestants à la veille de la Révolution," *Revue des études juives* 132 (1973): 79–93.

60. Michel Vovelle, *The Fall of the French Monarchy, 1787–1792* (Cambridge, Eng., 1987), p. 149.

61. Dardier, ed., *Paul Rabaut,* 2: 405.

62. Lynn Hunt, *Politics, Culture, and Class in the French Revolution* (Berkeley, 1984).

63. Schama, *Citizens,* p. 859. See also Antoine de Baecque, "L'homme nouveau est arrivé: La 'Régénération' du français en 1789," *Dix-huitième siècle* 20 (1988): 193–208.

64. François Furet and Denis Richet, *La Révolution française* (Paris, 1972), pp. 115–16.

65. Joan B. Landes, *Women and the Public Sphere in the Age of the French Revolution* (Ithaca, N.Y., 1988).

66. Merrick, *The Desacralization of the French Monarchy,* pp. 168–69.

67. Cited in Michel Péronnet, "Nos Seigneurs du Clergé de France en 1789," *Dix-huitième siècle* 20 (1988): 128.

BIBLIOGRAPHY

MANUSCRIPTS

(Individual collections are noted; particular folios are not designated.)
Archives du Département de la Gironde: C. 192; C. 198; C. 315; C. 4683
Archives du Département de l'Hérault: C. 232; C. 233; C. 236; C. 467
Archives Historiques de la Guerre (Paris): MR 1086 document 19
Archives du Ministère des Affaires Étrangères (AM, Paris): Correspondance
  politique, Pologne 236; Correspondance politique, Prusse 185
Archives Nationales (AN, Paris): O'452, O'453; TT 440, documents, 2, 8, 41,
  129, 143, 257; TT 441, documents, 141, 159, 180, 181, 187, 189, 190, 191, 192,
  193, 194, 268, 288, 312; TT 442, documents, 32, 70, 71, 72, 197, 200, 218; TT
  447, documents, 167, 169, 170, 173; Y 15813
Bibliothèque de l'Arsenal (Paris) 12022
Bibliothèque Nationale (BN: Paris): NAF 1799; FF 7047; FF 10,628; Lb. 38 659
Bibliothèque de Port-Royal (BPR, Paris): 547
Bibliothèque de la Société de l'Histoire du Protestantisme Français (B.S.H.P.F.,
  Paris): MS Coquerel 309, 310 B, 310 C, 311, 337; 358 III; Fonds Farelle, Lan-
  guedoc XIX, Cévennes 449; Collection 1085
Bibliothèque de l'Université de Genève (B.U.G.): Collection Antoine Court
  1/28; CF7; CF 29/3; 46; 47
British Museum (BM, London): Add. MSS 32,871; Add. MSS 32,872; Add.
  MSS 32,873; Add. MSS 32,874; Add. MSS 32,875; Add. MSS 32,997; Add.
  MSS 6839
Public Record Office: 30/8/85 I; 30/8/48 I
Archives Consistoriales de l'Eglise Réformée de Nîmes: B 33; B 91/20; C 8;
  L 47
Newberry Library (Chicago, Ill.): Case FRC 1151; Case FRC 1161; Case FRC
  3474; Case FRC 4623; Case FRC 4964; Case FRC 6495; Case FRC 8208

PRINTED PRIMARY SOURCES

Almon, John, *Anecdotes of the Life of the Right Hon. William Pitt.* 3 vols., London, 1810.
Anselme, P., and M. Du Foury. *Histoire généalogique et chronologique de la mai-
  son royale de France.* . . . Paris, 1726.
Argenson, René-Louis de Voyer, marquis d'. *Journal et mémoires du marquis
  d'Argenson.* Edited by E.-J.-B. Rathery. 9 vols. Paris, 1859–67.

Barbier, Edmond-J. F. *Journal historique et anecdotique du règne de Louis XV, 1718–1763.* Edited by A. de la Villegille. 8 vols. Paris, 1857–66.

Basnage, Henri, Sieur de Beauval. *Tolérance des Religions.* 1684. Edited by Elisabeth Labrousse. New York, 1970.

[Beaumont, chevalier de]. *L'accord parfait de la Nature, de la Raison, de la Révélation.* . . . Göttingen, 1755.

Bisset, Andrew, ed. *Memoirs and Papers of Sir Andrew Mitchell.* 2 vols. London, 1850.

Boutaric, M. E. *Correspondance secrète inédite de Louis XV sur la politique étrangère avec le comte de Broglie, Tercier.* . . . 2 vols. Paris, 1866.

Boutry, Maurice. *Choiseul à Rome: Lettres et mémoires inédits, 1754–1757.* Paris, n.d.

Bradshaw, John, ed. *The Letters of Philip Dormer Stanhope, Earl of Chesterfield.* 3 vols. London, 1893.

Broglie, comte de. *Politique de tous les cabinets de l'Europe pendant les règnes de Louis XV et de Louis XVI.* Hamburg, 1794.

[Chevrier, François Antoine]. *Testament politique du maréchal duc de Belle-Isle.* Paris, 1762.

Choiseul, Etienne François. *Mémoires du duc de Choiseul.* Preface by Jean-Pierre Guicciardi. Paris, 1983.

Climenson, Emily, J., ed. *Elizabeth Montagu, The Queen of the Blue Stockings: Her Correspondence from 1720 to 1761.* 2 vols. London, 1906.

Collé, Charles. *Journal historique ou Mémoires critiques et littéraires.* 3 vols. Paris, 1807.

Collection générale des décrets rendus par l'Assemblée nationale. 15 vols. Paris, 1790.

Condorcet, Marie Jean Antoine Nicolas de Caritat, marquis de. *Recueil de pièces sur l'état des protestants en France.* London, 1783.

Court, Antoine. *Lettre d'un patriote sur la tolérance civile des protestants de France et sur les avantages qui en résulteroient pour le Royaume.* N.p., 1756.

———. *Le patriote français et impartial ou réponse à la Lettre de M. l'Evêque d'Agen à M. le Controleur Général contre la tolérance des Huguenots, en datte du 1 mai 1751.* 2 vols. Villefranche, 1753.

Court de Gébelin. *Les Toulousaines ou lettres historiques et apologétiques en faveur de la Religion Réformée.* . . . Edimbourg [Lausanne], 1763.

Covel, John. *Some Account of the Present Greek Church.* Cambridge, Eng., 1722.

Dardier, Charles, ed. *Paul Rabaut, ses lettres à divers.* 2 vols. Paris, 1892.

Duclos, M. *Mémoires secrets sur le règne de Louis XIV, la régence et le règne de Louis XV.* 2 vols. Paris, 1805.

Dutens, Louis. *Memoirs of a Traveller, Now in Retirement.* 4 vols. London, 1806.

Flammermont, Jules, and Maurice Tourneux, eds. *Rémonstrances du Parlement de Paris au XVIIIe siècle.* 3 vols. Paris, 1888–98.

Gardy, Frédéric, ed. *Correspondance de Jaques Serces*. 2 vols. London, 1956.

General Court-Martial. Published by Authority, London, 1758.

Hugues, Edmond, ed. *Les Synodes du Désert: Actes et réglements des synodes nationaux et provinciaux tenus au Désert de France de l'an 1715*. 3 vols. Paris, 1891.

Koser, R., ed. *Politische Correspondenz Friedrich Des Grössen*. Vol. 14. Berlin, 1886.

[Lafayette, Marquis de]. *Mémoires, correspondance et manuscrits du général Lafayette*. 6 vols. Published by his family. Paris, 1837–38.

Lettre de M. l'Evêque d'Agen à M. Le Controleur Général contre la tolérance des Huguenots. N.p., 1751.

Luynes, Charles-Philippe d'Albert, duc de. *Mémoires du duc de Luynes, sur la cour de Louis XV, 1735–1738*. Edited by L. Dussieux and E. Soulié. 17 vols. Paris, 1860–65.

Malesherbes, Chrétien Guillaume de Lamoignan de. *Mémoire sur le mariage des Protestants*. N.p., 1785.

Masson, Frédéric, ed. *Mémoires et lettres de François Joachim de Pierre Cardinal de Bernis (1715–1758)*. 2 vols. Paris, 1878.

[Molines]. *Lettre curieuse et intéressante aux Catholiques romains et aux Protestants*. Saint-Quentin, 1757.

Monclar, Jean-Pierre-François Ripert de. *Mémoire théologique et politique au sujet des mariages clandestins des protestants en France*. N.p., 1755, 1756. Recent scholarship suggests that this work was actually written in the context of a Protestant group in association with C. F. Baer, minister of the Chapel of Sweden in Paris, and a M. Perrier from Nîmes (Poujol, "Aux sources de l'Edit de 1787," p. 362).

"Note d'un traitre fournissant à l'Intendant du Languedoc des indications sur les ministres du désert et leurs familles, 1751(?)." *B.S.H.P.F.* 7 (1858): 461–65.

Ozanam, Didier, and Michel Antoine, eds. *Correspondance secrète du comte de Broglie avec Louis XV (1756–1774)*. 2 vols. Paris, 1956.

Pichéral-Dardier, A., ed. *Paul Rabaut, ses lettres à Antoine Court (1739–1755)*. 2 vols. Paris, 1884.

Pièces originales et procédures du procès fait à Robert-François Damiens, tant en la prévôté de l'Hôtel qu'en la cour du parlement. Paris, 1757.

Pilatte, Léon, ed. *Edits Déclarations et Arrests concernant la religion réformée, 1662–1751*. Paris, 1885.

Pitt, William. *Authentic Memoirs of the Right Honourable the late Earl of Chatham*. London, 1778.

———. *Correspondence of William Pitt, Earl of Chatham*. Edited by John, Earl of Chatham. 2 vols. London, 1888.

Pompadour, Madame de. *Mémoires de Madame la Marquise de Pompadour . . . Ecrites par elle-même*. Liege, 1756.

[Rabaut de Saint-Etienne]. "Opinion de M. Rabaut de Saint-Etienne sur la motion suivante de M. le comte de Casteltane, 'Nul homme ne peut être inquieté pour ses opinions, ni troublé dans l'exercise de sa religion.'" In *Procès-verbal de l'Assemblée nationale,* vol. 3, p. 7. Paris, 1789.

Ravaisson-Mollien, François. *Archives de la Bastille, d'après des documents inédits.*. 19 vols. Geneva, 1866–1975.

[Richelieu, duc de]. *Mémoires du maréchal duc de Richelieu: Pour servir à l'histoire des Cours de Louis XIV, de la minorité et du Règne de Louis XV.* 9 vols. Paris, 1793.

Rousseau, Jean-Jacques. *The Confessions of Jean-Jacques Rousseau.* Translated by J. M. Cohen. New York, 1978.

Russel, Lord John. *Correspondence of John, Fourth Duke of Bedford.* 3 vols. London, 1843.

Sedgwick, Romney. "Letters from William Pitt to Lord Bute: 1755–1758." In *Essays Presented to Sir Lewis Namier,* edited by A.J.P. Taylor; London, 1956.

Simon, Richard. *Additions aux Recherches curieuses sur la diversité des langues et religions d'Edward Brerewood.* Edited by Jacques Le Brun and John Woodbridge. Paris, 1983.

Soulavie, J. L. *Mémoires historiques et anecdotes de la cour de France pendant la faveur de la marquise de Pompadour.* Paris, 1802.

———. *Suite des mémoires du maréchal duc de Richelieu.* Paris, 1791.

Turgot, Anne Robert Jacques. *Le Conciliateur ou Lettres d'un ecclésiastique à un magistrat sur les affaires présentes.* N.p., 1754, 1788.

Walpole, Horace. *Letters from Hon. Horace Walpole to George Montagu, Esq., from the Year 1736 to the Year 1770.* London, 1819.

———. *The Letters of Horace Walpole, Fourth Earl of Oxford.* Edited by Paget Toynbee. 4 vols. Oxford, 1903.

———. *Memoirs of King George II.* Edited by John Brooke. 3 vols. New Haven, Conn., 1985.

———. *Memoirs of the Reign of King George the Second.* Edited by Lord Holland. 3 vols. London, 1846.

Yorke, Philip C., ed. *The Life and Correspondence of Philip Yorke Earl of Hardwicke, Lord High Chancellor of Great Britain.* 3 vols. Cambridge, Eng., 1913.

PRINTED SECONDARY SOURCES

Adams, Geoffrey. *The Huguenots and French Opinion, 1685–1787: The Enlightenment Debate on Toleration.* Waterloo, Ontario, 1991.

———. "Monarchistes ou républicains?" *Dix-huitième siècle* 17 (1985): 83–95.

d'Amat, Roman, ed. *Dictionnaire de biographie française.* Paris, 1961.

d'Anglas, Boissy. *Discours et opinions de Rabaut-de-Saint-Etienne suivis de ses deux dérniers écrits et précédés d'une notice sur sa vie.* Paris, 1827.

Anquez, Léonce. *Histoire des assemblées politiques des réformés de France (1573–1622)*. Geneva, 1970 [1859].

Antoine, Michel. *Louis XV*. Paris, 1989.

Arduin, Françoise. "Un subdélégué de Libourne au XVIIIe siècle: Léonard Bulle (1748–1773)." *Revue historique de Bordeaux et du Département de la Gironde* 16 (1923): 26–36, 102–10, 168–74, 209–33, 275–96.

Armogathe, Jean-Robert. *Croire en liberté: L'Eglise catholique et la révocation de l'Edit de Nantes*. Paris, 1985.

Aston, Nigel. *The End of an Elite: The French Bishops and the Coming of the Revolution, 1786–1790*. Oxford, 1992.

Ayling, Stanley. *The Elder Pitt, Earl of Chatham*. London, 1976.

de Baecque, Antoine. "L'homme nouveau est arrivé: La 'Régénération' du français en 1789." *Dix-huitième siècle* 20 (1988): 193–208.

Baker, Keith M. *Inventing the French Revolution: Essays on French Political Culture in the Eighteenth Century*. Cambridge, Eng., 1990.

———. "Politics and Public Opinion under the Old Regime: Some Reflections." *Press and Politics in Pre-Revolution France*, edited by Jack Censer and Jeremy Popkin, pp. 204–46. Berkeley, 1987.

———. "Politique et opinion publique sous l'Ancien Régime." *Annales: Economies, Sociétés, Civilisations* 42 (January–February 1987): 41–71.

Beik, William. *Absolutism and Society in Seventeenth-century France: State Power and Provincial Aristocracy in Languedoc*. New York, 1985; Cambridge, Eng., 1992.

Bell, David. *Lawyers and Citizens: The Making of a Political Elite in Old Regime France*. New York, 1994.

Benedict, Philip. "Catholics and Huguenots in Sixteenth-Century Rouen: The Demographic Effects of the Religious Wars." *French Historical Studies* 9 (fall 1975): 209–34.

———. *The Huguenot Population of France, 1600–1685: The Demographic Fate and Customs of a Religious Minority*. Philadelphia, 1991.

———. "La population réformée française de 1600 à 1685." *Annales: Economies, Sociétés, Civilisations* 42 (November–December 1987): 1433–65.

Benoist, Elie. *Histoire de l'Edit de Nantes contenant les choses les plus remarquables qui se sont passées en France avant et après sa publication*. 5 vols. Delft, 1693–95.

Benoît, Daniel. *L'état religieux du protestantisme français dans la seconde moitié du XVIII siècle*. Montauban, 1909.

———. *Les frères Gibert: Deux pasteurs du Désert et du Réfuge (1722–1817)*. Toulouse, 1889.

———. "Ribaute Charon, Voltaire et Rousseau." *Recueil de l'Académie des sciences, belles-lettres et arts de Tarn-et-Garonne* 21 (1905; published 1906): 41–56.

Benoît, Daniel and Emile du Cailar. *Gal-Pomaret, Pasteur de Ganges: Son temps, son ministère, ses écrits*. Paris, 1899.

Bercé, Yves-Marie. *History of Peasant Revolts: The Social Origins of Rebellion in Early Modern France*. Translated by Amanda Whitmore. Ithaca, N.Y., 1990.

Besterman, Theodore. *Voltaire*. 3d. ed. Chicago, 1976.

Bien, David. *The Calas Affair: Persecution, Toleration, and Heresy in Eighteenth-Century Toulouse*. Princeton, N.J., 1960.

——. "Catholic Magistrates and Protestant Marriages in the French Enlightenment." *French Historical Studies* 2 (fall 1962): 409–29.

Birn, Raymond. "Malesherbes and the Call for a Free Press." In *Revolution in Print: The Press in France, 1775–1800*, edited by Robert Darnton and Daniel Roche, pp. 50–66. Berkeley, 1989.

Bluche, François. *Les Magistrats du parlement de Paris au XVIIIe siècle*. Paris, 1960.

——. *La vie quotidienne au temps de Louis XVI*. Paris, 1980.

Blumenkranz, Bernard, and Albert Soboul, eds. *Les Juifs et la Révolution Française: Problèmes et aspirations*. Toulouse, 1976.

Bois, Jean-Pierre. *Maurice de Saxe*. Paris, 1992.

Bosher, J. F. *The French Revolution: A New Interpretation*. London, 1989.

——. "The Political and Religious Origins of La Rochelle's Primacy in Trade with New France, 1627–1685." *French History* 7 (September 1993): 286–312.

Bost, Charles. *Histoire des Protestants de France*. Seine-et-Oise, 1926.

——. *Les prédicants du Bas Languedoc*. Paris, 1912.

Brown, Peter Douglas. *William Pitt, Earl of Chatham: The Great Commoner*. London, 1978.

Browning, Reed. *The Duke of Newcastle*. New Haven, Conn., 1975.

Butler, Rohan. *Choiseul*. Vol. 1, *Father and Son 1719–1754*. Oxford, 1980.

Cahen, Léon. *Les querelles religieuses et parlementaires sous Louis XV*. Paris, 1913.

Campardon, Emile. *Madame de Pompadour et la cour de Louis XV au milieu du dix-huitième siècle*. Paris, 1867.

Capefigué, Jean Baptiste Honoré Raymond. *Oeuvres de Capefigué: Louis XV et la société du XVIIIe siècle*. Brussels, 1845.

Capon, G., and R. Yves Plessis. *Paris galant au dix-huitième siècle: Vie privée du prince de Conty Louis-François de Bourbon (1717–1776)*. Paris, 1907.

Carbonnier, Jean. "Sociologie et psychologie juridiques de l'Edit de Révocation." In *La Révocation de l'Edit de Nantes et le protestantisme français en 1685*, edited by Roger Zuber and Laurent Theis, pp. 31–57. Paris, 1986.

Censer, Jack R. *Prelude to Power: The Parisian Radical Press, 1789–91*. Baltimore, 1976.

Cerny, Gerald. *Theology, Politics and Letters at the Crossroads of European Civilization: Jacques Basnage and the Baylean Huguenot Refugees in the Dutch Republic*. Dordrecht, 1987.

Chalamet, Marc. *Un collaborateur d'Antoine Court—Pierre Peirot Pasteur du Désert (1712–1772)*. Paris, 1923.

Chaponnière, Paul. *Voltaire chez les Calvinistes*. Paris, 1936.

Charteris, Evan. *William Augustus Duke of Cumberland and the Seven Years' War*. London, 1920.

Chartier, Roger. *The Cultural Origins of the French Revolution*. Translated by Lydia G. Cochrane. Durham, N.C., 1991.

Chaussinand-Nogaret, Guy. *The French Nobility in the Eighteenth Century: From Feudalism to Enlightenment*. Translated by William Doyle. Cambridge, Eng., 1985.

Chavannes, Jules. "Une école libre de théologie des temps passés: Notes historiques sur le séminaire protestant à Lausanne." *Le Chrétien Evangélique: Revue religieuse de la Suisse Romande* 15 (1872): 33–45, 73–88, 119–30; 168–81.

Chédozeau, Bernard. "Les grandes étapes de la publication de la Bible catholique en français du concile de Trente au XVIIIe siècle." In *Le Grand Siècle et la Bible*, edited by Jean-Robert Armogathe, pp. 341–60. Paris, 1989.

Chisick, Harvey. "Pamphlets and Journalism in the Early French Revolution: The Offices of the *Ami du Roi* of the Abbé Royou as a Center of Royalist Propaganda." *French Historical Studies* 15 (fall 1988): 623–45.

Clark, J.C.D. *The Dynamics of Change: The Crisis of the 1750s and English Party Systems*. Cambridge, Eng., 1982.

———. *English Society 1688–1832: Ideology, Social Structure and Political Practice During the Ancien Régime*. Cambridge, Eng., 1985.

Clark, John G. *La Rochelle and the Atlantic Economy during the Eighteenth Century*. Baltimore, 1981.

Cognet, Louis. *Le jansénisme*. Paris, 1968.

Coquerel, Charles. *Histoire des églises du désert chez les protestants de France depuis la fin du règne de Louis XIV jusqu'à la révolution française*. 2 vols. Geneva, 1841.

Cottret, Bernard. *Terre d'exil: L'Angleterre et ses réfugiés, 16e–17e siècles*. Paris, 1985.

Cottret, Monique. "Aux origines du republicanisme janseniste: Le mythe de l'église primitive et le primitivisme des lumières." *Revue d'histoire moderne et contemporaine* 31 (1984): 99–115.

Crahay, Roland, ed. *La tolérance civile*. Brussels, 1982.

Cranston, Maurice. *Jean-Jacques: The Early Life and Work of Jean-Jacques Rousseau, 1712–1754*. Bungay, Suffolk, 1983.

———. *Philosophers and Pamphleteers: Political Theorists of the Enlightenment*. Oxford, 1986.

Crouzet, Denis. *Les guerriers de Dieu: La violence au temps des troubles de religion*. 2 vols. paris, 1990.

Crow, Thomas E. *Painters and Public Life in Eighteenth Century Paris*. New Haven, Conn., 1985.

Dann, Uriel. *Hanover and Great Britain, 1740–1760: Diplomacy and Survival.* London, 1991.

Dardier, Charles. "Voltaire agissant en faveur des protestants en 1754." *B.S.H.P.F.* 32 (1883): 528–29.

Darnton, Robert. *Bohème littéraire et révolution: Le monde des livres au XVIIIe siècle.* Paris, 1983.

———. "Philosophy under the Cloak." In *Revolution in Print: The Press in France, 1775–1800,* edited by Robert Darnton and Daniel Roche, pp. 27–49. Berkeley, 1989.

Dartique, J.-Albert. "Rabaut de Saint-Etienne à l'Assemblée Constituante de 1789." Thesis, Faculty of Protestant Theology, Montauban, 1903.

Dedieu, Abbé. *Histoire politique des protestants français, 1715–1794.* 2 vols. Paris, 1925.

De Félice, G. *Histoire des Protestants de France depuis l'origine de la Réformation jusqu'au temps présent.* Paris, 1850.

De la Garde, Henry. *Le Duc de Rohan et les Protestants sous Louis XIII.* Geneva, 1978 [1884].

De la Groce, Agnès. *Camisards et dragons du Roi.* Paris, 1950.

Del Perugia, Paul. *Louis XV.* Paris, 1975.

Delumeau, Jean. "La difficile émergence de la tolérance." In *La Révocation de l'Edit de Nantes et le protestantisme français en 1685,* edited by Roger Zuber and Laurent Theis, pp. 359–74. Paris, 1986.

———. *Naissance et affirmation de la Réforme.* Paris, 1965.

Desan, Suzanne. *Reclaiming the Sacred Lay Religion and Popular Politics in Revolutionary France.* Ithaca, N.Y., 1990.

Desgraves, Louis. *Répertoire des ouvrages de controverse entre Catholiques et Protestants en France: 1598–1685.* 2 vols. Geneva, 1984–85.

Dévic, C., and J. Vaissette. *Histoire générale du Languedoc.* 14 vols. Toulouse, 1878.

Deyon, Solange. "Protestants, avant et après la révocation." *Revue d'histoire et de philosophie religieuses* 66 (July–September 1986): 277–86.

Dez, Pierre. *Histoire des Protestants et de l'Eglise Réformée de l'Isle de Ré.* La Rochelle, 1926.

Diefendorf, Barbara. *Beneath the Cross: Catholics and Huguenots in Sixteenth-Century Paris.* New York, 1991.

———. "Recent Literature on the Religious Conflicts in Sixteenth-Century France." *Religious Studies Review* 10 (October 1984): 362–671.

Dodge, Guy Howard. *The Political Theory of the Huguenots of the Dispersion with Special Reference to the Thought and Influence of Pierre Jurieu.* New York, 1972 [1947].

Douen, O. "Jean Gardien Givry de Vervins, l'un des prémiers pasteurs du Désert dans le Nord de la France, 1691." *B.S.H.P.F.* 9 (1860): 174–92.

Doyle, William. *Origins of the French Revolution.* Oxford, 1982.

———. *The Oxford History of the French Revolution.* Oxford, 1990.

Dubief, Henri. "La réception de l'Edit du 17 novembre 1787 par les Parlements." *B.S.H.P.F.* 134 (April–June, 1988): 281–93.

Ducasse, A. *La guerre des Camisards.* Paris, 1947.

Dupont, André. *Rabaut Saint-Etienne, 1743–1793.* Strasbourg, 1946.

Durrlemen, Freddy. *Eloge et condamnation de la Révocation de l'Edit de Nantes.* Carrières-sous-Poissy, 1985.

Egret, Jean. *The French Prerevolution, 1787–1788.* Translated by Wesley D. Camp. Chicago, 1977.

Ellis, Harold. *Boulainvilliers and the French Monarchy: Aristocratic Politics in Early Eighteenth-Century France.* Ithaca, N.Y., 1988.

Escheverria, Durand. *The Maupeou Revolution: A Study in the History of Libertarianism in France, 1770–1774.* Baton Rouge, La., 1985.

Estèbe, Janine. "Vers une autre religion et une autre église (1536–1598)." In *Histoire des protestants en France,* edited by Robert Mandrou, pp. 45–116. Toulouse, 1977.

Farge, Arlette. *Fragile Lives: Violence, Power and Solidarity in Eighteenth Century Paris.* Translated by Carol Shelton. Cambridge, Mass., 1993.

Farge, Arlette, and Jacques Revel. *Logiques de la foule: L'affaire des enlévements d'enfants, Paris 1750.* Paris, 1988.

Farge, James K. *Orthodoxy and Reform in Early Reformation France: The Faculty of Theology of Paris, 1500–1543.* Leiden, 1985.

Fauchois, Yann. "Jansénisme et politique au XVIIIe siècle: Légitimation de l'état et délégitimation de la monarchie chez G. N. Maultrot." *Revue d'histoire moderne et contemporaine* 34 (1987): 473–91.

Feuerwerker, D. *L'émancipation de Juifs en France de l'Ancien Régime à la fin du Second Empire.* Paris, 1976.

Ford, Franklin L. *Robe and Sword: The Regrouping of French Aristocracy after Louis XIV.* Cambridge, Mass., 1953.

Frèche, Georges. "Contre-Réforme et dragonnades (1610–1689): Pour une orientation statistique de l'histoire du Protestantisme." *B.S.H.P.F.* 119 (April–June 1973): 362–83.

Furet, François. *Penser la Révolution française.* Paris, 1978.

Furet, François, and Denis Richet. *La Révolution française.* Paris, 1972.

Furet, François, et al. *Livre et société dans la France du XVIIIe siècle.* 2 vols. Paris, 1965–70.

Gargett, Graham. *Voltaire and Protestantism.* Oxford, 1980.

Garrisson, Janine. *L'Edit de Nantes et sa révocation: Histoire d'une intolérance.* Paris, 1985.

Garrisson-Estèbe, Janine. *Tocsin pour un massacre.* Paris, 1973.

Gazier, A. *Histoire générale du mouvement janseniste depuis ses origines jusqu'à nos jours*. 2 vols. Paris, 1923.

Gelbart, Nina. *Feminine and Opposition Journalism in Old Regime France: The Journal des Dames*. Berkeley, 1988.

————. "'Frondeur' Journalism in the 1770s: Theatre Criticism and Radical Politics in the Prerevolutionary French Press." *Eighteenth-Century Studies* 17 (summer 1984): 493–514.

Gembicki, Dieter. *Histoire et politique à la fin de l'Ancien Régime: Jacob-Nicholas Moreau, 1717–1803*. Paris, 1979.

Gerson, Noel Bertram. *The Edict of Nantes*. New York, 1969.

Godard, Philippe. *La querelle des réfus de sacrements, 1730–1765*. Paris, 1937.

Godechot, Jacques. *The Counter-Revolution: Doctrine and Action 1789–1804*. Translated by Salvator Attanasio. Princeton, N.J., 1981.

————. *The Taking of the Bastille, July 14th, 1789*. Translated by Jean Stewart. London, 1970.

Göhring, Martin. *Rabaut Saint-Etienne: Ein Kämpfer an der Wende zweier Epochen*. Berlin, 1935.

Golden, R. M., ed. *The Huguenot Connection: The Edict of Nantes, Its Revocation, and Early French Migration to South Carolina*. Dordrecht, 1988.

Goldmann, Lucien. *Le Dieu caché: Etude sur la vision tragique dans les Pensées de Pascal et dans le théâtre de Racine*. Paris, 1956.

Goncourt, Edmond, and Jules Goncourt. *Madame de Pompadour*. Paris, 1888.

Goodman, Dena. "Enlightenment Salons: The Convergence of Female and Philosophic Ambitions." *Eighteenth-Century Studies* 22 (spring 1989): 329–50.

Gordon, Daniel. "'Public Opinion' and the Civilizing Process in France: The Example of Morellet." *Eighteenth-Century Studies* 22 (spring 1989): 302–28.

Gould, William, ed. *Lives of the Georgian Age, 1714–1837*. New York, 1978.

Gray, Janet. *The French Huguenots: Anatomy of Courage*. Grand Rapids, Mich., 1981.

Greengrass, Mark. *The French Reformation*. Oxford, 1987.

Grosclaude, Pierre. "Comment MALESHERBES élabore sa doctrine sur le problème des Protestants." *B.S.H.P.F.*, 103 (July –September, 1957): 149–72.

————. *Malesherbes, témoin et interprète de son temps*. Paris, 1961.

————. "Une négociation prématurée: Louis Dutens et les protestants français, 1775–1776." *B.S.H.P.F.* 104 (April–June, 1958): 73–93.

Gruder, Vivian. "Paths to Political Consciousness: The Assembly of Notables of 1787 and the 'Pre-Revolution in France.'" *French Historical Studies* 13 (spring 1984): 323–55.

Guéhenno, Jean. *Jean-Jacques Rousseau*. Translated by John Weightman and Doreen Weightman. 2 vols. New York, 1967.

Guirard, G. Edouard. "Le séminaire de Lausanne et le pastorat en France pendant la période du Désert 1715–1787 (d'après les manuscrits Court)." Thesis: University of Geneva, 1913.

Gwynn, Robin D. *Huguenot Heritage: The History and Contribution of the Huguenots in Britain*. London, 1985.

Haase, Erich. *Einführung in die Literatur des Refuge: Der Beitrag der französischen Protestanten zur Entwicklung analytischer Denkformen am Ende des 17*. Jahrhunderts. Berlin, 1959.

Habermas, Jürgen. *L'espace public*. Paris, 1986.

Hanley, Sarah. *The Lit de Justice of the Kings of France: Constitutional Ideology in Legend, Ritual and Discourse*. Princeton, N.J., 1983.

Hardman, John. *Louis XVI*. New Haven, Conn., 1993.

Hardy, James. *Judicial Politics in the Old Regime: The Parlement of Paris during the Regency*. Baton Rouge, La., 1967.

Hatton, Ragnhild. *George I, Elector and King*. Cambridge, Mass., 1978.

Heller, Henry. *The Conquest of Poverty: The Calvinist Revolt in Sixteenth Century France*. Leiden, 1986.

———. *Iron and Blood: Civil Wars in Sixteenth-Century France*. Montreal, 1991.

Herman, Arthur. "The Huguenot Republic and Antirepublicanism in Seventeenth-Century France." *Journal of the History of Ideas* 53 (1992): 249–69.

Hertzberg, Arthur. *The French Enlightenment and the Jews*. New York, 1968.

Heyck, Thomas William. *The Peoples of the British Isles: A New History*. 2 vols. Belmont, Calif., 1992.

Heyd, Michael. "La réaction à l'enthousiasme et la sécularisation des sensibilités religieuses au début du dix-huitième siècle." In *Sécularisation*, edited by Michèle Mat, pp. 5–38. Brussels, 1984.

Hovyn de Tranchère, J., ed. *Le dessous de l'histoire curiosités judiciaires administratives, politiques et littéraires*. Paris, 1886.

Hudault, Joseph. *Guy-Jean-Baptiste Target et sa contribution à la préparation de l'Edit de novembre 1787 sur l'état civil des protestants*. Paris, 1966.

Hugues, Edmond. *Antoine Court: Histoire de la restauration du Protestantisme en France au XVIIIe siècle d'après des documents inédits*. 2 vols. Paris, 1872.

———. "Un épisode de l'histoire du protestantisme au XVIIIe siècle." *B.S.H.P.F.* 26 (1877): 289–303, 338–50.

Hunt, Lynn. *Politics, Culture, and Class in the French Revolution*. Berkeley, 1984.

Imbart de la Tour, P. *Les origines de la Réforme*. 4 vols. 2d ed. Melun, 1946.

Jackson, Richard A. "Peers of France and Princes of the Blood." *French Historical Studies* 7 (spring 1971): 27–46.

Jacob, Margaret. *The Radical Enlightenment: Pantheists, Freemasons and Republicans*. London, 1981.

Johnson, Hubert C. *Frederick the Great and His Officials*. New Haven, Conn., 1975.

Joutard, Philippe. "Les déserts (1685–1800)." In *Histoire des protestants en France*, edited by Robert Mandrou, pp. 189–262. Toulouse, 1977.

———. "1685: Une fin et une nouvelle chance pour le protestantisme français." In *Le Réfuge huguenot*, edited by M. Magdelaine and R. von Thadden, pp. 13–30. Paris, 1985.

———. *La légende des Camisards: Une sensibilité au passé*. Paris, 1977.

———. "The Revocation of the Edict of Nantes: End or Renewal of French Protestantism?" In *International Calvinism*, edited by Menna Prestwich, pp. 339–68. Oxford, 1985.

Joynes, Daniel Carroll. "Parlementaires, Peers, and the *Parti Janséniste*: The Refusal of Sacraments and the Revival of the Ancient Constitution in Eighteenth Century France." In *Proceedings of the Eighth Annual Meeting of the Western Society for French History, October 23–25, 1980 Eugene, Oregon*, edited by Edgar Leon Newman, pp. 229–38. Las Cruces, N.M., 1981.

Judge, H. G. "Louis XIV and the Church." In *Louis XIV and the Craft of Kingship*, edited by John C. Rule, pp. 240–64. Columbus, Ohio, 1969.

Kahn, Léon. *Les Juifs pendant la Révolution*. New York, 1968.

Kaiser, Thomas E. "Rhetoric in the Service of the King: The Abbé Dubos and the Concept of Public Judgment." *Eighteenth-Century Studies* 23 (winter 1989–90): 182–99.

Kantorowicz, Ernst H. *The King's Two Bodies: A Study in Medieval Political Theory*. Princeton, N.J., 1957.

Kelly, George A. "From *Lèse-Majesté* to *Lèse-Nation*: Treason in Eighteenth-Century France." *Journal of the History of Ideas* 42 (1981): 269–86.

———. "The Machine of the Duc d'Orléans and the New Politics." *Journal of Modern History* 51 (December 1979): 667–84.

———. *Mortal Politics in Eighteenth-Century France*. Waterloo, Ontario, 1986.

Kennedy, Emmet. *A Cultural History of the French Revolution*. New Haven, Conn., 1989.

Kennett, Lee. *The French Armies in the Seven Years' War*. Durham, N.C., 1967.

Keohane, Nannerl O. *Philosophy and the State in France: The Renaissance to the Enlightenment*. Princeton, N.J., 1980.

Kern, Hélène. "Le séminaire de Lausanne et le Comité Génevois." *B.S.H.P.F.* 108 (October–December, 1962): 192–218.

Kettering, Sharon. *Judicial Politics and Urban Revolt in Seventeenth-Century France: The Parlement of Aix, 1629–1659*. Princeton, N.J., 1978.

Kingdon, Robert. *Geneva and the Coming of the Wars of Religion in France, 1555–1563*. Geneva, 1956.

———. *Geneva and the Consolidation of the French Protestant Movement, 1564–1572*. Geneva, 1967.

———. *Myths about the St. Bartholomew's Day Massacres 1572–1576*. Cambridge, Mass., 1988.

Klaits, Joseph. *Printed Propaganda under Louis XIV: Absolute Monarchy and Public Opinion*. Princeton, N.J., 1976.

Kleinman, Ruth. "Changing Interpretations of the Edict of Nantes: The Administrative Aspect, 1643–1661." *French Historical Studies* 10 (fall 1978): 541–71.

Knachel, Philip A. *England and the "Fronde": The Impact of the English Civil War and Revolution on France*. Ithaca, N.Y., 1967.

Kossmann, Ernst. *La Fronde*. Leiden, 1954.

Kreiser, B. Robert. *Miracles, Convulsions, and Ecclesiastical Politics in Early Eighteenth-Century Paris*. Princeton, N.J., 1978.

Labatut, Jean-Pierre. *Les ducs et pairs de France au XVIIe siècle*. Paris, 1972.

Labrousse, Elisabeth. "The Political Ideas of the Huguenot Diaspora (Bayle and Jurieu)." In *Church, State, and Society under the Bourbon Kings of France*, edited by Richard M. Golden, pp. 222–83. Lawrence, Kan., 1982.

———. *La Révocation de l'Edit de Nantes: Une foi, une loi, un roi?* Payot, 1985.

———. "Understanding the Revocation of the Edict of Nantes from the Perspective of the French Court." In *The Huguenot Connection: The Edict of Nantes, Its Revocation, and Early French Migration to South Carolina*, edited by R. M. Golden, pp. 49–62. Dordrecht, 1988.

———. "The Wars of Religion in Seventeenth-Century Huguenot Thought." In *The Massacre of St. Bartholomew: Reappraisals and Documents*, edited by Alfred Soman, pp. 243–55. The Hague, 1974.

Landes, Joan B. *Women and the Public Sphere in the Age of the French Revolution*. Ithaca, N.Y., 1988.

Laplanche, François. *L'Écriture, le sacré et l'histoire: Érudits et politiques protestants devant la Bible en France au XVIIe siècle*. Amsterdam, 1986.

Launay, Michel. *Rousseau*. Paris, 1968.

Lauriol, Claude. *La Beaumelle: Un protestant cévenol entre Montesquieu et Voltaire*. Geneva, 1978.

———. "L'Edit de 1787 and la tolérance à la fin de l'Ancien Régime." *B.S.H.P.F.* 134 (April–June 1988): 425–433.

Le Brun, Jacques. "La conscience et la théologie moderne." In *La Révocation de l'Edit de Nantes et le protestantisme français en 1685*, edited by Roger Zuber and Laurent Theis, pp. 113–33. Paris, 1986.

Lefèvre, Georges. *The Coming of the French Revolution*. Translated by R. R. Palmer. Princeton, N.J., 1947.

Lemaire, André. *Les lois fondamentales de la monarchie française d'après les théorticiens de l'Ancien Régime*. Paris, 1975 [1907].

Léonard, Emile. *Histoire ecclésiastique des réformés français au XVIIIe siècle*. Paris, 1940.

Ligou, Daniel. "L'Eglise Réformée du Désert: Fait economique et social." *Revue d'Histoire Economique et Sociale* 32 (1954): 146–67.

Lods, Armand. "Biographie: Les partisans et les adversaires de l'Edit de Tolérance: Etude bibliographique et juridique 1750–1789." *B.S.H.P.F.* 36 (1887): 551–65.

———. *Essai sur la vie de Rabaut de Saint-Etienne, Pasteur à Nîmes, Membre de l'Assemblée Constituante et de la Convention nationale (1743–1793)*. Paris, 1893.

———. "Quelques notes sur les opinions politiques de Rabaut de Saint-Etienne." *La Révolution française* 40 (January–June 1901): 353–57.

Loft, Lenone. "Brissot and the Jewish Question." Paper presented at the International Congress on the History of the French Revolution, Georgetown University, Washington, D.C., May 6, 1989.

Lüthy, Herbert. *La Banque Protestante en France de la Révocation de l'Edit de Nantes à la Révolution*. 2 vols. Paris, 1961.

Luttrell, Barbara. *Mirabeau*. Carbondale, Ill., 1990.

Mackay, Ruddock. *Admiral Hawke*. Oxford, 1965.

Magdelaine, M., and R. von Thadden, eds. *Le Réfuge huguenot*. Paris, 1985.

Mandrou, Robert. "Pourquoi se réformer." In *Histoire des protestants en France*, edited by Mandrou, pp. 7–44. Toulouse, 1977.

Mann, M. *Erasme et les débuts de la réforme française (1517–1536)*. Paris, 1934.

Margerison, Kenneth. "History, Representative Institutions, and Political Rights in the French Pre-Revolution (1787–1789)." *French Historical Studies* 15 (spring 1987): 68–98.

Martimort, Aimé Georges. *Le gallicanisme de Bossuet*. Paris, 1953.

Martin, Odile. *La conversion protestante à Lyon (1659–1687)*. Geneva, 1986.

———. "Prosélytisme et tolérance à Lyon du milieu du XVIIe siècle à la Révocation de l'Edit de Nantes." *Revue d'histoire moderne et contemporaine* 25 (1978): 306–20.

Martin, Victor. *Le Gallicanisme politique et le clergé de France*. Paris, 1929.

Mason, Haydn. *Voltaire: A Biography*. Baltimore, 1981.

Maza, Sarah. "Politics, Culture, and the Origins of the French Revolution." *Journal of Modern History* 61 (December 1989): 704–23.

———. "Le Tribunal de la Nation: Les mémoires judiciares et l'opinion publique à la fin de l'ancien régime." *Annales: Economies, Sociétés, Civilisations* 42 (January–February, 1987): 73–90.

Mazoyer, Louis. "L'Application de l'Edit de 1787 dans le Midi de la France." *B.S.H.P.F.* 74 (1925): 141–76.

Menard, Jean. *Pascal*. Translated by Claude Abraham and Marcia Abraham. University, Ala., 1969.

Merrick, Jeffrey. "Conscience and Citizenship in Eighteenth-Century France." *Eighteenth-Century Studies* 21 (fall 1987): 48–70.

———. "The Coronation of Louis XVI: The Waning of Royal Ritual." In *Proceedings of the Eighth Annual Meeting of the Western Society for French His-*

tory, October 23–25, 1980, Eugene Oregon, edited by Edgar Leon Newman, pp. 191–204. Las Cruces, N.M., 1981.

———. *The Desacralization of the French Monarchy in the Eighteenth Century.* Baton Rouge, La. 1990.

———. "'Disputes over Words' and Constitutional Conflict in France, 1730–1732." *French Historical Studies* 14, (fall 1986): 497–520.

Middleton, Richard. *The Bells of Victory: The Pitt-Newcastle Ministry and the Conduct of the Seven Years' War, 1757–1762.* Cambridge, Eng., 1985.

Mitford, Nancy. *Madame de Pompadour.* New York, 1984.

Monod, Albert. *Les sermons de Paul Rabaut: Pasteur du Désert (1738–1785).* Mazamet, 1911.

Moote, A. Lloyd. *The Revolt of the Judges: The Parlement of Paris and the Fronde, 1643–1652.* Princeton, N.J., 1971.

Morris, Madeleine F. *Le Chevalier de Jaucourt: Un ami de la terre.* Geneva, 1979.

Motley, Mark. *Becoming a French Aristocrat: The Education of the Court Nobility, 1580–1715.* Princeton, N.J., 1990.

Mours, Samuel. *Les Eglises Réformées en France: Tableaux et cartes.* Paris, 1958.

Mours, Samuel, and Daniel Robert. *Le protestantisme en France du XVIIIe siècle à nos jours.* Paris, 1972.

Mousnier, Roland. *The Assassination of Henry IV: The Tyrannicide Problem and the Consolidation of the French Absolute Monarchy in the Early Seventeenth Century.* Translated by Joan Spencer. London, 1973.

Namier, Lewis. *The Structure of Politics at the Accession of George III.* London, 1961.

Nathans, Benjamin. "Habermas's 'Public Sphere' in the Era of the French Revolution." *French Historical Studies* 16 (spring 1990): 620–44.

Necheles, Ruth F. "The Abbé Grégoire's Work in Behalf of Jews, 1788–1791." *French Historical Studies* 6 (fall 1969): 172–84.

Negre, Léopold. *Vie et ministère de Claude Brousson d'après des documents pour la plupart inédits.* Paris, 1878.

Nicholls, D. "The Nature of Popular Heresy in France, 1520–1542." *Historical Journal* 26 (1982): 261–75.

Nixon, Edna. *Voltaire and the Calas Case.* New York, 1961.

de Nolhac, Pierre. *Madame de Pompadour et la politique.* Paris, 1928.

"Note sur les Galériens Protestants (1683–1775)." *B.S.H.P.F.* 116 (April–June 1979): 178–231.

O'Brien, Charles. "The Jansenist Campaign for Toleration of Protestants in Late Eighteenth-Century France: Sacred or Secular?" *Journal of the History of Ideas* 46 (1985): 523–38.

———. "Jansenists on Civil Toleration in Mid-Eighteenth Century France." *Theologische Zeitschrift* 37 (1981): 71–93.

O'Connor, John T. "Republican Conspiracies in the Old Regime." Paper

presented at the International Congress on the History of the French Revolution, Georgetown University, Washington, D.C., May 6, 1989.

Orcibal, Jean. *Louis XIV et les protestants*. Paris, 1951.

———. *Saint-Cyran et le jansénisme*. Paris, 1961.

Ozouf, Mona. "'Public Opinion' at the End of the Old Regime." *Journal of
Modern History* 60, supp. (September 1988): S1–S22.

Pajol, Le comte. *Les Guerres sous Louis XV. Vol. 4, 1749–1759*. Paris, 1885.

Palmer, Robert. *Catholics and Unbelievers in Eighteenth Century France*. Princeton, N.J., 1939.

Pappas, John. "La répression contre les protestants dans la seconde moitié du
siècle, d'après les registres de l'ancien régime." *Dix-huitième siècle* 17 (1985):
111–28.

Péronnet, Michel. "Les assemblées du clergé et les protestants." *Dix-huitième
siècle* 17 (1985): 141–50.

———. *Les Evêques de l'ancienne France*. 2 vols. Lille, 1977.

———. "Loménie de Brienne, archevêque de Toulouse, principal ministre
du roi, et l'Edit de Non Catholiques de novembre 1787." *B.S.H.P.F.* 134
(April–June 1988): 261–80.

———. "Nos Seigneurs du Clergé de France en 1789." *Dix-huitième siècle* 20
(1988): 119–31.

Perrault, Gilles. *Le secret du roi*. Paris, 1992.

Peters, Marie. *Pitt and Popularity: The Patriot Minister and London Opinion during the Seven Years' War*. Oxford, 1980.

Plongéron, Bernard. "Une image de l'église d'après les 'Nouvelles Ecclésiastiques': 1728–1790." *Revue d'histoire de l'Eglise de France* 16 (1967): 241–68.

Plumb, J. H. *The First Four Georges*. London, 1977.

Poland, Burdette. *French Protestantism and the French Revolution: A Study in
Church and State, Thought and Religion, 1685–1815*. Princeton, N.J., 1957.

Pomeau, René. *La religion de Voltaire*. Paris, 1969.

Popkin, Jeremy. "Pamphlet Journalism at the End of the Old Regime."
Eighteenth-Century Studies 22 (spring 1989): 351–67.

———. "The Prerevolutionary Origins of Political Journalism." In *The French
Revolution and the Creation of Modern Political Culture*, vol. 1, *The Political Culture of the Old Regime*, edited by Keith Baker, pp. 203–23. Oxford, 1987.

———. *The Revolutionary News: The Press in France, 1789–1799*. Durham,
N.C., 1990.

———. *The Right-Wing Press in France, 1792–1800*. Chapel Hill, N.C., 1980.

Poujol, Jacques. "Aux sources de l'Edit de 1787: Une étude bibliographique."
B.S.H.P.F. 133 (July–September 1987): 343–84.

Poujol, Robert. "La surveillance des protestants en Hautes-Cévennes (1705–
1760)." *Dix-huitième siècle* 17 (1985): 129–39.

Prestwich, Menna. "The Huguenots under Richelieu and Mazarin, 1629–61:

A Golden Age?" In *Huguenots in Britain and Their French Background, 1550–1800: Contributions to the Historical Conference of the Huguenot Society of London, 24–25 September 1985*, edited by Irene Scouloudi, pp. 175–97. Totowa, N.J., 1987.

Prestwich, Menna, ed. *International Calvinism*. Oxford, 1985.

Queniart, Jean. *La Révocation de l'Edit de Nantes: Protestants et catholiques français de 1598 à 1685*. Paris, 1985.

Rabaud, Camille. *Paul Rabaut, Apôtre du Désert*. Paris, 1920.

Renaudet, Augustin. *Pré-réforme et humanisme à Paris pendant les premières guerres d'Italie (1494–1517)*. 2d. ed. Paris, 1953.

Rétat, Pierre, ed. *L'attentat de Damiens: Discours sur l'événement au XVIIIe siècle*. Paris, n.d.

Rex, Walter. *Essays on Pierre Bayle and Religious Controversy*. The Hague, 1965.

Richter, Melvin. "Despotism." In *Dictionary of the History of Ideas*, edited by Philip P. Wiener, vol. 2, pp. 1–18. New York, 1973.

Riley, James C. *The Seven Years' War and the Old Regime in France: The Economic and Financial Toll*. Princeton, N.J., 1986.

Ritter, Gerhard. *Frederick the Great: A Historical Profile*. Berkeley, 1970.

Robert, Daniel. "La fin du 'Désert héroïque'— Pourquoi Jean-Louis Gibert a-t-il émigré (1761–63)?". *B.S.H.P.F.* 98 (October–December 1951): 238–47.

Roche, Daniel. "Censorship and the Publishing Industry." In *Revolution in Print: The Press in France, 1775–1800*, edited by Robert Darnton and Daniel Roche, pp. 3–26. Berkeley, 1989.

———. *The People of Paris: An Essay in Popular Culture in the Eighteenth Century*. Berkeley, 1987.

Roelker, Nancy Lyman. *Queen of Navarre: Jeanne d'Albret, 1528–1572*. Cambridge, Mass., 1968.

Salmon, J.H.M. *Renaissance and Revolt: Essays in the Intellectual and Social History of Early Modern France*. Cambridge, Eng., 1987.

Samoyault, Jean-Pierre. *Les bureaux du sécretariat d'état des affaires étrangères sous Louis XV*. Paris, 1971.

Sauzet, Robert. "Les evêques du Bas-Languedoc et la Révocation." In *La Révocation de l'Edit de Nantes et le protestantisme français en 1685*, edited by Roger Zuber and Laurent Theis, pp. 75–86. Paris, 1986.

Schama, Simon. *Citizens: A Chronicle of the French Revolution*. New York, 1989.

Schickler, Baron F. de. *Les Eglises du Réfuge en Angleterre*. 3 vols. Paris, 1892.

Schwartz, Hillel. *The French Prophets: The History of a Millenarian Group in Eighteenth-Century England*. Berkeley, 1980.

Scoville, W. C. *The Persecution of Huguenots and French Economic Development, 1680–1720*. Berkeley, 1960.

Sedgwick, Alexander. *Jansenism in Seventeenth-Century France: Voices from the Wilderness*. Charlottesville, Va., 1977.

————. "Seventeenth-Century French Jansenism and the Enlightenment."
In *Church, State, and Society under the Bourbon Kings of France*, edited by
Richard M. Golden, pp. 125–47. Lawrence, Kan., 1982.

Simanyi, Tibor. *Madame de Pompadour: Eine Biographie*. Düsseldorf, 1979.

Skinner, Quentin. *The Foundations of Modern Political Thought*. Vol. 2, *The Age
of Reformation*. London, 1978.

Smith, D. W. *Helvétius: A Study in Persecution*. Westport, Conn., 1982.

Snoeks, Remi. *L'argument de tradition dans la controverse eucharistique entre catholiques et réformés français au XVIIe siècle*. Louvain, 1951.

Soboul, Albert. *Histoire de la révolution française*. Vol. 1, *De la bastille à la gironde*.
Paris, 1962.

Spector, Robert. *English Literary Periodicals and the Climate of Opinion during the
Seven Years' War*. The Hague, 1966.

Stephan, Raoul. *Histoire du protestantisme français*. Paris, 1961.

Stone, Bailey. *The French Parlements and the Crisis of the Old Regime*. Chapel
Hill, N.C., 1986.

————. *The Parlement of Paris, 1775–1789*. Chapel Hill, N.C., 1981.

Sutherland, N. M. *The Huguenot Struggle for Recognition*. New Haven, Conn.,
1980.

————. *The Massacre of St. Bartholomew and the European Conflict, 1559–1572*.
London, 1973.

Swann, Julian. "Parlement, Politics and the Parti Janséniste: The Grand Conseil Affair, 1755–1756." *French History* 6 (December 1992): 435–61.

Taber, Linda. "Religious Dissent within the Parlement of Paris in the Mid-
Sixteenth Century: A Reassessment." *French Historical Studies* 16 (spring
1990): 684–99.

Tackett, Timothy. *Priest and Parish in Eighteenth-Century France: A Social and
Political Study of the Curés in a Diocese of Dauphiné, 1750–1791*. Princeton,
N.J., 1977.

————. *Religion, Revolution and Regional Culture in Eighteenth-Century France:
The Ecclesiastical Oath of 1791*. Princeton, N.J., 1986.

Taveneaux, René. *Jansénisme et politique*. Paris, 1965.

Trench, Charles Chenevix. *George II*. London, 1973.

Tüchle, Herman, C. A. Bouman, and Jacques Le Brun. *Réforme et contre-
réforme*. Vol. 3 of *Nouvelle Histoire de l'Eglise*. Paris, 1968.

Tulau, G., ed. "La flotte anglaise sur les côtes d'Aunis et de Saintonge en
1757." *Revue maritime et coloniale* 114 (July–September 1892): 111–18.

Tunstall, W. C. B. *Admiral Byng and the Loss of Minorca*. London, 1928.

————. *William Pitt, Earl of Chatham*. London, 1938.

Valensise, Marina. "The French Constitution in Prerevolutionary Debate."
Journal of Modern History 60, supp. (September 1988): S22–S57.

Van Kley, Dale. "Church, State, and the Ideological Origins of the French

Revolution: The Debate over the General Assembly of the Gallican Clergy in 1765." *Journal of Modern History* 51 (December 1979): 629–66.

——. *The Damiens Affair and the Unraveling of the Ancien Régime, 1750–1770.* Princeton, N.J., 1984.

——. "The Estates General as Ecumenical Council: The Constitutionalism of Corporate Consensus and the *Parlement's* Ruling of September 25, 1788." *Journal of Modern History* 61 (March 1989): 1–52.

——. "The Jansenist Constitutional Legacy in the French Prerevolution." In *The French Revolution and the Creation of Modern Political Culture,* vol. 1, *The Political Culture of the Old Regime,* edited by Keith Baker, pp. 169–201. Oxford, 1987.

——. *The Jansenists and the Expulsion of the Jesuits from France, 1757–1765.* New Haven, Conn., 1975.

——. "New Wine in Old Wineskins: Continuity and Rupture in the Pamphlet Debate of the French Prerevolution, 1787–1789." *French Historical Studies* 17 (fall 1991): 447–65.

——. "The Religious Origins of the Patriot and Ministerial Parties in Pre-Revolutionary France: Controversy over the Chancellor's Constitutional *Coup,* 1771–1775." *Historical Reflections / Réflexions historiques* 18 (summer 1992): 17–63.

Van Kley, Dale, and Jeremy Popkin, "The Pre-Revolutionary Debate," sec. 5. In *The French Revolution Research Collection.* Oxford, 1990.

Vienot, J. *Histoire de la réforme française: Des origines à l'Edit de Nantes.* Paris, 1926.

Vovelle, Michel. *The Fall of the French Monarchy, 1787–1792.* Cambridge, Eng., 1987.

——. *Piété, baroque et déchristianisation en Provence au XVIIIe siècle.* Paris, 1973.

——. *Religion et Révolution: La déchristianisation de l'an II.* Paris, 1976.

Vuilleumier, Henri. *Histoire de l'Eglise réformée du pays du Vaud sous le régime Bernois.* 4 vols. Lausanne, 1933.

Waddington, Fr. "Projet d'émigration du pasteur Gibert pour les protestants de la Saintonge et des provinces voisines d'après des documents inédits, 1761–1764." *B.S.H.P.F.* 6 (1858): 370–81.

Waddington, Richard. *Louis XV et le Renversement des Alliances.* Paris, 1896.

Weber, Hermann. "Le sacre de Louis XVI." In *Actes du colloque international de Sorèze: Le règne de Louis XVI et la Guerre d'Indépendance américaine.* Dourgne, 1977.

Weiss, Charles. *History of the French Protestant Refugees.* Edinburgh, 1854.

Wemyss, Alice. *Les Protestants du Mas-d'Azil: Histoire d'une résistance 1680–1830.* Toulouse, 1961.

White, Antonia. *The Memoirs of Chevalier d'Eon.* London, 1970.

Whitworth, Rex. *Field Marshal Lord Ligonier: A Story of the British Army, 1702–1770.* Oxford, 1958.

Williams, Alan. *The Police of Paris: 1718–1789.* Baton Rouge, La., 1979.

Williams, Basil. *The Life of William Pitt, Earl of Chatham.* 2 vols. New York, 1913.

Williams, William H. "The Significance of Jansenism in the History of the French Catholic Clergy in the Pre-Revolutionary Era." *Studies in Eighteenth-Century Culture,* edited by Roseann Runte, vol. 8, pp. 289–303. Madison, Wis., 1978.

Wilson, Arthur M. *Diderot.* New York 1962.

Woodbridge, John. "La conspiration du prince de Conti." *Dix-huitième siècle* 17 (1985): 97–109.

———. "L'influence des philosophes français sur les pasteurs réformés du Languedoc pendant la deuxième moitié du dix-huitième siècle." Thesis, University of Toulouse, 1969.

———. "The Reformed Pastors of Languedoc Face the Movement of Dechristianization (1793–1794)." In *Sécularisation,* edited by Michèle Mat, pp. 77–89. Brussels, 1984.

———. "An 'Unnatural Alliance' for Religious Toleration: The Philosophes and the Outlawed Pastors of the 'Church of the Desert.'" *Church History* 42 (December, 1973): 505–23.

Yardeni, Myriam. "Les Juifs dans la polémique sur la tolérance des protestants à la veille de la Révolution." *Revue des etudes juives* 132 (1973): 79–93.

ANONYMOUS PRINTED SOURCES

Candid Reflections on the Report (As Published by Authority) of the General Officers Appointed by his Majesty's Warrant of the First of November last, to enquire into the CAUSES of the FAILURE of the late Expedition to the Coasts of FRANCE. London, 1758.

Discours sur l'édit de bienfaisance: A l'usage des Protestans de la Campagne. N.p., 1788.

Galérie de l'ancienne cour, ou Mémoires anecdotes pour servir à l'histoire des règnes de Louis XIV et de Louis XV. 4 vols. N.p., 1788.

A Genuine Account of the Late Grand Expedition to the Coast of France, under the Conduct of the Admirals Hawke, Knowles, & Broderick, and of General Mordaunt . . . By a Volunteer . . . London, 1757.

Mercure historique et politique. October and November, 1757.

The Report of the General Officers, Appointed By his MAJESTY's Warrant of the First of November 1757, to enquire into the Causes of the Failure of the late Expedition to the Coasts of FRANCE. London, 1758.

The Secret Expedition Impartially Disclosed. . . . London, 1757.

Vie privée et politique de Louis-François-Joseph, Prince de Conti, Prince du Sang par J. P★★★. Paris, 1790.

INDEX

Alembert, Jean Le Rond d', 149
Algre (Reformed minister), 61
Allamand, François-Louis, 20
Alleurs, comte des, 28
Almon, John, 203 n.49
Anson, Lord George, 91, 94, 102, 106, 108,
    123, 126
Antoine, Michel, x–xi, 136
Argenson, marquis d', 28, 29, 55, 67, 70, 71,
    72, 76, 172
Arnauld, Antoine, 35, 36, 194 n.35
Arouet, François-Marie. See Voltaire
Ashburnham, Lord, 103
Aston, Nigel, 212 n.99
Aubie, François, 118, 119
Augustine, Saint, 33
Austria, treaty with France, 45–46, 57

Baër, Karl Friedrich, 149
Baillon, Jean, 16, 66
Bailly, Jean Sylvain, 167
Baker, Keith, xvi
Barbier, Edmond, 73
Barentin, Minister of Justice, 164
Barnave, Antoine-Pierre, 168, 179
Barrington, Mr., 94
Basnage, Jacques, 191 n.70
Bastille, taking of, 168–69
Bâville, intendant of Languedoc, 8
Bayle, Pierre, 6, 19
Beaumarchais, Pierre-Augustin Caron de,
    138
Beaumelle, Laurent Angliviel de La, 149
Beaumont, Christophe de, 39, 40, 77
Beckford, William, 141–42, 207 n.22
Bedford, duke of, 104, 123
Belle-Isle, maréchal de, 97, 209 n.68
Benedict, Philip, 4
Benedict XIV, Pope, 40
Bénézet, François, 14
Bernis, abbé de, 79, 138
Berryer, Nicolas-René, xii, xiv; as liaison

for spies on Conti, 69, 71, 78, 79, 80,
    81–82, 83, 84, 85, 86, 93, 136, 151, 200 n.26
Betrine, Pastor, 138–39
Beza, Theodore, 185 n.5
Bien, David, 154
Blachon, Jean, 22
Blair, Mr., 126
Blancmesnil, Seigneur de. See Lamoignon,
    Guillaume
Bonnaud, Jacques-Julien, 177
Bosher, J. F., 168
Bourbon, duc de, 9
Bourbon-Orléans, Louise-Diane de, 26
Boyer, M., 61
Breteuil, baron de, 157, 158
Briçonnet, Guillaume, 2
Brissot, Jacques-Pierre, 181
Broglie, comte de, 28, 29, 76, 137, 169
Brousson, Claude, 8
Bulle, Antoine, 117–18, 119
Bulle, Léonard, 117
Bussey, François de, 200 n.37
Bute, Lord, 121
Byng, Admiral, 95, 122–23

Calas, Jean, 146
Calas, Marc-Antoine, 146
Calas Affair, 145–46
Calvin, John, 2, 5, 34
Calvinism, 2, 4–5; and Jansenism, 34–35.
    See also Protestants, French
Cambon (Reformed minister), 61, 62
Camisards, Guerre des. See Guerre des
    Camisards
Camus, Armand-Gaston, 167, 168, 179
Capon, G., x
Catholics, See Roman Catholics
Cavalier, Henri (Latour), 18, 61, 62
Caveirac, M., 68
Cayla, M. du, 61, 91–92
Cerceau, Antoine du, 25, 26
Chaise, Père de la, 36
"Chaloux," Pastor, 60

Chapelle, Armand de la, 20
Chartier, Roger, xvi, 173 213 nn.23, 24
Chaumont, 77
Chaumont, Claude, 146
Chayla, abbé du, 8
Chesterfield, Lord, 122, 124, 205 n.25
Choiseul, Etienne-François, duc de, 26, 28,
   136, 150, 195 n.47
Church of the Desert, 11, 19, 22, 51, 185 n.1
Claude, Jean, 194 n.35
Clement XI, Pope, 36, 37
Clerk (Clarke), Robert, 98, 103, 104, 105,
   129, 133
Clevland, John, 91
Coffin, Charles, 39
Cole, M., 91
Collé, Charles, 74–75
Committee of Geneva, 11
Committee of Lausanne, 11
Condé, Louis II de Bourbon, Grand, 25, 44
Condé, prince de, 3
Condorcet, marquis de, 145
Conti, Armand de Bourbon, prince de, 25,
   44
Conti, Louis-Armand II, prince de, 25
Conti, Louis-François de Bourbon, prince
   de: agents involved with, 89–93; charac-
   ter of, 24–25; conspiracy against Louis
   XV, ix–xi, xii, xiv–xv, 46–47, 49–50,
   161–62; court influence of, 66–69; as
   Damiens' judge, 74–79; early years of,
   25–26; and French foreign policy, 29;
   intelligence reports on, 79–88; and Jansenists, 31–33, 43, 44; and "Messieurs de
   Paris," 53–55; as military leader, 27–28,
   69–70; as Protestant ally, 138–39; and
   Rabaut, 23, 50–53, 56–57, 58, 59, 60, 62;
   rebellion proposed by, 55–60, 73, 136;
   and refusal of sacraments controversy,
   39–41; relationship with Louis XV,
   69–71, 76, 136, 137, 171–72; secret activities of, 28–29
Conti, princesse de, 25
Conway, Harry, 103, 104, 106, 122, 128, 129,
   130
Cornwallis, General, 106
Coslin, Madame de, 30, 46, 56
Coste (Reformed pastor), 13–14
Court, Antoine, 51, 52, 56, 61, 116, 142–43,
   148, 181–82, 197 n.14; and Jean-Louis
   Gibert, 17–18; and the prince de Conti,

53, 54, 55; as Protestant leader, 10–11; and
   Paul Rabaut, 19–21, 57–58
Court de Gébelin, 52, 55, 57–58, 66, 142–43,
   148, 181–82, 196 n.4
Cromwell, Oliver, 44, 161
Cumberland, duke of, 64, 65; and Secret
   Expedition, 95, 97, 98, 102, 104, 105–6,
   108–9, 111, 130–31

Damiens, Robert François: stabbing of
   Louis XV, ix, x, xiv, xv, 71, 72–74, 172,
   199 n.7; trial of, 74–79, 92–93
Dardier, Charles, 10
Darnton, Robert, 174–75
Debosc, M., 54
Declaration of 1724, 9–10, 13, 158
Declaration of the Rights of Man and Citizen,
   The, 180, 181, 182–83
Desmont, Olivier, 154
Desmoulins, Camille, 165
Devonshire, William Cavendish, fourth
   duke of, 95, 104, 120, 201 n.1
Diderot, Denis, 138, 147
Diefendorf, Barbara, 2–3
Dreux-Brézé, marquis de, 167
Duclos, M., 30
Dugas, Pierre, 17, 62, 85
Dulthiez, Pastor, 56
Dupplin, Lord, 104
Dutens, Louis, 26, 89–90, 139
Duval, Pastor, 54

Edict of Fontainebleau, 7, 9, 10
Edict of Nantes, 3; revocation of, 7–10, 158
Edict of Toleration, 145, 158–59, 176–77,
   180, 212 n.99
Edwards, John, 91
Eiser, John, 128
Eon, chevalier d', 28, 137
Epinay, prince d', 26
Eprémesnil, d', 159
Estates General, 162–64, 166. *See also* Third
   Estate
Etaples, Jacques Lefèvre d', 2

Fénelon, François, 37
Ferrières, Maistre de, 76
Flecher. *See* Molines
Fleury, Joly de, 15, 148–49
Fox, Henry, 94, 123
Frappier, Michel, 118

Frederick II, king of Prussia, 48–49, 63, 65, 66, 73, 77; military victories of, 141, 142; and Secret Expedition, 95, 96, 97, 101–3, 105, 106, 107, 120–21

Frégère, Isabeau, 118

Gabriac (pastor), 62

Gachon, Jean, 180

Gallicanism, 37

Gal-Pomaret, pastor, 154

Garrisson, Janine, 5

Gautier, Dominique, 76

George II, and Secret Expedition, 95, 96–97, 98, 100, 101, 102, 105–6, 107, 123, 124, 125, 128, 129–30

Gibert, Etienne, 17, 144, 150

Gibert, Jean-Louis, xiii, 51, 59; and Herrenschwand, 84, 85, 86, 87; and William Pitt, 143; and prince de Conti, 89; as Protestant leader, 144, 150; and Secret Expedition, 88, 99, 114, 119–20, 132; as threat to Catholics, 16–18, 20, 22, 61, 62, 66, 116, 136

Greengrass, Mark, 3

Grégoire, abbé, 181

Grenville, George, 123

Grimm, Friedrich, 149

Guerre des Camisards, 8–9, 10, 19–20

Hardwicke, Lord, 94, 101, 102, 103, 104, 105, 107, 122, 123, 130, 141, 143

Hauranne, Duvergier de, abbé de Saint-Cyran, 33

Havrincourt, marquis d', 28

Hawke, Sir Edward, 104, 105, 106, 108, 120, 121, 123, 124, 125, 126, 129, 130, 131, 132–33, 202 n.28

Healy, Mr., 91

Henley, Sir Robert, 94

Henry of Navarre, 3

Herrenschwand (spy), xiv, 69, 111, 120, 151, 200 n.26, 209 n.68; as spy on Conti's activities, 58–59, 62, 79–88, 89, 92, 99, 136, 138, 173

Holdernesse, Lord, ix, 92, 93, 97, 99, 101, 102, 104, 120, 131, 135, 140, 173

Huguenots, French, xi, xiv, xv, 1–2, 21, 48, 162, 191 n.72; oppression of, 5–6, 215 n.57. *See also* Protestants, French

Hugues, Edmond, xi, 200 n.26

Hulin (agitator), 168

Innocent X, Pope, 35

Jansen, Cornelius, 33

Jansenists: beliefs of, 33–35, 194 n.32; as conspirators, 215 n.50; and Louis XIV, 36–37; and pamphlets on religious toleration, 177–79; parlements as allies of, 38–39; and prince de Conti, 31–33; and refusal of sacraments controversy, 39–41, 154–55

Jaucourt, Louis de, 147

Jenkinson, Charles, 123

Joutard, Philippe, xi–xii, 20

Joynes, Daniel Carroll, 41

Jurieu, Pierre, 19

Kaiser, Thomas, xvi

Knowles, Admiral, 104

Knyphausen, Baron, 66–67, 97

Labrousse, Elisabeth, 6, 186 n.15

La Chapelle (priest), 76–77

Lafayette, marquis de, 157, 158

Lagarde, Soulier de Puechmille, 14, 61–62, 65, 189 nn.42, 50

Lamoignon, Guillaume, Seigneur de Blancmesnil, xii, 198 n.1

La Nible. *See* Duval, Pastor

La Rochelle, expedition to. *See* Secret Expedition

La Touche, chevalier de, 28

Latour. *See* Cavalier, Henri

La Tour, Simon de, 25, 32, 77

Launay, Governor de, 168

Lavergne. *See* Thibaut, prieur d'Auriac de Boursan

Le Blanc, Sieur, 73, 77

Leboeuf, Michel, 117

Le Brun, Jacques, xvi, 35

Le Cointe, Jean-Louis, xiv, 50–51, 53, 78, 80, 81, 82, 120, 138, 196 n.4

Lefebvre, Guillaume, 13

Legge, Mr., 94

Le Gouvé, Jean-Baptiste, 76

Léonard, Emile, 185 n.1

Le Paige, Adrien, 32, 41–42, 44, 57, 66, 70, 138, 157, 162, 170, 172, 206 n.4

Lerner, Robert, xvi

Ligne, prince de, 25, 44

Ligonier, Jean-Louis, 66, 97–98, 99,

Ligonier, Jean-Louis *(cont'd)*
    100–101, 103, 104, 107, 108, 113, 120, 125,
    126–27, 128, 132, 133–34, 203 n.50
Linange, Van den Enden, comte de, 19, 96
Linguet, M., 176
Locke, John, 149
Louis XIV: campaign against Jansenists,
    36–37, 43–44; Protestantism under, 4, 5,
    9, 157; revocation of Edict of Nantes, 7,
    35–36
Louis XV: as admirer of Conti, 25, 27;
    comparisons with Louis XVI, 170–73;
    Conti conspiracy against, ix–xi, xii,
    xiv–xv, 49–50, 55–60, 182; Damiens'
    stabbing of, 72–74, 77–78, 136, 161, 172;
    and Jansenists, 39–41; *lit de justice* of, 172;
    melancholy state of, 135–36; Protestants'
    loyalty to, 48–49, 115–16, 162, 182; and
    public opinion, 173–75; relationship with
    Conti, 69–71, 76, 136, 137, 171–72; sacra-
    mental policy of, 152–54; and Secret
    Expedition, 110, 115, 117; toleration of
    Protestants, 144–45, 150–54, 159–60, 182
Louis XVI, 28; challenges to authority of,
    167–70; comparisons with Louis XV,
    170–73; economic crisis faced by, 162–64;
    and public opinion, 175; toleration of
    Protestants, 145, 156, 157–58, 159, 160
Luther, Martin, 2
Lutherans, 2
Luynes, duc de, 29, 30, 64, 67, 79

Machiavelli, Niccolò, 200 n.28
Maintenon, Madame de, 5, 36
Mairobert, Pidansat de, 174
Majal, Matthieu, 13
Malesherbes, Chrétien-Guillaume de
    Lamoignon de, 31, 139, 157, 158, 174, 179
Mansfield, Lord, 109
Marguerite, duchesse d'Alençon, 2
Maria Teresa of Austria, 45
Marillac, intendant of Poitou, 6
Marlborough, duke of, 126
Marron, Paul-Henri, 181
Maupeou, M., 74–75, 170
Maupeou revolution, 138
Maza, Sarah, xvi
Mazal, Abraham, 8, 9
Meister, Jakob Heinrich, 156
Mercier, Louis-Sébastien, 174
Mericourt, Le Fuel de, 174

Merrick, Jeffrey, xii–xiii, xvi, 31, 145, 155,
    183
Merton (pastor), 62
"Messieurs de Paris," 53–55
Metayer, Jacques, 146
Metayer, Pierre, 146
Michelet, Jules, 11
Mirabeau, Honoré-Gabriel Riqueti, comte
    de, 167, 168, 179, 183
Mirepoix, duc de, 60–61, 63, 67–69, 73–74,
    197 n.34
Mitchell, Andrew, 97, 101, 106, 107, 121, 131,
    132, 140
Molines (pastor), 14
Molinism, 34
Moltou, Paul, 147
Moncan, M. de, 62, 74, 144
Monin, Nicolas, 29, 50, 70, 137
Montagu, George, 65
Montalembert, Marc-René, marquis de, 76
Montclar, Jean-Pierre-François Ripert de,
    31–32, 149
Montesquieu, Baron, 147, 148
Mordaunt, John: charges against, 122–23,
    125, 126–28, 129; as leader of Secret Ex-
    pedition, 99, 103, 104, 105, 106–7, 114,
    120, 122, 124, 130, 131–32, 133, 139, 205 n.28
Moreau, Jacob-Nicholas, 40
Morély, Jean, 2, 185 n.5
Moultou, Paul, 52
Mounier, Jean-Joseph, 166
Mourny, M. de, 64

Nantes, Edict of. *See* Edict of Nantes
National Assembly, 167–68, 216 n.57
Necker, Jacques, 164, 168
Newcastle, duke of, 94, 95, 97, 109, 120–21,
    130, 141, 143; and failure of Secret Expe-
    dition, 122, 126, 128–29; on William Pitt,
    123–24, 125; and planning of Secret
    Expedition, 101, 102, 103, 104, 105, 108
Nicole, Pierre, 194 n.35
Noailles, maréchal de, 28, 36, 192 n.12
"Nogaret," Pastor, 112

O'Brien, Charles, 33
O'Connor, John, xvi, 96
Orcibal, Jean, 7
Ordinance of 1750, 13, 15
Orléans, duc d', 42, 139

Orléans, Louis-Philippe Joseph, duc d',
  164–66, 169–70, 214 n.36
Orléans, Philippe d', 9
Ozouf, Mona, xvi

Paix d'Alès, 4
pamphlets on religious toleration, 175–79
Pappas, John, 145, 149–50
Pâris, François de, 38
Paris, Parlement of, 36–37, 39, 41–42, 66,
  158, 159
Pascal, Blaise, 35
Pasquier, M., 74–75
Paumy, M. de, 27
Pellison-Fontanier, Paul, 5
Peters, Marie, 125
Phillips, William, 127
Pitt, William, ix, xi, xv, 86, 91, 93; and fail-
  ure of Secret Expedition, 114, 121–23,
  124–26, 129, 139–40, 142; and planning of
  Secret Expedition, 94–97, 100–102,
  103–9, 113; as political survivor, 140–43
Plessis, R. Yves, x
Pompadour, Madame de, ix–x, xii, xiv, xv,
  27, 43, 45–46, 55, 67, 68, 69, 70, 135, 136,
  193 n.20; relationship with prince de
  Conti, 29–30, 137; suspicions of Conti,
  78, 79, 82, 83
Pompignan, Lefranc de, 55
Potter, Thomas, 122, 124
Pradel, Jean, 51, 54, 67, 197 n.14
Prévost, abbé, 148–49
Prévôt, Sr. Barret, 64
Prévot, Sr. Trigant, 118
Prince, M. de, 110
Protestants, French: class distinctions
  among, 12, emigration of, 6–7, 21; under
  Louis XVI, 156–57; and monarchy, xi,
  4–5, 19–20, 48–49, 162; oppression of, 5–
  6, 9–10, 13, 14–16, 21–22, 145; and Secret
  Expedition, 109–12, 115–20, 133–34; as
  threat to monarchy, 56–66, 178–80; as
  threat to Roman Catholics, 2–3, 4–5; tol-
  eration of, xiii, xiv, 3–4, 7–8, 12, 31–32,
  144–54, 156–60, 175–79, 180–83; Voltaire
  as supporter of, 146–47
Puech (Reformed minister), 61

Quesnel, Pasquier, 36, 40

Rabaut, Paul, xv, 11, 15, 16, 19–21, 22, 67,
  68, 86, 97, 116, 136, 151, 152, 190 n.67,
  209 n.65; and "Messieurs de Paris,"
  53–55; and prince de Conti, 23, 24,
  46–47, 50–53, 56–57, 58, 59, 60, 62,
  63–64, 80, 83, 87; on Voltaire, 147–48
Rabaut Saint-Etienne, 156–57, 178, 179,
  180–81, 183
Ranc, Louis, 13
Ranum, Orest, xvi
Reformation, French, 1–2. *See also* Protes-
  tants, French
Reformed churches, restoration of, 10–16
republicanism, 4, 179, 186 n.15
Réveillon Riots, 163
Richelieu, duc de, 15–16
Richer, Edmond, 194 n.32
Ritter, Gerhard, 141
Rochefort, expedition to. *See* Secret Expe-
  dition
Roger, Jacques, 13
Roman Catholicism, as state religion of
  France, 158–60
Roman Catholics: and Declaration of 1724,
  9–10; in eighteenth-century France, xiii;
  Protestantism as threat to, 2–3, 4–5
Rousseau, Jean-Jacques, 138, 146–47,
  208 n.48
Roux, Jean, 62
Royer, Jean, 66
Ruff, Julius, xvi
Rulhière, Claude-Carloman de, 157, 174,
  178, 179

Sackville, Lord, 126
Saint Bartholomew's Massacre, 3
Saint-Florentin, comte de, 15, 49–50, 60,
  61, 66, 68, 69, 73, 97, 112, 116, 152,
  189 n.50, 197 n.34; fears of Protestant
  rebellion, 63
Saint-Priest, 73, 74, 197 n.34
Saint-Simon, 9
Saint-Vincent, Robert de, 158, 170, 178
Saxe, maréchal de, 27, 192 n.11
Schama, Simon, 169
Secret Expedition: English reaction to failure of, 120–34; execution of, 112–13; failure of, 114, 131–34, 142; fear of retribution for, 115–20, 133–34; French response
  to, 109–12; Louis XV's fears of, 136; planning of, 94–109

Séguier, Esprit, 8
Sennecterre, maréchal de, 110, 116
Serces, Jaques, 116, 143
Seven Years' War, 48
Severt, M., 74–75
Shelburne, Lord, 122
Soulavie, J. L., 26, 78–79, 92
Starhemberg, George Adam von, 45
Superville, Pastor de, 17, 18
Symmer, Mr., 97, 121, 132

Taafe, Theobald, 90–91, 92, 200 n.36
Tackett, Timothy, xvi
Teissier, Pastor, 16
Tellier, Père, 36
Temple, Lord, 94
Tercier, Jean-Pierre, 29, 70, 137
Thévenin, Matthieu, 118
Thévenin family, 118–19
Thibaut, prieur d'Auriac de Boursan, 64, 65, 111
Thierry, Joseph, 98, 103, 105, 129, 143–44
Third Estate, 163, 166, 176; as challenger of Louis XVI, 167–70
Thomond, maréchal de, 49, 111, 112, 116, 152
Tourny, M. de, 111, 112, 116, 117, 119
Treaty of Versailles, first, 46
Turgot, M., 148–49, 156

Unigenitus Dei Filius, 36–39, 40, 154, 155, 159, 162, 195 n.47

Van den Enden, comte de Linange. See Linange, Van den Enden, comte de
Van Kley, Dale, xii–xiii, xvi, 76, 154, 155, 170
Vergennes, comte de, 137
Vernet, Alexandre, 22
Versailles, first Treaty of, 46
Vesenobre (Reformed pastor), 13–14
Voisins, Gilbert de, 153
Voltaire, 138, 145–46, 147–49, 178

Waldegrave, General, 126
Walpole, Horace, 65, 98, 122, 128, 129, 135, 140, 141
Washington, George, 157
Weber, Hermann, 156
Westminster Convention, 48
Whitworth, Rex, 203 n.50

Young, Arthur, 166, 175–76

Zalusky, M., 76

Library of Congress Cataloging-in-Publication Data

Woodbridge, John D., 1941–
  Revolt in prerevolutionary France : the Prince de Conti's conspiracy against Louis XV, 1755–1757 / John D. Woodbridge.
    p.   cm.
  Includes bibliographical references and index.
  ISBN 0-8018-4945-4
  1. Conti, Louis François de Bourbon, prince de, 1717–1776.
2. Louis XV, King of France, 1710–1774 — Assassination attempt,
1757.   3. Offenses against heads of state — France.   4. Nobility —
France — Biography.   I. Title
DC135.C58W66   1995
944'.034 — dc20   94-21460